Big Dan Brouthers

Big Dan Brouthers
Baseball's First Great Slugger

Roy Kerr

McFarland & Company, Inc., Publishers
Jefferson, North Carolina, and London

LIBRARY OF CONGRESS CATALOGUING-IN-PUBLICATION DATA

Kerr, Roy, 1947–
    Big Dan Brouthers : baseball's first great slugger / Roy Kerr.
    p.   cm.
    Includes bibliographical references and index.

    ISBN 978-0-7864-7560-5
    softcover : acid free paper ∞

    1. Brouthers, Dan, 1858–1932.   2. Baseball players—United States—Biography.   I. Title.
    GV865.B754K47 2013   796.357092—dc23   [B]   2013036338

BRITISH LIBRARY CATALOGUING DATA ARE AVAILABLE

© 2013 Roy Kerr. All rights reserved

No part of this book may be reproduced or transmitted in any form or by any means, electronic or mechanical, including photocopying or recording, or by any information storage and retrieval system, without permission in writing from the publisher.

On the cover: Dan Brouthers of the Detroit Wolverines, Goodwin & Company baseball card, 1888 (Library of Congress)

Manufactured in the United States of America

McFarland & Company, Inc., Publishers
  Box 611, Jefferson, North Carolina 28640
  www.mcfarlandpub.com

For Bill and Marie Jenkinson,
Dan Brouthers' Greatest Fans

Table of Contents

Acknowledgments ix
Preface 1
ONE. The Wappingers Falls Boy: 1858–1880 3
TWO. The Champion Batsman of the Country: 1881–1885 27
THREE. Big Dan: 1886–1888 48
FOUR. Old Jed: 1889–1891 76
FIVE. Big Brother with the Stick: 1892–1895 96
SIX. The Sage of Wappingers Falls: 1896–1906 119
SEVEN. The Once Famous Ball Player: 1907–1932 152

Epilogue: The Grand Old Man of the Game 177
Appendix A: Dan Brouthers' Nicknames 183
Appendix B: Dan Brouthers' Longest Hits 185
Appendix C: Dan Brouthers' Major League Statistics 188
Chapter Notes 191
Bibliography 199
Index 203

Acknowledgments

Many people helped make this book possible. Ed Borsoi, Bill and Marie Jenkinson, and Leon and Margaret Lyday reviewed and critiqued the text with care and insight. Deb Payne at SABR and Nora Galbraith at Florida Southern College's Roux Library patiently and expeditiously responded to all my microfilm requests. Mark Rucker of Transcendental Graphics and the staffs of the Baseball Hall of Fame and the Wappingers Falls Historical Society provided a number of marvelous lesser-known photos. The "two Marys," who staff the office at St. Mary's Catholic Church in Wappingers Falls, graciously provided access to church records relating to the Brouthers family. Sandra Vaccio, president of the Wappingers Falls Historical Society, granted me access to various resources that were essential to my research.

The assistance of two colleagues proved indispensable to the completion of this project. In addition to reviewing the text, baseball historian Bill Jenkinson allowed me full access to his remarkable Dan Brouthers player files and home run logs, served as my research partner in Wappingers Falls, and enthusiastically lent his decades of expertise to the task at hand. Rena Corey, author, lecturer, and former Wappingers Falls Historical Society archivist, was the ideal on-site contact person wished for by every prospective biographer. A tireless researcher, Rena threw herself into the task of recovering Dan Brouthers' personal history with boundless energy and optimism, and was an invaluable partner during the preparation of the manuscript. Bill and Rena did much more than provide research assistance — they were co-collaborators in the Dan Brouthers project from start to finish.

Preface

> Past are the times when Dan Brouthers strode on his terrible way. While pitchers, quaking before him would send in a fast ball — and pray.— *Sporting Life*, May 28, 1904

History has been a careless guardian of the facts surrounding Dan Brouthers' life and career, perpetuating inaccuracies and falsehoods that continue to appear in modern profiles of the great slugger. Born Dennis Booder, the future Hall of Famer's surname was an Anglicized version of its original Gaelic, *O'Bruádair*. During the first decade of his career, he was alternately referred to in the press as Booder, Bruder, Bruther, Bruthers, Broeders, Boedders and Brothers, until Brouthers became the agreed-upon form. While playing for Detroit in the late 1880s, admiring sportswriters added to the confusion by coining the nickname "Dan" or "Big Dan" for him, which soon alternated indiscriminately with Brouthers' given name, Dennis, in game accounts.

In July 1877, while still a semi-pro player, Brouthers was involved in a collision on the diamond that took the life of the other player. For more than a half-century, mangled press versions of the accident completely misrepresented the specifics of the tragedy and assigned incorrect names to the victim, his team and home town. It was also reported that a traumatized Brouthers resigned from the game for two years after the incident, when in reality he was back on the diamond the following spring.

Every standard source for baseball information states that Brouthers batted and fielded left-handed. Evidence from photographs and illustrations of his era, however, prove that while he did hit left-handed, he fielded right-handed. At the height of his career, Brouthers was described as being an awkward hitter, a clumsy fielder and a poor baserunner. The "awkward" hitter won five batting and seven slugging titles, ranks first among nineteenth-century players in slugging, and is ninth all-time in batting average. The "clumsy" fielder led the league in putouts and fielding percentage, and was the era's most celebrated and successful practitioner of the hidden ball trick. The "poor" baserunner averaged 25 steals a season after the stolen base became an official statistic in 1886.

Clearly, it is time for a new historical perspective on this Hall of Fame member. The present study, in addition to correcting the many errors about Dan Brouthers that have crept into the literature, provides a comprehensive review of his life and career, from his youth as an apprentice in a print and dye factory to his final days as an attendant at the Polo Grounds. Brouthers is one of the few men who played organized baseball in five decades, and at age 53 he was still banging out hits and stealing bases in a semi-pro league. His major league career spanned 16 years, and in his prime he was considered the greatest hitter in baseball. He hit for average and power, and was one of the most difficult men to strike out in the history of the game. He was the first player to win consecutive batting and slugging titles and the first to be walked intentionally on a regular basis. The consensus among his peers was that no one hit the ball harder or farther. Appendix B provides a chronological listing of his longest hits.

One of the most intriguing discoveries about "Big Dan" is the more than four dozen nicknames invented by the press to express wonder at his size, strength and hitting prowess — a quantity and variety exceeded by no other player in baseball history. Appendix A catalogues these epithets by date and source, and all chapter titles are nicknames once used by sportswriters to describe Dan Brouthers. Viewed collectively, these condensed verbal portraits provide a unique glimpse of "the Champion Batsman of the World," "the Mighty Irish King," "the Fence-Smasher of the 80s" and "the Grand Old Man of the Game," who was one of the most talented and respected players of his era.

A Note on Spelling, Punctuation and Usage

Spelling, punctuation and usage in Dan Brouthers' day varied widely from today's standards. Baseball, for example, was spelled as two words (*base ball*) until the end of the 19th century. Center field was written *centrefield* or *centre field*. Ballparks such as the South End Grounds were referred to as the South End *grounds*. Hitters were called *batsmen*. Fans were known as *kranks* or *cranks*, and when they criticized a player, they "*guyed*" him. The unusual name of Dan Brouthers' home town, Wappingers Falls, which derives from a Native American term, was regularly misspelled in the press either as *Wappinger* Falls or *Wappinger's* Falls. In all quoted press accounts recorded in this volume, the original spelling, punctuation and usage have been maintained except in cases in which clarification was deemed necessary.

ONE

The Wappingers Falls Boy: 1858–1880

I never thought I was good.... I always thought that I ought to do better.—Dan Brouthers, *Poughkeepsie Eagle-News*, October 18, 1929.

The majestic Hudson River, which flows for 300 miles from its source in the Adirondacks to the southern tip of Manhattan, has for centuries served as both an important means of transport and a magnet for commerce. Such activities reached their peak in the mid-nineteenth century, when fleets of steamboats plied the river, moving travelers about New York State and delivering raw materials and manufactured goods to market in New York City.

In the late eighteenth century, small villages sprang up in close proximity to the Hudson, wherever its feeder tributaries dashed over waterfalls on their way to join the great river. The falls initially provided power to operate simple machines that ground wheat and cut lumber. Economic activity quickened in pace and complexity after the completion of the Erie Canal in 1823, which enabled coal extracted from Pennsylvania mines to be barged across New York State to the Hudson's shores and then shipped throughout the Hudson Valley. Coal soon replaced water power as the primary energy source, leading to heightened regional manufacturing productivity. Coal's superiority over charcoal in the iron-smelting process caused a local boom in the mining and refining of iron ore, resulting in the manufacture of wire, nails, cast-iron stoves and other practical items.

The development of the iron-refining industry in Beekman, New York, a hamlet ten miles southeast of Poughkeepsie in the mid–Hudson Valley, is intimately linked to the personal history of adventurer Daniel DeLaney. Born in County Kilkenny, Ireland, in 1801, DeLaney was "pressed into service in the British Navy, jumped ship in South America, made his way to New York, married ... and at some time prior to 1852, arrived in Beekman, evidently as a farm hand."[1] While working the land on the nearby shores of Sylvan Lake, DeLaney discovered significant iron ore deposits. Using money from his wife's dowry, he purchased property around the lake and went into the open-pit mining business.

In order to obtain laborers for his mining venture, "DeLaney periodically travelled to New York City where he recruited Irish immigrants straight off the boat and brought them to Sylvan Lake. Soon the miners had wives and the colony of Catholics in Beekman started to grow."[2] In 1858, DeLaney donated land to build St. Denis Catholic Church in the village.

One of DeLaney's early recruits to the iron ore pits was Irishman Michael Brooder, who by 1860 had settled in Beekman with his wife, Annie, and four children: Martin, Ellen, Dennis and James. Dennis, nicknamed "Denny," was born in the same year as the founding of St. Denis Church, and may well have been named in honor of its patron saint. Years later, while playing baseball in the National League, "Denny" would be known as Dan.

Census data lists Michael Brooder's occupation in Beekman as an "iron furnace man."[3] This important and dangerous job first required feeding coal fires for several days to keep the iron ore at a continuous temperature of 2,500 degrees, until the impurities had been removed. Then, using a long iron rod, the furnace man

Dan Brouthers, circa 1887. In his late twenties and in the prime of his career, a dapper Dan poses with hand in jacket. The pose, popular in eighteenth-century English portraiture, was considered an appropriate stance for men of breeding (Transcendental Graphics/www.theruckerarchive.com).

ONE. *The Wappingers Falls Boy: 1858–1880*

broke open the clay door in the hearth and directed the molten iron's flow out onto the casting floor. Here it entered a series of sand trenches, where it hardened into bars called "pigs" or "pig iron."

By 1870, Brooder, now referred to as Michael *Bruder*, had fathered a fifth child, Margaret, switched to a less dangerous and less physically demanding job, and moved two miles north to the town of Fishkill Plains (the name derives from the Dutch, *vis kill*, meaning a stream full of fish). He was now employed at a "Print Works,"[4] and his eldest son, Martin, 15, was working in a cotton mill.

Confusion over the spelling and pronunciation of foreign-sounding surnames like Bruder (or Brooder), was common in the nineteenth century, and many were routinely altered by immigration officers when foreigners entered the Unites States. Bruder's original Irish patronym, O'Bruádair, is historically significant, since it suggests kinship to Daíbhi (David) O'Bruádair, born in County Cork in 1624 and today considered the most influential Gaelic poet of the seventeenth century.

In ensuing years, Michael's second-eldest son, Dennis, frequently witnessed creative attempts to spell his last name after becoming a professional baseball player, until *Brouthers* became the standard version around 1880. While most evidence indicates that the name was pronounced *"Brew-thers,"* a later variant, *Broedders*, and one of his later baseball nicknames, "Big-Brother-with-the-Stick," suggests that it may also have been pronounced "Brothers." On at least one occasion, as we shall see, the name was spelled *Brothers* in sports reports of the era.

Sometime after 1870, the family resettled a few miles west, in the village of Wappingers Falls, where the "print works" that employed Michael was located. Here the children were educated in rudimentary fashion and began their own work careers. Dennis continued to reside in this village for nearly a half-century, becoming so linked to his home town that versions of its name were often used in the national press to refer to its most famous citizen. He was alternately known, for example, as "the Wappingers Falls boy,"[5] "the Wappingers Falls terror,"[6] "the sage of Wappingers Falls,"[7] "Old Wappinger,"[8] or "the Wappingerian."[9]

Located eight miles southeast of Poughkeepsie, Wappingers Falls' history is typical of myriad small Hudson River Valley towns that owe their existence to their proximity to the Hudson River and to nearby streams whose waterfalls were harnessed to create energy. The residents named the village after its original inhabitants, the Wappinger Indians. Why the name *Wappinger* was not made possessive in the normal fashion of adding an apostrophe + s (*Wappinger's*) is unclear, but the unique spelling appears as early as 1689 on a survey

Wappingers Falls, New York, 1862. Brouthers and his family moved here from East Fishkill, New York, in the mid–1870s. Brouthers would live in the village for nearly a half-century (courtesy Wappingers Falls, New York, Historical Society).

of the area.[10] For years, national news items dealing with the village's most famous resident, Dennis Brouthers, often incorrectly spelled both the great slugger's last name and his hometown in the same article.

At Wappingers Falls, the upper Wappingers Creek tumbles 50 feet over a waterfall and continues on for another two miles until reaching the Hudson River at New Hamburg. In the early nineteenth century it was a tiny village, consisting of "several saw and grist mills, seven dwellings, and no stores, churches or schools."[11] A calico dye and printing mill — the "print works" that eventually employed Michael Bruder — was established in the 1830s, bringing rapid growth to the area. The factory, known in different eras either as the Garner or the Dutchess print works, was modernized in the 1860s, about the time Michael Bruder began working there, and its power source was switched from water to coal-fired steam boilers. The print works' finished products were barged down the lower Wappingers Creek to the Hudson, and there shipped by rail or steamboat to other parts of the Hudson Valley and across the country. By 1900, business was booming, and the enterprise employed over 1,200 workers.

Dennis Brouthers joined his father there in his early teens,[12] earning ten dollars for "a sixty-hour week with no vacation pay or unemployment insurance or paid holidays."[13] The work day began at 6:20 A.M. and ended at 6 P.M., with an hour lunch break and a half-day's work on Saturday. Living in

ONE. *The Wappingers Falls Boy: 1858–1880*   7

nearby company housing, the Bruder family managed to eke out a decent living, but the conditions of daily life were primitive. Company houses had no running water or sewer systems, and heating and cooking were done with coal or coke, "which created ashes that had to be carried out of the house each day."[14] Drinking water was carried by pail from public water wells in town, and kerosene lamps were used for lighting. Caring for her husband and five children and enduring the harsh Hudson Valley winters proved too difficult an existence for Michael's Irish-born wife Annie, who died in Wappingers Falls before her 48th birthday.

By his late teens, Dennis, standing 6'2" and weighing 200 pounds, was considered a giant by the standards of the day. At some point he switched jobs, moving on to the Sweet-Orr company, one of two businesses in the village that used the print works' finished product, dyed cloth, to produce durable denim overalls and jackets.[15] There, Dennis' physique, youth, and lack of experience relegated him to performing heavy labor, such as shoveling or hauling coal and ashes, moving heavy machinery, or boxing and transporting finished textile goods. In the spring, summer and fall, he spent what little spare time he had on the weekends playing baseball, a sport that had captured the imagination of the country.

Sweet-Orr overall factory, Wappingers Falls, New York, 1876. Founded by Irish immigrants, Sweet-Orr was the first firm in the U.S. to produce denim overalls. Dan Brouthers worked here until he became a professional ballplayer. Instead of uniforms, the Wappingers Falls Actives, Brouthers' first team, wore Sweet-Orr overalls supplied for free by the company (courtesy Wappingers Falls, New York, Historical Society).

By the 1830s, young men up and down the East Coast were playing varying types of ball and stick games for recreation in their leisure hours. Each neighborhood or town club played according to its own rules. In 1845, Alexander J. Cartwright, a member of Manhattan's amateur Knickerbocker Base Ball Club, developed a set of regulations for the game. Over the course of the next decade they were revised, published and adopted by most East Coast teams and by others as far away as Detroit. Rules standardization fostered increased competition, initially between teams from different towns, and later between clubs from different states. In 1857, representatives from 16 amateur clubs established the National Association of Base Ball Players, or NABBP, the country's first national sports organization. A decade later it had over 100 members.

It did not take long for baseball fever to work its way up the Hudson to Poughkeepsie and Wappingers Falls. In 1859, Poughkeepsie resident Joseph H. Cogswell started a baseball club and played first base for the nine. By the time Dennis Brouthers reached his mid-teens in the mid–1870s, Poughkeepsie had four teams: the Volunteers, the Mutuals, the Athletics and the Stars, and Wappingers Falls had at least three: the Actives, Monitors, and Enterprise.[16]

In the short span of time between Brouthers' birth and the beginning of his playing career, baseball transformed from an amateur to a professional sport. Fierce competition between town clubs and rivalries with teams from neighboring towns led to the practice of paying superior players for their services or importing and paying star athletes from elsewhere when possible.

The trend toward professionalization of the sport was bolstered by the excitement and interest created by a two-year cross-country challenge tour undertaken by one of the first all-professional teams, the Cincinnati Red Stockings, in 1869 and 1870. Traveling the country from Boston to San Francisco in 1869, the Reds played 57 games and won them all. Competing mainly in the Midwest and along the East Coast, the 1870 team finished with a record of 67 wins, seven losses and one tie.

Thanks to this remarkable ball-playing exhibition, every city and town now wanted its own professional team. In 1871, the first professional league, the National Association of Professional Base Ball Players (NAPBBP) was formed. In 1876 it was replaced by the National Association of Base Ball Clubs, today's National League. A year later, a rival professional league, the International Association, was created. The advent of fixed schedules and the rivalries forged by playing the same opponents regularly added new dimensions to the sport. The professionals' salaries were paid by enclosing their ballparks and charging admission to attend the games.

Despite such events, as Dennis Brouthers reached his mid teens, professional league play was still the exception rather than the rule, in particular outside the larger cities, where hundreds of amateur, semi-professional and independent professional clubs continued to compete in a less-well-regulated and more loosely-arranged fashion. Team rosters and schedules were fluid in this broader arena, with clubs from different towns or areas agreeing to compete by word of mouth or by general invitations issued in the press.

On the East Coast, the *New York Clipper*, a bi-weekly newspaper that combined coverage of theater and the arts with sports reporting, served as the prime intermediary for such contests. In one 1877 press notice, for example, the Keystone Club of Manhattan announced its wish to play "the Actives of Wappingers Falls, the Bridge City team of Poughkeepsie, the Lone Star [club] of Catskill, the Nolans of Albany, the Haymakers of Troy and the Rings of Cohoes."[17] In a kind of free-for-all democratic process, box scores in the *Clipper* from such amateur or semi-professional contests, when available, were randomly mixed with scores from the professional teams. Game accounts of contests between small-town amateur or semi-pro teams were not always noted in local newspapers, however, since reporters were few and coverage was casual.[18]

Opinions differ on the exact year Dennis Brouthers began his playing career with the semi-pro Wappingers Falls Actives. A brief biography of the young slugger appearing in the *Clipper* in 1880,[19] whose probable source was Brouthers himself, cited 1877 as his rookie year in organized ball. Midway through his major league career (1887), the *Boston Globe* gave the year as 1876.[20] After his death in 1932, it was suggested that Brouthers began play in 1875.[21] There may be some truth in each version, since he did not become a starter on his home town team on the first day he walked on the field.

Despite his size and strength, Brouthers was not a natural athlete. His powerful upper body teetered on the support of slender legs and very small feet (he wore size seven shoes). His speed and range of movement on the field were negatively affected by his "knock-knees," a condition that causes the legs to turn inward and the knees to touch while the feet remain wide apart. Self-conscious and defensive about this condition throughout his career, Brouthers remarked after retiring that "There's no need to knock a fellow because he's knock-kneed."[22] Long after he became an established National League star, news reports continued to classify his fielding as ragged[23] and his hitting stance as awkward.[24]

A Brouthers contemporary who was a fellow ballplayer and life-long friend observed that in addition to such physical issues, Dennis' initial skill level at the sport was not high. Late in life, Wellington "Wallie" Lansing, who played on Poughkeepsie's first professional team in 1873, recalled that

The [Wappingers Falls] Actives [Club] was the first of the small town teams to make an extended tour [,] and on a trip to Mattawan, a substitute was needed. The team looked over Brouthers' brawn and decided he was the man. But he failed miserably. In nine innings of play he failed to touch the ball once while at the bat, and his fielding ... was atrocious.... Needless to say, he was dropped.[25]

Undaunted by his poor early performance, Brouthers sought to improve his offense by hiring "two boys at 10 cents a day to pitch to him and chase flies for hours after each day's work."[26] He followed this routine diligently, but it brought little success until he analyzed his approach at the plate and realized its defect: "I found out ... that just before my swing I took my eye from the ball and looked at the bat."[27] The future Hall of Famer had discovered the most basic rule in hitting: Keep your eye on the ball.

In the field, Brouthers started out as a pitcher, and as a semi-professional enjoyed considerable success. The rules of the era required him to throw underhanded from within a six-foot-by-six-foot "pitcher's box," whose front edge was 45 feet from home plate. By 1879, his first year as a professional, the box became a rectangle when its width was reduced to four feet. The primary action of the early game of baseball in the 1840s and 1850s was between the striker (hitter)

The photograph (above) and illustration (opposite) confirm that, contrary to popular belief that he was a pure lefty, Brouthers actually threw right-handed (both images Transcendental Graphics/www.theruckerarchive.com).

and the fielders. Consequently, the pitcher's original role was simply to lob an underhanded throw to the striker to initiate the hitting and fielding action.

Modern baseball records sources, based on normally reliable informants like Connie Mack[28] and Hall of Fame historian Ernest Lanigan,[29] all claim that Dan Brouthers both hit and threw left-handed. In fact, while he did hit lefty, photos and illustrations of him at first base verify that he actually threw right-handed.

In the thirty years that transpired between the Knickerbocker era and Brouthers' semi-pro years, pitchers transformed the game and their role in it by developing the fastball, the curve and the change-up. After an 1873 rule change allowing a wrist snap when throwing the ball, a pitcher's delivery resembled that of a modern-day fast-pitch softball pitcher. Reputed to have "great speed and a baffling curve,"[30] Brouthers had just enough lack of control to strike fear in the hearts of unprotected batters standing 45 feet away at home plate.

Although he pitched a few times in later years and occasionally played the outfield, by 1880 he had settled in at first base, a logical choice given his height. Most position players fielded barehanded until the mid–1880s, but by the late 1870s catchers were experimenting with heavy work gloves for protection behind the plate, and some pitchers and first basemen were wearing skin-tight dress gloves. When he began his professional career, Brouthers fielded barehanded, regardless of his position. By mid-career, in the late 1880s, first baseman Brouthers wore fingerless gloves resembling today's handball gloves on each hand.

While it is unclear exactly how much time Brouthers spent sharpening his game skills before becoming a regular with the Wappingers Falls Actives, the three-year time frame (1875–1877) suggested in the previously mentioned reports of his baseball beginnings does not seem farfetched, given what he needed to accomplish. By 1877, however, he was the Actives' regular pitcher. Pitching rotations were unknown in the era, and it was assumed that a single pitcher would start and finish almost every game. Short playing schedules and the required underhand pitching motion made this expectation feasible. During the 1877 National League season, for example, Tommy Bond of the league champion Boston Red Caps pitched 58 of the team's 61 games, and Jim Devlin of the second-place Louisville Grays pitched all 61 of his team's contests.

The Wappingers Falls Actives were an unusual sight on the diamond, since they played not in uniforms but "in overalls supplied by the Sweet-Orr factory,"[31] Brouthers' employer. One of the earliest known game accounts that mentions Dennis Brouthers was published in the *New York Clipper* and noted that in a July 1877 contest that was called due to rain after eight innings between the Enterprise and the Actives, both of Wappingers Falls, "Bruther" pitched for the Actives, picked up a hit, scored a run, and made an error in a 2–2 tie.[32]

Besides traveling up and down the Hudson playing regional rivals, the Actives were "active" in promoting visits to Wappingers Falls from teams as far away as New York City. In one invitation posted in the *Clipper*, for example, the team expressed interest in playing "all first class clubs," noting as an incentive that they had "a good inclosed [sic] grounds [and thereby the ability to charge admission] and draw large crowds."[33]

During one such home contest in July 1877, an on-field accident involving 19-year-old Brouthers nearly ended his career. In the fifth inning of a game against the visiting Harlem Clippers at Wappingers Falls,

> Bruthers, the pitcher of the club, had succeeded in reaching the third base, and in attempting to reach the home plate before a ball thrown from the field could be caught by John Quigley, the catcher of the Clippers, who is a small man (about 19 years of age) and [who] was standing in a stooping posture ... [Quigley] was struck on the left side of the forehead in a terrible manner by Bruthers' knee. He fell over on the ground and was picked up and stood still for a few moments, but in a short time was taken [to] one side and laid down on the grass, and then the terrible injuries he had sustained became apparent, blood in large quantities streaming from the wounds.[34]

A local physician who was attending the game, Dr. James M. Cosgrove (originally mis-identified as Dr. *Congreve* in local accounts of the incident), had the stricken player carried to his home and sent word for a second physician from Poughkeepsie, a Dr. Cooper, to come to his assistance. The two soon discovered that "the upper portion of the orbit of the fontal bone had

ONE. *The Wappingers Falls Boy: 1858–1880* 13

been knocked in, injuries which the physicians thought must prove fatal."[35] Meanwhile, the young catcher's mother, a widow with several other small children, was sent for. Young Quigley, who worked in "a kindling wood establishment in Harlem,"[36] was the only wage-earner in the family.

A few days later, the second attending physician, Dr. Cooper, operated on Quigley, removing several bone fragments from his skull and sewing up the wound with silver thread. Initial reports were positive: "Quigley was perfectly rational and ready to converse with all who were allowed to enter his room. He says he is ready and anxious to play again as soon as he can get out. Mr. Bruther, who ran into him, has been in attendance on him since the accident."[37] The catcher's condition gradually worsened, however, probably due to the onset of infection. After lingering near death for over a month, Quigley died in Poughkeepsie on August 12.

The death shocked both teams and the local community. *The Dutchess Farmer*, a Poughkeepsie weekly, praised the Actives team for all its efforts on Quigley's behalf: "The Active Base Ball Club, of Wappingers Falls, purchased a coffin for Mr. Quigley, and bore the expenses of sending the remains to Harlem. The members of the club deserve credit for the attention they bestowed upon the unfortunate young man in their endeavors to mitigate his sufferings and minister his wants."[38]

Brouthers, who routinely was described during his career as good-natured[39] and sensitive,[40] was overwhelmed with remorse over the affair, yet still had to endure a formal inquest on the accident on the day after Quigley's death. "Coroner Bailey held an inquest yesterday upon the body of Quigley, the base ball player, the Jury returning a verdict according to the facts, and fully exonerating the ball player, Bruthers, from all blame. During the inquest there was a war of words between physicians in attendance and others, but no serious outbreak occurred."[41] Despite the favorable ruling, Brouthers retired from play for the rest of the season, with the intention of giving up the game for good. In early September, a benefit game for Quigley's mother was played in the Bronx between the deceased catcher's club, the Clippers, and another local team, the Harlems. It was reported that "a good sum of money was realized."[42]

The specter of John Quigley's death haunted Brouthers for the rest of his life, and not only from his own recollections of the incident. Much to his distress, the tragedy was periodically revisited in the press, particularly when he changed teams. With the passing years, the accounts became more distorted, often misnaming the victim and providing completely spurious details of the accident. By 1924, for example, the account published in the *Buffalo Express* bore no resemblance to the actual events: "Dan Brouthers came into prominence as a ball player in 1877. In a game one day, when sliding into second base, he fell on second baseman McGlynn, and the ponderous weight of Big Dan practically crushed the life out of McGlynn, for he died from the injuries a few days afterward. Brouthers retired from the game after that accident."[43]

Despite the immediate personal trauma caused him by Quigley's untimely death, Brouthers returned to the Actives in 1878. In mid-summer, the *Clipper* provided a brief report of his 10–1 pitching victory over the Stottsville team: "The Stottsville club visited Wappinger Falls, NY, June 29, and were beaten by the Actives of that place."[44] Listed as "D. Bruther" in the box score, Dennis batted third and went hitless, but scored a run in the victory. His younger brother James covered shortstop for the Actives. As we shall see, for years after becoming a big league star, Dennis made continued attempts — most of them unsuccessful — to help his less-talented sibling reach the majors.

The Stottsville nine hailed from the village of the same name located 50 miles up the Hudson from Brouthers' home town. Although Stottsville was much smaller than Wappingers Falls, a description of the village written in 1878, the same year as the Actives-Stottsville game mentioned above, reveals that its founding and growth bore a striking similarity to the history of the Actives' home town:

> Stottsville is a flourishing manufacturing village of half a thousand inhabitants in the southeastern part of the town [of Stockport], about four miles from the city of Hudson. Claverack creek here makes a descent of fifty-three feet in three successive falls, affording excellent water-power, which is all used in operating *Stott's Woolen Mills*. These extensive mills are the result of the enterprising spirit of Jonathan Stott ... who located here in 1828, and began the manufacture of flannels.... His mills soon became the controlling industry of the place, which caused his name to be bestowed upon it.... Jonathan Stott died in May, 1863, but the business has since been successfully carried on by his sons and grandsons ... from twelve thousand to fourteen thousand yards of flannels and other goods are manufactured daily, giving employment to several hundred operatives.[45]

As similar as Stottsville and Wappingers Falls were in their history, the former village had an advantage that the latter lacked with regard to its baseball team. Two members of the Stott family, identified only as center fielder C. Stott and second baseman W. Stott, who probably were the grandsons of the town's founder, were avid baseball men and played on the village team. The fact that this tiny, out-of-the-way spot, perhaps less than one-fifth the size of Wappingers Falls, could regularly attract teams from New York City and Brooklyn (at the time still an independent city) for games at its home grounds, strongly suggests that its ball club benefited from the largesse of the Stott family in developing its schedule of opponents and compensating them for their travel and efforts on the field.

ONE. *The Wappingers Falls Boy: 1858–1880* 15

The Actives and the Stottsville nines met for a second time in early July at the latter's home grounds. On this occasion, they defeated the Wappingers Falls club, 2–0, although losing pitcher "D. Bruther" gave up just two hits and contributed two hits for the Actives.[46] The two Stott family members on the home team liked what they saw in the rival pitcher, and by August had convinced him to leave the Actives and join the Stottsvilles. Given the painful memory of the Quigley accident that he recalled each time he played at his home grounds, he jumped at the opportunity to be able to distance himself from the scene of the tragedy.

In his first known appearance with the Stottsvilles, on August 23, 1878, Brouthers pitched for the home team, losing 2–1 and going hitless against a visiting Jersey City nine. The following day, also at Stottsville, he lost a 4–3, ten-inning contest against local rival Hudson. The most significant aspect of this game was the emergence of Dennis Brouthers the hitter. He collected six hits, including a four-bagger — his first known home run — in a losing effort. Playing at Hudson a few days later, he banged out five hits while leading the Stottsvilles to a 6–4 victory.[47]

There is scant news of Brouthers' whereabouts again until spring 1879, when a note in the *Clipper*, referring to him as "Broeders," indicated that by late June he had switched positions from pitcher to first base and had moved on to another team up the Hudson, at Troy. "The consolidated Haymakers-Hudson club of Troy is composed of the following players: Hayes, catcher; Valentine, pitcher, *Broeders*, West and Curran on the bases, Latham, shortstop; with Taylor, Stevins and Lavin in the outfield."[48] (emphasis added).

The Haymakers and the Hudsons, originally two independent teams, competed in the New York State Association, and had apparently combined squads on a temporary basis in early June. The Haymakers had played at least one exhibition game against Troy's National League team, the Troy Citys, early in the spring. Brouthers' performance in that contest must have impressed Troy manager Horace Phillips, for it was soon reported that "Brouthers has been engaged by the Troy Citys, taking Shoupe's place, who has been released. Brouthers is six feet high, weighs 210 pounds, and is a heavy left-handed batsman."[49] This is the first known instance in which Dennis' last name was spelled *Brouthers* in a newspaper.

Playing a reduced schedule for two seasons, the young factory worker from Wappingers Falls had gone from the sandlots to the premier professional league in the country. His stay there on this occasion, however, would unfortunately be brief.

The 1879 National League was a far cry from its modern counterpart. Of more than a dozen cities granted franchises during the league's first four years, only one, Chicago, had turned a profit, and only two, Boston and Chicago, had survived since the inaugural season. Start-up costs, scandals caused by player dishonesty, low attendance due to a high admission fee (50 cents) and a blanket prohibition against Sunday ball and liquor sales had all combined to take their toll on the young league. Its brief history, tainted by a series of club expulsions due to insolvency or corruption, presented a distinctly unsavory image to the public and to potential future investors.

For League President William Hulbert, Troy's strong industrial base, distinguished baseball pedigree, and proximity to the state capitol of Albany, suggested at least the possibility of success for a team there, and the city was granted a franchise in 1879. Another Hudson Valley town that benefited from the availability of Pennsylvania coal via the Erie Canal, Troy turned to iron and steel production in the 1820s, and became the region's leading manufacturer of church bells. It acquired its nickname, "The Collar City," from the local invention of detachable collars and cuffs, and its economy further diversified when the city became a national leader in this light industry. By the end of the nineteenth century, 90 percent of all detachable collars were made in Troy.[50]

Like other towns up and down the Hudson, Troy had contracted baseball fever before the Civil War. In 1860, a Troy team gained admission to the amateur National Association of Base Ball Players. A few years later, the lowly Lansingburg Unions team, based in North Troy, sailed down the Hudson and defeated the mighty Brooklyn Atlantics on their opponent's home grounds. After the stunning victory, the Brooklyn press, smarting from the defeat of their home club by a team of rural yokels, christened them "the Haymakers." Undaunted, Lansingburg adopted the new nickname with gusto, appearing in club photos brandishing pitchforks. In 1871, a professional Haymakers team representing Troy proper joined the first major league, the National Association of Professional Base Ball Players, but folded in its second season due to lack of funds. Finally, in 1879, a Troy franchise known as the Troy Citys returned to the professional ranks in the National League under the leadership of Horace Phillips.

Forgotten today, Troy's manager, "Hustling Horace" Phillips was one of the era's more idiosyncratic managers. Born in Ohio and raised in Philadelphia, he was just five years older than Dennis Brouthers when hired to manage the Troy Citys. The handsome, smooth-talking Phillips possessed superior skills of communication and persuasion, and he was an expert at manipulating the media of his day—the newspapers—to suit his own purposes. He used such skills to gain appointment as Troy's first National League manager in 1879, despite scant prior experience.

Phillips began his career in 1877 as manager and substitute-player for

ONE. *The Wappingers Falls Boy: 1858–1880*

two Philadelphia teams associated with the League Alliance, a collection of teams from the Northeast and Midwest that were loosely aligned as minor league clubs under the National League. He spent 1878 in a similar role for two International Association teams, the Hornellsville, New York "Hornells" and the Binghamton Crickets. Two of his Binghamton players, pitchers Jim Whitney and John Ward, later enjoyed successful careers in the National League, with Ward's efforts ultimately earning him a plaque at Cooperstown. Phillips himself played in only a handful of games during these seasons, and spent the rest of his career as a non-playing manager.

His curious professional behavior over the next few years followed a similar pattern. Moving from city to city, he first spent enormous amounts of energy (hence his nickname, "Hustling Horace") successfully developing the financial backing for a new baseball team, and then went about the business of recruiting players. In the latter endeavor he often left behind a trail of angry teams whose players jumped their contracts — thanks to Phillips' encouragement — to play for his new team.

His troubles with financial backers typically began when he either developed conflicts over control of the team or was accused of misusing club funds. He then would quit or be fired, only to move on to another city and start the work of organizing yet another team. In interim periods in which he found himself temporarily out of baseball, he found employment as a hotel clerk, usually in Philadelphia or Chicago. There at the front desk, he cheerfully planned his next baseball adventure.

In his most successful scheme, he collaborated in 1882 with Cincinnati sportswriter O. P. Caylor to create the American Association, a rival national organization and the first serious threat to the National League's professional baseball monopoly. During his last six years in baseball, Phillips successively managed Pittsburgh's entry in the American Association for three years, and the Iron City's National League team for another three years. By the late 1880s, however, it became apparent that his mercurial personality and obsessive behavior were signs of mental illness. A decade after taking charge of the Troy Citys, he was declared legally insane and institutionalized in Philadelphia for the rest of his life. As the *New York Times* subsequently noted, a significant part of Phillips' later delirium was related to baseball:

> In an offhand way, Mr. Phillips informed the [hotel] clerk that he was worth millions upon millions, and was seeking investments. As the sole owner of all the baseball clubs in the country, he proposed to make many innovations in the national game and have it conducted on a more liberal basis. This he related in a matter-of-fact way, and the ordinary listener would have supposed he was entirely rational.[51]

Hustling Horace Phillips died in the Philadelphia Hospital for the Insane in 1896.

Young Dennis Brouthers was one of many players who apparently were mesmerized by Horace Phillips' powers of persuasion. His naive faith in his first National League manager resulted in a trying, two-year baseball odyssey, during which he briefly played twice for Troy and also for four other teams. This experience proved to be a critical career detour, one that delayed his ultimate arrival on the scene as the most feared hitter in baseball.

The 1879 Troy Citys were the weakest team in the National League. Seven of its starters were rookies. The remaining players, pitcher George Bradley and third baseman Herm Doscher, had a combined seven years experience in the National Association. Troy compiled a horrendous 19–56 record in its first year, winning just seven games on the road. Twenty-three men appeared on the team roster over the course of the season, including six pitchers. George Bradley was the only Troy player to lead the league in any category — most pitching losses (40).

By mid–June, the Troy Citys' disastrous record forced the club's owners to begin shuffling substitutes in and out of the lineup in search of a winning combination. The most successful of these new men was Dennis Brouthers. Batting sixth and playing first base, he debuted for Troy on June 23 against the Syracuse Stars, collecting one hit, a double, and scoring a run. In the final two games of the three-game home series against the Stars, he contributed to two wins with four hits, including a double. The following day, the *Troy Daily Times* assessed his debut with the home team positively: "Broedders, the new first baseman, played splendidly. He put out 14 men, making only one error, and that doubtless caused by excessive nervousness in the first inning. He is a strong batter, and will make a valuable acquisition to the nine, provided he can sustain the reputation so well established yesterday."[52] The teams then traveled to Syracuse for a series of games, and here on July 2, he established a record: "Broedders made the longest hit ever seen on the Syracuse grounds yesterday. The ball struck the centre field fence within a foot of the top and rebounded to the infield. If the ball had gone a foot higher, Broedders would have made a home run."[53] This blow was the first of dozens that would establish new long-ball distance records in parks across the country.

Brouthers led Troy's offense in July and August, collecting 46 hits in 39 games for a respectable .274 batting average. Despite his playing less than half the season, his four home runs placed him third in the league in that category. Two weeks after nearly clearing the fence at Syracuse, he hit the first of his 107[54] major league four-baggers in Cincinnati off Will White on July

ONE. *The Wappingers Falls Boy: 1858–1880* 19

19, during an 11-inning, 7–6 loss to the Reds. The second, off Boston's Tommy Bond on July 31, came at home during a 19–3 defeat by the Red Caps. In reporting this home run, the *Troy Daily Times*, which had been referring to the young first baseman as *Broedders*, changed the spelling of his name to *Bruthers*: "Bruthers made a home run, batting the ball over the right field fence."⁵⁵ By mid–July, one of Troy's local papers was proudly reporting what the *Buffalo Express* was saying about Brouthers' power hitting: "When he hits the ball, it goes like a shot from a Parrot gun, and woe betide the player who essays to stop it."⁵⁶ The young first baseman's third and fourth home runs were hit on successive days off Providence's ace, Bobby Matthews at Troy. On August 6, he first homered off Mathews, and the *New York Clipper's* report of the blast offered yet another spelling of the young slugger's name. "Brouthers alone batted him [Matthews] and made the only run for the home nine, he completing the circuit of the bases on his hit over the centre-field fence in the sixth inning."⁵⁷ Mathews again mastered the Troys the following day, 13–9, but Brouthers collected two hits, one of them by "knocking the ball over the centre-field fence for a home run in the fifth inning."⁵⁸

The league's home run leader in 1879 was Boston's Charley Jones, an eight-year veteran of the National Association and the National League, who slugged nine four-baggers in 83 games for the Red Caps. Rookie Dennis Brouthers hit four in just 39 contests for Troy, and had performed the impressive feat of hitting two of his total in successive games.

Defensively, Brouthers' performance was underwhelming. In his first experience as a full-time first baseman, he committed 33 errors in 37 games, and his fielding average, .926, was 49 points lower than Chicago's league-leader Cap Anson at the position. In one three-game stretch in mid–August, he committed six errors, including three in a game against Boston on August 11, prompting the *Troy Daily Times* to observe that the team effort was "weakened by the exceptionally bad play of Brouthers."⁵⁹ His prior full-time role as a pitcher with semi-pro teams clearly had not prepared him to play first base at the professional level.

Young Brouthers also pitched three games for Troy, with mediocre results. He debuted on July 30 against Boston, after starting pitcher George Bradley was called home due to "the death of his child the day preceeding."⁶⁰ Brouthers lost this first game, 8–3, surrendering 11 hits but giving up only two earned runs. He returned to the box again against Boston in relief of Bradley on August 20. "Brouthers pitched the last three innings, but this change did no good, for the Bostons hit him safely seven times."⁶¹ Despite this poor performance, he was called upon again to pitch against Boston the next day this time as a starter, with the same result. He surrendered 16 runs (six of which were earned) on 17 hits, walked four and struck out two in the loss.

Although the rookie's work at first base was unsteady and his substitute pitching weak, his offensive success, as demonstrated by his team leadership in home runs, batting average and slugging (over 100 points higher than any other team starter), all while playing little more than half the season, convinced him that he had earned a spot on the Troy Citys for the 1880 season. To his surprise and disappointment, however, he was released before the last week of the 1879 campaign.

Circumstances suggest that Brouthers' poor defensive play may have been partially caused by factors not related to the rookie's catching and throwing skills, but rather to his relationship with his new manager. About the same time in June that Troy's owners began looking for substitute players (including Brouthers himself), press rumors indicated that they were also seeking a new manager — one who could direct the team while on the field as a player. "It is said that the Troy Citys are after Bob Ferguson, late of the Springfields."[62]

Unlike Horace Phillips, the 34-year-old Ferguson, a Brooklyn native, had an impressive baseball resume, having served as captain of the Brooklyn Atlantics in the 1860s and as a player-manager for two National Association teams in the 1870s. Versatility was his middle name. Baseball's first switch-hitter, he excelled as a defensive player, both as a catcher and at most infield positions. As Captain of the Atlantics nine years earlier, he made baseball history by scoring the winning run in the 11th inning against the touring Cincinnati Red Stockings, thus ending the Reds' 97-game winning streak.

Ferguson and Phillips represented two different approaches to the art of managing, which, like other aspects of the nineteenth-century game, was in a state of transition during major league baseball's first quarter-century. While Ferguson managed from the field as a player, Phillips' role more closely resembled that of today's teams' business manager. There were several successful examples of the latter model, including Frank Bancroft, who managed five National League teams in the 1880s, Jim Mutrie, who led the Giants to successive pennants in 1888 and 1889, and Frank Selee, whose Boston clubs of the 1890s won several championships. Such skippers relegated most on-field decision-making to a team captain. Horace Phillips followed this tradition at Troy, naming pitcher George Bradley to that position.

Contrastively, there were numerous successful player-managers of the Bob Ferguson- mold during the nineteenth century. These included Boston's Harry Wright in the 1870s, the Chicago White Stockings Cap Anson in the 1880s and the Cleveland Spiders' Patsy Tebeau in the 1890s.

By early August 1879, the Troy City trustees had decided that a more

ONE. *The Wappingers Falls Boy: 1858–1880*

hands-on approach was necessary for the team. "Manager H.B. Phillips of the Troy Club has tendered his resignation and Bob Ferguson has been engaged to captain and manage the Troys."[63] Playing third base, Ferguson debuted on August 7 during a 13–9 loss to Providence, and had his first look at young Brouthers, who collected two hits, including the previously mentioned home run over the center field wall at Troy, scored two runs, and made two errors at first base.

From the day Ferguson took control as manager, Brouthers' hitting, as well as his defense, became erratic. Two of the three disastrous outings he experienced in the pitcher's box against Boston occurred during this period, and he suffered through a trio of three-error games at first base. Offensively, he went hitless in six of his last seven games with the club. Such a complete breakdown may simply have been bad luck, but it may also have been caused by other factors.

The new Troy manager and his rookie from Wappingers Falls had radically different personalities. The crusty Ferguson was bad-tempered, had an authoritarian leadership style, and routinely berated players for poor performance. After his sudden death 15 years later at age 49, his *Sporting Life* obituary noted that he was "impulsive, rather quick tempered, and often talked too sharply to his men when irritated."[64]

The young Brouthers, in contrast, was extremely self-conscious and sensitive, characteristics that were exacerbated by the terrible Quigley incident that had occurred two years earlier. On one occasion during his brief stay with the Troy Citys, for example, the rookie burst into song while celebrating with team captain George Bradley, and afterward asked Bradley what he thought of his singing. The veteran responded in a sarcastic but humorous vein, "Dan, your voice needs a very heavy coat of cultivation, at present you sing a good deal like the bird they call the pig."[65] Instead of laughing along with Bradley, Brouthers was mortified at the comment, prompting a sportswriter to observe that he "must be of a very sensitive disposition, if he can not put up with a little joke or two when he knows them to be true."[66]

Several years after Brouthers retired from the major leagues, a former teammate, Art Irwin, commented on how the slugger's sensitive nature had affected him once while playing for Boston.

> One of the most sensitive ball tossers that ever brooded over a knock or criticism was Dan Brouthers. Dan Brouthers played first base for our [American] Association team in 1891. He had an awfully yellow day in the game against the Browns, and two muffs [errors] of thrown balls by him cost us a game, if one player can lose a game. [Boston sportswriter and former first baseman] Tim Murnane came out with a shot at Dan [in the *Boston Globe*] the next morning, and among

other flowery things suggested that Dan needed hinges on his knees and a new set of Gray [sic] matter. "I knew that stiff was a knocker," said Dan. "What did I ever do to him that he should set his hammer at me ... I'm hanged if I'll play another game in this city." Dan kept his word so far as that week was concerned. That roast came out Tuesday and he laid off for the rest of the week.[67]

Brouthers' reaction to the first of these incidents, which took place in his rookie year when he was just 21, is perhaps understandable, given his age and inexperience. As a 33-year-old, 13-year major league veteran, however, his response to the Murnane criticism in the *Boston Globe* demonstrates the persistence of his extreme sensitivity, even after years of playing experience. These examples suggest that after playing day-to-day for the genial Horace Phillips, who watched the games from the grandstand, Brouthers might have struggled significantly under authoritarian player-manager Bob Ferguson, who was known for fiercely and openly criticizing his players when they made errors, performed erratically, or failed to produce at the plate.

Disappointed by Horace Phillips' departure and intimidated by Ferguson's dictatorial demeanor, the rookie played poorly in his last month on the team. He certainly wished he were playing elsewhere, and news from Baltimore suggested that such an option might be forthcoming. Although Troy newspapers reported that deposed manager Phillips would spend the rest of the season umpiring, a week after his Troy departure the *Clipper* noted that "H. B. Phillips has taken Myers and Shetsline of the [Philadelphia] Athletics to Baltimore with him, where he is to manage a nine for the remainder of the season. The Athletics are very indignant at the action of the Troy's ex-manager."[68] The speed with which Phillips organized a team in Baltimore suggests that he had been planning the move for some time, and perhaps even hinted at his plans to Troy players before his departure.

A month later, after his original Baltimore financial backers pulled their money out of the new team, Phillips, undaunted, announced that the club had decided to continue "on the co-operative" plan (sharing expenses and revenues),[69] and would do a northern tour in late September to end the season, visiting Philadelphia, Jersey City, and Poughkeepsie. These sites were carefully chosen by "Hustling Horace" as locations where he might continue to recruit more players (including Brouthers, who was a stone's throw from Poughkeepsie, at Wappingers Falls) for Baltimore's 1880 season. Showing the supreme confidence that was his hallmark, Phillips then named H. C. Myers, who earlier had deserted the Athletics to join him in Baltimore, as captain and manager of the as yet non-existent 1880 team. He then reported that prominent Baltimore citizens had vowed to put the new club in the National

ONE. *The Wappingers Falls Boy: 1858–1880*

Association (not to be confused with the 1871–1875 National Association, which was a major league; the 1880 NA was not a major).

In early spring 1880, Phillips' marketing skills were once again evident in two letters that he posted to the *Clipper*, communications that the New York City paper dutifully published. The first announced that he was still seeking recruits for his team, and asked several players, including Providence's Bobby Mathews, Troy's C. E. Reilley and Dennis Brouthers, to contact him at once, indicating "their very lowest terms."[70] The second, a week later, further signaled to the baseball world that he was now negotiating with several players, including catcher Pat Deasley and Dennis Brouthers, and indicated that that "the majority have already signed contracts."[71] A short time later he revealed that he had secured membership for the team in the National Association.

Phillips new Baltimore club, now with Dennis Brouthers holding down first base, began 1880 with a pre-season northern exhibition tour. Besides scheduling games with Association rivals on the trip, the unflappable Phillips had arranged contests with three National League teams, including the Troy club from which he had resigned the previous year. Offensively, Dennis Brouthers continued where he left off the previous year (prior to the arrival of Bob Ferguson at Troy). It was his surprisingly good fielding, however, that now drew press notice. After a 12-inning, 4–2 loss to Worcester, in which he contributed a double and recorded 21 putouts, it was noted that "Brouthers and [short stop] John Richmond excelled in fielding for the visitors."[72]

At Troy on April 20 and 21, the newly-minted Baltimores were soundly whipped, 21–1 and 9–6, by Bob Ferguson's team, which now featured two future Hall of Famers: pitcher Mickey Welch and infielder Roger Connor. Brouthers collected three hits in the two contests, including a double, and committed an error in the second game. In the surprise of the spring, the unheralded Baltimores then caught the reigning National League champion Providence Grays napping, defeating them on their home grounds, 4–1, on April 28. Brouthers played errorless ball at first and did most of the offensive damage, contributing three hits, including a double. Upon the team's return to Baltimore, his torrid hitting was touted in the press. "Brouthers led the batting averages by a large majority in the Baltimore northern trip."[73]

The Baltimores officially opened the National Association's season at home on May 14 with a 17–16 win over Albany, led by Dennis Brouthers, who collected four hits and scored three runs. Albany's starter, Tim Keefe, who soon would transfer to Bob Ferguson's Troy team, was at the beginning of a long, successful career in which he would record 342 wins and ultimately earn a plaque at Cooperstown. He was relieved late in the contest by another legendary player, Lip Pike, a star of the 1860s and 1870s, whose nickname, the "Iron Batter," hinted at his fame, and who at this juncture was in the twilight of his career.

Although Brouthers' fine playing continued, his team and the National Association were in deep financial trouble. Predictably, Horace Phillips was one of the first to see the handwriting on the wall. On June 1, citing owner interference, he resigned his position at Baltimore and promptly headed north, with the intention of forming yet another team. "Phillips claims several of the [Baltimore club] directors wanted to 'run the machine.' He is now in Rochester, NY, where he expects to manage a club."[74]

In the same fashion as he had in Baltimore, Phillips, with the financial help of Rochester patent-medicine mogul Asa Sole, seemingly pulled a new team out of the air. In just a week, his new club, the Rochester Hop Bitters (named after owner Sole's successful elixir), played its first game, temporarily assisted by the participation of several Rochester University players. Just as it had with Dennis Brouthers at Baltimore, Phillips' slick talk and promises convinced another young future star and future Hall of Fame inductee, catcher/infielder Buck Ewing, to leave his semi-pro Cincinnati Buckeyes team and join the new Rochester nine.

Brouthers barnstormed with the Baltimore squad until the National Association disbanded on June 28, and then joined Phillips in Rochester, bringing along four of his Baltimore teammates. If the naive first baseman had any hopes that his erstwhile manager had finally settled down with the intention of finishing the season with the same club, such hopes soon would be dashed.

With the demise of the National Association, the Rochesters barnstormed in Massachusetts and New York State, playing former Association rivals, National League teams like Worcester and Buffalo, and even traveling to Canada to play the Guelph nine, previously a member of the defunct International Association. Brouthers averaged a hit a game in these contests and connected for two home runs, both against Buffalo. In the second of these contests, on July 12, his four-bagger "won the game for the Rochesters."[75]

A death blow was dealt the Hop Bitters in late July, however, when manager Phillips abandoned the team, absconding with the remainder of the club's meager financial assets, a sum of approximately $1,400. The desperate Rochesters, now broke and leaderless, scheduled a series of games at the Union Grounds in Brooklyn against their former National Association rivals, the Washington Nationals.

After four games played before dwindling Brooklyn crowds, games in which Brouthers banged out five hits, a group from the Rochester nine, including Buck Ewing and Brouthers, devised a new plan of action designed to see them through the waning weeks of the season. They joined another rag-tag group of players from other disbanded teams, formed a new nine, and headed for Troy with the intention of putting on exhibition games at the Troy Citys' home grounds while the team was on a late-season western tour. Their hope was to secure a tryout with the National League squad on its return. "A nine including Larkin, pitcher, Ewing, catcher, Brouthers, Briody and Sharpe on the bases, Ahern, shortstop, with Latham, Harbridge and Higham in the outfield, will play amateur games under the auspices of the Troy club during the absence of the latter professional team."[76] Strictly speaking, these were not *amateur* contests as reported in the *Clipper*, since the custom in Troy was to invite semi-pro teams to play games on the Troy Citys' home grounds at a reduced admission price while the National League club was on a Western tour.

A year after being released by Troy, Brouthers, thanks to Horace Phillips, was now reduced to trying to catch on again with crusty manager Ferguson. Seven of the nine players who had made the trek to Troy, including Brouthers, were given tryouts during the team's final home games. Only one, Buck Ewing, managed to get a contract with Troy for the following year.

Playing three games on the opposite side of the infield from his bogeyman, third baseman Ferguson at Troy, Brouthers once again collapsed, committing three errors. Although he had been hitting splendidly under trying circumstances during the month after Horace Phillips' desertion from the Hop Bitters, he could now summon none of that skill to impress Ferguson, and managed just two singles in 12 at-bats for a .167 average. At season's end, no one needed to inform him that he would not be invited back to Troy for the 1881 season.

The fates played another cruel trick on young Brouthers just after his tryout with Troy began. As one of its regular sports features each week, the *Clipper* published a brief biography and an accompanying line-drawing portrait of current baseball notables, including managers, owners, established stars and up-and-coming players. In late August, 1880, Dennis Brouthers was the *Clipper*'s featured player. Noting that he was "recently re-engaged by the Troys,"[77] the short article reviewed his prior playing experience and offered a detailed description of his physical proportions: "He is over six feet in height, with massive limbs of such magnitude and muscle that in good condition, without an ounce of superfluous flesh about him, he weighs over 200 lbs."[78] The *Clipper*'s evaluation of the rookie's first base play was more guarded: "Although not the most graceful in style, he is still an uncommonly useful man to have at that position."[79]

By the time some readers had a chance to review this assessment in the *Clipper*, the first baseman's tryout with Troy was already over. It would be a long winter for Brouthers back home in Wappingers Falls, especially after the embarrassment of being having first been praised in an important New York City paper and then given his second release by Troy.

The first chapter of Dennis Brouthers' long baseball career bears a strong resemblance to the plot of a melodramatic Victorian novel. It is the tale of a sensitive young lad of modest circumstances and as yet modest abilities, who attempts to make his way in the baseball world. He finds his progress impeded, however, first by a wily shyster and future madman (Horace Phillips), and then by an imperious, intimidating personality (Bob Ferguson). Despite such trying circumstances, young Dennis Brouthers, like the classic Dickensian hero, soon would transcend such impediments and emerge as "the champion batsman of the country,"[80] the "terror of all pitchers,"[81] and the "mighty Irish King"[82] of the national pastime.

Two

The Champion Batsman of the Country: 1881–1885

> Brouthers is the great home run man. —*Buffalo Daily Courier*, July 30, 1881

Years after Dennis Brouthers retired from the major leagues, an anonymous reporter, described as "one of baseball's historians,"[1] declared that after the young slugger's release by Troy in 1880, he was ready to give up baseball. "After Brouthers had failed with the Troy club he went back home to his old job of laying sewer pipe, resolved to quit the game for good."[2] Nothing could have been further from the truth. In the spring of 1881, Brouthers was covering first base for a new professional team in New York, not digging ditches in Wappingers Falls.

During his first tryout with Troy in 1879, Brouthers briefly made the acquaintance of "Honest John" Kelly, a light-hitting backup catcher who played in a few games for both the Syracuse Stars and Troy that year. Troy manager Bob Ferguson may not have been impressed with Brouthers at the time, but Kelly was. In March 1881, news broke that Kelly, a New York City native, had organized a new team in the Big Apple, one that planned to compete with a second new club, the Metropolitan, for the favor of the city's fans.

Kelly's team was at a disadvantage even before the season started, since the Metropolitan club already had a season under its belt, and would play its games at the convenient Polo Grounds, at 5th Avenue and 110th Street in Manhattan, which had been converted to a baseball venue the previous fall. Kelly's fledgling New Yorks, in contrast, were forced to look elsewhere for a location to play their "home" contests.

> New York will be represented this season on the ball field by two first-class nines, the Metropolitan and the New York, the latter being the name of a professional

team recently organized by John Kelly, formerly catcher of the Flyaways of this city.... He will catch for the nine.... The ground has not been selected, but will probably be the Union [Grounds], Brooklyn. Arrangements are also being made for the professional nine to play two days each week at Newark, New Jersey, provided a suitable inclosed [sic] ground can be obtained.[3]

Commenting on the team's roster in April, the *Clipper* introduced a new spelling for Dennis's surname when it announced that "Brothers, the big batsman, will play for the New York Club."[4]

Brouthers spent only a few weeks on the New Yorks, averaging more than a hit a game. On May 5, he returned to the pitcher's box, losing 17–13. to the Brooklyn Atlantics. "In the absence of Leary, who at his special request was engaged by the Metropolitan club, Brouthers pitched and Sweeny caught for the New Yorkers."[5] A few days later, Kelly's club gave up the ghost as a Manhattan team and announced it was moving to Hoboken. Unaccountably, it

Dan Brouthers, Buffalo Bisons, 1882. In his first full big league season, Brouthers led the National League in batting, slugging, on-base percentage and hits. Early in the season, the league experimented briefly with player uniforms by assigning a different color or pattern shirt and hat to each field position. Here Brouthers wears the red and white stripes of a first baseman. The new uniforms, unpopular with both players and fans, were discarded by mid-season (National Baseball Hall of Fame Library, Cooperstown, New York).

Two. *The Champion Batsman of the Country: 1881–1885* 29

also changed its name to the Jersey City Browns. Aware of the team's planned departure to New Jersey, Brouthers transferred to the team against whom he had recently pitched. "Brouthers ... late of the New York Club, will hereafter play with the Atlantics of Brooklyn."⁶

In the midst of this new cycle of professional uncertainty that must have seemed eerily familiar to Brouthers, word arrived of the return of a well-known figure to the baseball scene. Having made restitution to Rochester Hop Bitters' owner Asa Sole for the funds he stole from the team, Horace Phillips was back in the game, and once again looking to sign Dennis Brouthers. "Baseball in Philadelphia seems to be booming. The Athletics have secured the exclusive use of Oakdale Park for four days each week.... Brouthers and Hayes of the Brooklyn Atlantics are wanted by the Athletics to strengthen them. All communication for the Athletics should be addressed to H. P. Phillips, Manager, 258. N. Ninth St., Philadelphia."⁷

Fortunately, Brouthers could no longer be seduced by Phillips' powers of persuasion. After playing a few games for the Atlantics, he received and accepted an offer from Buffalo's National League team. The Bisons remembered him well from the previous season, when they had scheduled three exhibition games with regional rival Rochester during Brouthers' stay with the team. Buffalo lost all three contests, thanks in great part to Brouthers, who scored five runs in the Hop Bitters' victories and contributed seven hits, including a double and two home runs.

The Bisons' new manager, Jim O'Rourke, had a simple plan for winning ballgames: "overwhelm opponents with heavy hitting."⁸ Seeking to implement this strategy, Buffalo hired the man whose bat had made the team look so bad the previous season. "The Buffalos have engaged Brouthers, late of the Atlantics, to play first base. He will strengthen the nine at the bat."⁹

Buffalo was a newcomer on the professional scene, having fielded its first pro team in 1877. The Bisons won the pennant the following year in the short-lived International Association, thanks to the splendid pitching of rubber-armed rookie Jim "Pud" Galvin. "It is doubtful if any pitcher in baseball history ... had a year to match Galvin's 1879 iron-man performance. Of the total 116 league and non-league games played by the Bisons, he pitched in 101, of which 96 were complete. He won 72 games, lost 25, and tied three."¹⁰ Over the course of the next 14 seasons, Galvin registered 364 victories, becoming the first pitcher to reach the 300-win plateau. He was elected to the Hall of Fame in 1965. Player/manager Jim O'Rourke had transferred to Buffalo from Boston for the 1881 season, bringing with him Irish-born Curry Foley, a talented utility player who hit .292 for the Red Caps in 1880. He also lured 34-year-old veteran Jim White, a .330 hitter for Cincinnati in 1880, back to

Buffalo Bisons' Team Photo, 1882. Four future Hall of Famers appear in the photograph: Jim O'Rourke, center, Jim "Pud" Galvin, to the right of O'Rourke, Dan Brouthers, below and to the left of Galvin, and Jim "Deacon" White, below and to the right of Brouthers (National Baseball Hall of Fame Library, Cooperstown, New York).

his home state. White, known as "the Deacon" for his abstemious personal habits, had primarily been used by the Reds as a catcher, but he could also play the infield and outfield well.

In addition to pitcher Galvin, the returning Bisons included infielders Jack Rowe and Hardy Richardson, both of whom had made their professional debuts with the team in 1879, and light-hitting, slick-fielding veteran infielder "Wee Davy" Force, who at 5' 4" was one of the smallest men ever to play major league baseball. Within a few years, an infield consisting of White, Richardson, Rowe and Brouthers would become known nationally as "The Big Four" while playing for the Detroit Wolverines.

Burly and loquacious, "Orator" Jim O'Rourke hailed from Bridgeport, Connecticut, and in his day sported baseball's most impressive Victorian handlebar moustache. A multi-position player with a lifetime batting average of .310, he started his professional career with Boston in 1872, and did not hang up his spikes until 1909. In the intervening quarter-century, he played on two championship Giants teams, earned a law degree from Yale University, and founded the Connecticut League, where he played and managed for years. O'Rourke made baseball history twice. In 1876 he became the first man to get a hit in a National League game. Twenty-eight years later, at age 54, he became the oldest man to collect a hit in a major league contest, after John McGraw invited him to catch a game for the Giants in 1904. Orator Jim was elected to the Hall of Fame in 1945, the same year in which his 1881 Buffalo recruit, Dennis Brouthers, received his Cooperstown plaque.

Despite reports that Dennis Brouthers would play first base for the Bisons, Jim O'Rourke had promised the position to Curry Foley as a condition for joining him on the Buffalo nine. Consequently, Brouthers spent his first 35 games either in left or right field, positions he had never previously covered. He made his first appearance as a Bison in right field at Providence on May 30. Batting third in the order, he collected a single in four at-bats and played errorless ball in the field. On June 9, ten days after joining the team, both his hitting and fielding proved crucial in a 13-inning, 1–0 win over Boston. "Brouthers was the hero of the day, as, besides making the only run on a [after a] terrific three-bagger [and then scoring on a Hardy Richardson sacrifice], he effected a wonderful running catch, scooping the sphere with his left hand before it touched the ground, and thereby preventing the Bostons from scoring at least two runs."[11] The hometown *Buffalo Daily Courier*'s comments on the game proved prophetic: "Brouthers was due to find the ball, and in yesterday's game he arrived."[12]

Brouthers indeed had arrived offensively, but not defensively. By the end of June he was hitting .302 for the Bisons, but fielding just .842 in the outfield.[13] Success at the plate tended to make the press overlook his weak defense. After he committed three errors in left field but went 2-for-5 at the plate in an 8–7 win against Chicago on July 19, the *Clipper*'s only comment was that "Brouthers made a wonderful double play by catching a difficult fly with one [bare] hand while running backward."[14]

Brouthers might have had difficulty playing for Bob Ferguson when he was at Troy, but he had no problem playing against him. His first home run as a Bison came in a ten-inning, 8–7 win against Ferguson's Troy Citys. Playing errorless ball in his debut against his former team and manager, he also contributed a triple. A week later against Boston at Buffalo's Riverside Park, he recorded his first home-field four-bagger as a Bison, an inside-the-park blast, when he "hit the ball down to the roller in right and made a circuit of the bases."[15]

Although there were exceptions, as we shall see, most National League parks in Brouthers' era were cavernous affairs, particularly in the left and right field power alleys and in dead center field. Consequently, inside-the-park home runs were more common than today. Over the course of Brouthers' career, 21 of his total of 107 four-baggers were inside-the-park hits. Responding in a 1931 interview to a question about the number of home runs he hit in his career, he noted that there were plenty of the inside-the-park variety in his total. "There were so many of 'em [home runs] I can't remember ... but I do remember I did some running to beat the ball home. No walking around the bases when I was a young feller."[16] Due to his size, Brouthers typically was stereotyped by the press of his era as a slow runner. His 21 inside-the-park home runs and 25 steals per year average (achieved after the steal became an official statistic in the last half of his career) demonstrate that the opposite in fact was true.

Brouthers' most impressive display of power hitting in 1881 came during a three-game series at Detroit at the end of July, when he slugged a home run in each game. The first two came off Frank Mountain on July 28 and 29. The third was hit off George Derby on July 30. This feat, rare in any era but virtually unheard-of in that decade, even earned him high praise from the hometown Detroit fans: "The applause which greeted Brouthers' third home run, his third in the three games just played, was something tremendous. He was voted the best batsman in the country."[17] In a few years he would receive similar accolades from the Detroit fans, but on those occasions he would be wearing a Detroit uniform.

After he was switched to first base in mid–August, where he spent the remainder of the season, Brouthers' defense steadied and his hot hitting continued. Now more comfortable in the field, he raised his batting average to .319 and continued to draw notice for his long-ball hitting, including

Two. *The Champion Batsman of the Country: 1881–1885*

four-baggers against Chicago (9/9), Boston (9/27), and Philadelphia (10/10), and one in an exhibition game against the Newark Domestics (10/7). His performance both in the field and at the plate prompted the *Buffalo Daily Courier*, disappointed with the Bisons' overall 1881 play, to affirm that "Brouthers is about the only reliable man on our alleged ball club."[18] And reliable he was, finishing first in the league in home runs (8), slugging (.541), and extra-base hits (35), and eighth in hitting (.319).

Except with regard to defense, it is difficult to fathom the Buffalo press's near-blanket criticism of the Bisons' 1881 performance. Under Jim O'Rourke's leadership the team moved up from fifth to third place in the standings, and while they placed last in fielding, they ranked second in hitting. Pud Galvin won 28 games and registered a 2.37 ERA. In addition to Dan Brouthers' league-leading home run and slugging numbers, Jack Rowe hit .333, Hardy Richardson and Deacon White tied for fourth in RBI (53), Jim O'Rourke ranked fourth in runs (71), and Davy Force led the circuit's bare-handed second basemen in fielding (.937).

Winning the 1878 International Association pennant in Buffalo's second year as a professional club had apparently led to unrealistic expectations on the part of fans, owners and the Buffalo press after the team joined the ranks of the more competitive National League. Despite compiling a 206–169 won-lost record and finishing third in the league three times between 1881 and 1884, the club would be sold by its owners at the end of the 1885 season. Sportswriter Sam Crane, who had played for the Bisons in 1880, offered a simple explanation for the team's ultimate demise: "Buffalo failed to support their team.... I have frequently seen assemblages at games there of not more than ten people."[19]

Brouthers' spectacular turnabout in his first year with the Bisons coincided with the beginning of a transformative era in major league baseball. In the dozen years from 1881 and 1893, more changes occurred in playing regulations and more attempts were made to challenge the dominant organizational structure of the game than at any other time in the sport's history.

On the field, the pitcher's new role as a primary rather than a secondary participant in the game's action led to a series of rules that sought to strike a balance of power between him and the batter. Hitters got an advantage when the distance between home plate and the pitcher's box was increased, first to 50 feet (1882), then to 55 feet (1887) and finally to 60' 6" (1893). As compensation to the pitcher, the sidearm motion (1883) and then the overhand motion (1884) were legalized.

The number of strikes and balls was finally standardized to three and four respectively in 1889. Prior to that, the batter gained an advantage for a single year (1887) when four strikes were required for a strikeout and walks counted as hits. The pitcher, however, had the luxury of being able to throw as many as eight balls before a walk was issued. That number was reduced to four in 1889. Batters could request either a low or high pitch until 1887. Afterward, the strike zone doubled, becoming the area from the top of the shoulders to the bottom of the knees.

No fielders other than the pitcher, catcher and an occasional first baseman were using any type of hand protection in 1881. By 1893, players were using gloves at all positions. Stolen bases were officially recognized in 1886, and the "sacrifice hit" became part of the official record in 1889. From 1889 to 1893, ground balls, fly balls and bunts on which runners advanced counted as sacrifices, but they also counted as a time at bat.

Baseball's organizational structure was changing as fast at the rules in the game changed. Player, fan, and potential-franchise-owner dissatisfaction with the National League's monopoly reached the boiling point between 1881 and 1890. Since 1880, the league's best players had been frustrated in their efforts to increase their salary or sell their services to other teams due to the Reserve Clause, a league requirement stipulating that once a player signed with a team, he was bound to it until he was released. Initially, five players per team — each club's best men — were reserved. By 1885, that number was increased to 12, or virtually a team's entire roster.

In 1882, a group of entrepreneurs, including the seemingly ubiquitous Horace Phillips, capitalized on player frustration over the Reserve Clause by establishing a rival six-team league, the American Association, offering comparatively lucrative salaries to National League players who would agree to jump their league contracts. To entice fans, the Association set admission at 25 cents, half that of the National League, and permitted the sale of liquor at games. Even though the Association itself soon acquiesced to the Reserve Clause, it successfully challenged the National League for a decade, and in its final season, 1891, its Boston club signed then-veteran Dennis Brouthers, who led the Red Caps to the Association's last pennant by finishing first in batting average (.350), slugging (.512) and on-base percentage (.471).

Opposition to the Reserve Clause during the period found a staunch supporter in the person of Henry V. Lucas, an amateur Ohio player and son of a wealthy railroad baron, who established the Union League in 1884. It lasted just one season before collapsing.

The last nineteenth-century effort to wrest control of players' destinies from team owners occurred in 1890, with the birth of the aptly-named but ill-fated Players' League, which was controlled by players and their financial backers. Like the Union League, it lasted just a year. As we shall see, beginning

Two. *The Champion Batsman of the Country: 1881–1885*

in 1885, Dennis Brouthers was active in a players' union, the Brotherhood of Professional Baseball Players, which conceived and implemented the Players' League in 1890, and Brouthers' .330 batting average for Boston's Players' League club that year helped power the team to the league's only pennant.

Many players could not adapt to the swift pace of change in baseball during the 1880s, and fell by the wayside. Dennis Brouthers, the insecure, inconsistent player of 1880, not only survived the game's transformations over the next dozen years, but thrived amid the chaos of new rules and competing leagues, becoming recognized nationally as the game's greatest hitter.

No returning Buffalo players were tempted by salary offers from the new American Association in 1882, and the team's only significant acquisition was 35-year-old pitcher Hugh "One Arm" Daily, who was purchased from the independent Metropolitan club. In picking up Daily, the team was acknowledging the new trend of trying to conserve the ace pitcher's arm (in this case, Pud Galvin's) by employing a two-man rotation. Ironically, due to the Reserve Rule supported by Buffalo's owners, the team found it impossible to attract quality, experienced pitchers who were currently employed by the league. Given this state of affairs, they took a chance on Hugh Daily.

Known for his "profane outbursts toward the opposition, umpires, fans and teammates,"[20] the irascible Daily had lost his left hand as a teenager after being shot in the wrist. Although there was nothing wrong with Daily's left arm above the wrist, the press liked the sound of One Arm Daily better than One Hand Daily. The pitcher's physical deformity, bad temper, and blazing fastball could intimidate the steadiest hitter. "His stump covered with leather and secured with straps, he leaned into each batter menacingly, cursing and rolling the ball along his truncated arm.... Daily used a windmill-like double motion, the pitch coming in on the second arm swing and coinciding with a quick short stride at the plate."[21] In addition to his use of psychological intimidation, Daily was not above violating the underhand pitch rule, which would not be rescinded until the following year. "No sooner was the game started than the crowd began to jeer and hoot at Daily for having his arm raised above his hip."[22]

Daily probably would have made the roster of a major league team much earlier in his career were it not for a playing rule, in force until 1890, which prohibited lineup substitutions except in the case of a disabling injury to a player. This meant that if Daily needed to be relieved in a game, another member of the team *on the field* would be required to take his place, with Daily in turn substituting for that individual at his position. Teams understandably were unwilling to have a one-armed man in the field in the event that he was hit hard in the box and had to be replaced.[23]

After getting off to a decent start with Buffalo (14–9), Daily broke his middle finger when "struck by a hit ball"[24] in late July. He returned to the box in early August, too soon for his finger to have healed properly, and after winning just one game and losing three, did not pitch again in the last six weeks of the season. This left Pud Galvin as the team's only pitcher, and he dutifully worked in 20 of the teams last 23 contests, being relieved only three times by outfielder Blondie Purcell.

Dennis Brouthers served notice in the first game of 1882, a home field exhibition contest in April against a team from Delaware, that his previous year's performance was no fluke. Batting third in the lineup behind Blondie Purcell and Jim O'Rourke, he collected five hits in five trips to the plate, including a home run, "an immense drive over the lower right hand corner of the fence."[25] After a decent but unspectacular start during the first two weeks of the regular season, the impatient Buffalo press exhorted Brouthers, "Come Dan, show yourself."[26] This May 18 press plea was the first known instance in which the Wappingers Falls slugger was referred to as *Dan*. How *Dennis* evolved into *Dan* is open to conjecture, but the most logical assumption is that a shortened form of "Dennis" ("Den") gradually morphed into Dan. Regardless of its origin, the new first name was the one by which the slugger would be best known from that day forward.

Brouthers dutifully heeded the call to action from the Buffalo press, reeling off 17 hits in the next seven games, and by mid–June he was hitting .354. Overall, however, the team was in poor form, and after a road trip in which they lost a series to Providence and were swept by lowly Troy, the *Buffalo Daily Courier* lamented that "The Unchangeables, otherwise known as the Buffalo base ball club, are indeed a sorry sight to look upon."[27] Meanwhile, Brouthers' torrid power hitting continued. At Philadelphia in June, his home run over the right-center field fence was declared "the longest hit ever made on the grounds."[28] A month later, his four-bagger in the eighth inning at Detroit was described similarly as "one of the longest hits ever seen on the grounds."[29]

These efforts, however, pale in comparison to his performance in an exhibition game against the Philadelphia Quakers in Philadelphia on August 5. The Quakers would enter the National League in 1883 as the Phillies, and they spent the 1882 season preparing for their entry by scheduling games with current members of the league. Their home field, Recreation Park, was an anomaly, given its extremely short fences — 300' down the line in left field, 331' in center, and a short 247' down the line in right. Hitting there, however, was not as easy as it may appear, since the sun shone directly in the batter's eyes during regularly scheduled (afternoon) games, and the white outfield

Two. *The Champion Batsman of the Country: 1881–1885*   37

fences made it difficult for the hitter to pick up the ball coming out of the pitcher's hand."[30] Sometime after Brouthers' first home run there in June, the park adjusted its ground rules by requiring that every hit over the fence count as a double.

In the Bisons' 14–3 win against Philadelphia on August 5, Brouthers collected four doubles, three of which left the grounds. One of them would probably have cleared any fence in the country by a wide margin.

> Brouthers' big batting was the feature of the contest. He made four two-baggers, and knocked the ball over the fence three times. His last hit was the longest and highest ever seen on the ground, and probably the longest ever made. The ball went over the centre-field fence, fully one hundred feet above it, and landed far away in the vacant lots beyond the ball ground.[31]

The *Buffalo Daily Courier* added a descriptive detail of the towering blow: "One of his [Brouthers'] hits went over the center field fence higher than any spire of the little brick church nearby. It was the longest hit ever made on the grounds."[32] Reminiscing about the home run in 1897, Brouthers added a further detail. He affirmed that not only did the ball sail *as high* as the spire of the nearby church, but that its trajectory actually took it *over* the spire.[33]

Still marveling at this long home run nearly 30 years later, veteran Philadelphia sportswriter Frank L. Hough paid tribute to Brouthers:

> The old-time first baseman and swatter, whose drive over the little church on the other side of that old horse market ground [Recreation Park] is still the talk of the fans who were chasing the game up in the early 80s. That drive went over the roof of a church, struck the pavement a block above, caromed into the north-bound car track and rolled up the gate of West Laurel Hill Cemetery, being subsequently returned to the ground by a drayman.[34]

Brouthers' outstanding 1882 offensive performance was matched by an equally outstanding year in the field. Gone was the error-prone Troy player of three years earlier. In his first full season as a Bison, Brouthers played more games at first base than anyone in the league, and his .974 fielding percentage bested all others at the position.

When the pitching distance was increased from 45 to 50 feet in 1882, it was assumed that batting averages would rise around the league. With the exception of Brouthers, however, the veteran heavy hitters for the Bisons all saw a precipitous drop in their averages. Jack Rowe plunged from .333 to .266, and Richardson, White and O'Rourke saw their marks fall by an average of 23 points. The only two possible explanations for this anomaly are that the remaining Bisons all just had a bad year, or that most hitters were having trouble timing a ball pitched from a greater distance.

The team's overall offensive decline, the failure to find a consistent second pitcher to relieve Jim Galvin, and a horrendous schedule that kept the team on the road for the month of August, all prevented Buffalo from finishing higher than its 1881 third-place ranking. With the team mired in fifth place in late July, the *Buffalo Daily Courier* suggested that the team's poor performance was due to heavy drinking among the players. "We do not threaten, but only say that the Buffalos are paid to play and not to get drunk."[35] Brouthers, leading the league in hitting, was not implicated.

Buffalo team owners did little to improve their reputation around the league when they succeeded in transferring the team's final three home games against Chicago to their opponent's grounds in order to make greater profits there than at home (in the era, visiting teams shared game receipts). Chicago, locked in a tight battle for the pennant with Providence, swept the Bisons and secured the championship.

The performance of 24-year-old Dennis Brouthers, who was now increasingly known as Dan Brouthers, was the highlight of the 1882 Buffalo season. In his breakout year, he led the league in batting average (.368), slugging (.547), on-base percentage (.403), total bases (192) and hits (129), and tied for second in home runs (6). One sign of his growing national prominence was an invitation to barnstorm after the season's end with a "combination" team of veterans that included George Gore, Silver Flint and Mike Kelly from Chicago, and Providence's Jack Farrell. The team played a series of games in Philadelphia, Boston, Saint Louis and New Orleans.

As the 1882 season drew to a close, the Wappingers Falls slugger could reflect on how far his career had advanced in such a brief period of time. Just two years earlier he was released by Troy after his second tryout with the team. Now he was the champion batsman of the National League and one of the game's star players.

Although Buffalo maintained its winning ways in the 1883 and 1884 seasons, posting respective won-lost percentages of .536 and .577, the team could make no headway in the league standings, finishing fifth the first year and then third. Superior pitching made the difference for the teams that outpaced the Bisons during these years. Boston won 33 of its last 44 games to take the 1883 pennant, led by the strong arms of Jim Whitney and Charlie Buffinton, who combined for 62 wins. The following year, Providence's Old Hoss Radbourn defied the convention of the two-man rotation, leading the Rhode Island nine to the 1884 pennant with 59 wins, striking out 441 batters and posting a 1.38 ERA.

Buffalo experimented with eight different pitchers in tandem with Jim Galvin in 1883, but combined, they managed only six wins against 16 losses. Galvin performed heroically, appearing in 76 games, pitching 656⅓ innings,

Two. *The Champion Batsman of the Country: 1881–1885*

and compiling a 46–29 record with a 2.72 ERA. Despite the fact that most of the team recovered from its 1882 batting slump, the Bisons' total reliance on Galvin's arm and their horrible away record (16–32), the second worst in the league, sealed their fate as they slipped to fifth in the standings.

In 1883, Dan Brouthers became the first player to lead his league in hitting (.374) and slugging (.572) in consecutive years. He also led the league in hits (159), triples (17), and RBI (97), and was the only Bison to play in every game (98). While his home run count dropped to three (New York's Buck Ewing led the league with ten), his slugging average was little affected, since he pounded out 61 extra-base hits in 98 games and had nearly three dozen multiple-hit contests, including eight three-hit and two four-hit efforts.

Against Philadelphia on July 19, Brouthers became the seventh man in baseball history to connect for six hits in a game, slapping out two doubles and four singles and scoring three runs in a lopsided 25–5 victory. His diminutive Buffalo teammate, Davy Force (a lifetime .249 hitter) was the first man to accomplish the feat, while playing for the Philadelphia Athletics in 1876. One of Brouthers' home runs, hit in the last week of the 1883 season, was another inside-the-park special. "Brouthers distinguished himself by landing on the first ball pitched in the fourth for one of the longest drives made inside of the fence [in Boston] this season, clear to the right field corner, the ball reaching the plate instantly after the runner had crossed it."[36]

In early August, Brouthers was involved in an unusual defensive play against Providence. "Sweeney was put out at first in one of the Buffalo-Providence games last week by the ball lodging in Brouthers' shirt. It was thrown badly by [Davy] Force, and but for the accident an error would have been charged the shortstop. Strange things happen on the diamond."[37] This would not be the last time that the young first baseman would have a ball hidden on his person during a game. On other occasions, as we shall see, it was an intended subterfuge, not an accidental one, for in his era he was the foremost practitioner of the "hidden ball" trick. "Probably no man in the business ever attempted that play so often and got away with it [was successful with it] as big Dan Brouthers."[38]

Brouthers' quiet, unobtrusive demeanor, which tended to lull the runner into a false sense of security, helped contribute to his success with the play. His sheer size was also an asset. Since he fielded gloveless in his early years in the game, and any hand protection he wore later at first base was fingerless and pocketless, the only place he could hide the ball was under one of his massive arms.[39] In the gloveless era, only a man with a physique like his could be successful in making a baseball seem to disappear on his person long enough to catch an inattentive runner off base.

As his fame grew, the press began to christen Brouthers with colorful nicknames that emphasized his size, power, or work ethic. This practice began during his first tryout with the Troy team, when the *Buffalo Express* declared him to be "the Goliath of the League."[40] When he joined John Kelly's independent New York team in 1881, the *Clipper* introduced him as "the Big Batsman."[41] After a few successful seasons with Buffalo, the local press coined the expressions "Reliable Dan,"[42] "Big Brouthers,"[43] "The Giant,"[44] and "the Big 'Un"[45] to refer to the young star.

Players in the game that have responded to monikers like Hoss (Radbourn), Dizzy (Dean), Hammerin' Hank (Aaron), Scooter (Rizzuto), and Big Papi (Ortiz) remind us that nicknames have long been a colorful part of baseball. At no time, however, was this custom more prevalent than in the nineteenth century. During Dan Brouthers' career, for example, he regularly played against or alongside players like "One Arm" Daily, "Egyptian" Healy, "Chicken" Wolf, "Icebox" Chamberlain and "Blondie" Purcell. Every player of the period had one or two common or unusual nicknames, but Brouthers, either owing to his curiously named hometown, his physical strength, his good-natured disposition or his hitting prowess, earned over four dozen during the course of his long career. A full listing and chronology of his nicknames appears in Appendix A.

While writers continually talked about Brouthers, the quiet giant rarely talked to them. However, having learned a valuable lesson from Horace Phillips regarding the power of the press to shape public opinion, he occasionally overcame his natural reluctance to speak in order to promote the baseball career of his younger brother, James.

As previously indicated, James Brouthers played alongside his older brother for the Wappingers Falls Actives in the late 1870s. As soon as Dan became well-established in the major leagues — and personally aware of how difficult the route to a professional career could be — he began campaigning to get Jim a baseball contract, even if he had to minimize his own accomplishments in the process. "Dennis Brouthers, the champion League batsman of 1882, has a younger brother who promises to surpass him as a first-baseman and batsman. He is only twenty years old, but has shown rare fielding and batting skills in amateur games in Wappinger Falls, N.Y., their native place."[46]

Thanks to his older brother's intervention, James did make it to the minor leagues, but he subsequently bounced from team to team, rarely lasting more than a season. Whenever he was out of a job, Dan went to bat for him again by sending out more announcements to the press, being sure to include his own name in the process. "Brouthers has a younger brother who can play almost as good a game as Dan himself. He has been with the Albanys, but as they are [now] defunct, he is without a place. He is a first rate shortstop and third baseman."⁴⁷ By the late 1880s, sportswriters had tired of these promotional efforts. "While big Dan is a pretty good man in his place, he does not seem to be able to work his brother in for a cent. This thing of one man floating around on the reputation of another is no good in baseball matters."⁴⁸

Although Dan proved to be a wonderful ally for James, a flaw in the younger Brouthers' character led to the end of his baseball career. After he was released by a Jackson, Michigan, team in 1888, *Sporting Life* noted that "As for [James] Brouthers, he is a good ball player, but his appetite for drink has lost him many a good position and will continue to so long as he keeps it up."⁴⁹

Due to the team's fifth-place finish, Buffalo's attendance fell in 1883, and after a $15,000 total outlay, the franchise's end-of-season ledger listed a $199.60 loss for the year. In November, *Sporting Life* responded to this news by repeating the now familiar opinion that "Buffalo evidently is a poor ball town."⁵⁰

The following year, Buffalo's owners were faced with another financial dilemma — the need for a new ballpark — after the owner of the old grounds at Fargo Avenue and Rhode Island Street informed them he was dividing the site into building lots. A new location at Richmond and Summer Streets was leased for $1,500, and a new grandstand constructed at a cost of $6,000. Such costly but necessary financial outlays only served to heighten management's immediate demand for a profit-making team, a position that ultimately would lead to the franchise's demise.

The effect of the new rule allowing overhand pitching was felt around the league in 1884, with team batting averages falling to an all-time low of .247. The worst was yet to come for hitters, since this new style of delivering the ball would not give rise to its greatest proponents — flamethrowers like Kid Nichols, Amos Rusie and Cy Young — until early in the next decade. Buffalo hitters bucked the trend, hitting .262 (second to Chicago's remarkable .281), but an inability to find a strong second pitcher to spell ace Jim Galvin again kept the team out of contention. Philadelphia-born rookie Billy Serad was the choice for the second starter, but his 16–20 record and 4.27 ERA paled in comparison to Galvin, whose labors in the box resulted in a 46–22 record and a sparkling 1.99 ERA.

Offensively, third-year man Dan Brouthers began where he left off the previous year, but early on a serious illness, either influenza or malaria, kept him out of the lineup for a month. Although his home run production increased to 14 and he again was the league's leading slugger, Brouthers' batting average, still strong at .327, now ranked fifth in the league.

Until his illness struck in early May, he gave signs that he might be a candidate for the home run title as well as the slugging title. He started spring training with a four-bagger against the University of Virginia on April 16, and two days later in Allentown, Pennsylvania, "drew great applause by making two home runs on long hits to right and centre field."[51] At Brooklyn on April 25, "Brouthers opened the match with a clean home run."[52] Three days later at Holyoke, he went 5-for-5 and scored four runs. Three of the hits were home runs, described as "some of the longest hits seen on the grounds."[53] He tripled and doubled in each of the first two games of the regular season against Boston. The second triple on May 2 was achieved by driving the ball "to the flagstaff at the centre field fence,"[54] a distance of approximately 444 feet. The *Cleveland Herald* suggested that the powerful blow was a good luck sign for Buffalo: "Dan Brouthers hit the staff of the Boston pennant with a blow from his bat a few days ago. Is that a favorable omen for Buffalo?"[55]

Two weeks later, as the team prepared to leave on a Western tour, Brouthers complained of chills and fever and was left behind in New York. By the time he recovered, 22 games later, Buffalo was in fifth place. On his return on June 6, he "was too weak to do any effective work,"[56] but by June 14, the *Buffalo Daily Courier* reassured its readers that "Brouthers can strike as hard as ever,"[57] after his triple and home run helped win a game against Cleveland.

Brouthers' round-trippers continued at a measured pace for the remainder of the season. He hit three in July, including two in a game at Cleveland off Jim McCormick. "Especially was big Brouthers on his muscle. He hit mighty ones to the centre field corner, and over the left centre fence, each time the hit yielding four bases."[58] Three homers followed in August, and two more in September. He celebrated the closing of the season by hitting a trio of four-baggers in October, all in Buffalo's final series against Boston. In the last game, he played his first and last game as a third baseman, commiting two errors in the process. "A few changes were made in the positions, just for the fun of the thing. Brouthers took [Jim] White's position on third, while [Hardy] Richardson attended first and [Davy] Force covered second."[59]

While playing his normal position earlier in the season against Chicago, Brouthers surprised White Stockings outfielder Billy Sunday with his now-familiar ploy. "Brouthers, in one of the games with Chicago last week, worked a very old trick on [Billy] Sunday. The latter had made a good base hit and was safe at first. The guileless Daniel had thrown the ball to [pitcher] Serad (in his mind) when Sunday slipped off the bag. Dan jerked the ball from under his arm and touched him out before the Chicago right fielder knew what happened."[60]

Two. *The Champion Batsman of the Country: 1881–1885* 43

Brouthers' persistent hot hitting throughout the 1884 campaign led to the introduction of a new strategy to try to slow him down. In an 18–2 blowout loss to Detroit on June 19, "[Detroit pitcher Frank] Meinke sent Brouthers to first four times out of five yesterday. He was apparently a little afraid of Dan."[61] While renowned baseball historian Peter Morris has provided ample evidence that the intentional base-on-balls was rare in the 1870s and 1880s,[62] exceptions, as we shall see, were frequently made when the hitter in question was the best batsman in the league.

Now an established star with a bright future, Brouthers found a unique way to ring in the new year of 1885. On New Year's Eve, 1884, he married his hometown sweetheart, Mary Ellen Croak, at St. Mary's Catholic Church in Wappingers Falls. Born in Ireland, Mary Ellen was an infant when she arrived in the U.S. in 1860. The Croak family's first stop in America was Rochester, but parents James and Margaret, daughter Mary Ellen, and younger brother William had by the mid–1860s moved to Wappingers Falls, where James found employment at the Dutchess Print Works. Five more Croak children were born in the village. Like Dan, Mary Ellen, who was one year his junior, began work at the Dutchess Print Works after completing grade school. The pair grew up working together there and shared the common cultural and religious values of all Irish immigrants. The marriage was a good match. It lasted 48 years, until Dan's death in August 1932. Mary Ellen followed her husband to the grave two weeks later.

There is no record of Mary Ellen either accompanying her husband while he was on the road or attending a major league game in which he played. She was kept busy at home caring for their four children and assuming responsibility for household affairs during her husband's frequent long absences from home. As a young girl, however, she must have enjoyed joining the rest of the village watching her future husband pitch for the hometown Actives. After the family relocated to Manhattan three decades later, she spent her weekend afternoons proudly watching her son, Addison, play alongside his father on Dan's Manhattan semi-pro team, the Colts.

The cracks in the Buffalo baseball franchise's foundation had begun in 1883, when attendance, which initially was in the thousands, dropped to the hundreds, and a sniping local press began attributing poor on-field player performance to alcohol abuse. The unexpected expense of building a new park in 1884 led to unwillingness to spend the money necessary to acquire a veteran pitcher who could spell workhorse Jim Galvin.

As the 1884 season progressed, the national press began to report conflicts between the players and manager O'Rourke. "Every member of the Buffalo team, it is said, has soured on Jim O'Rourke, the captain, for the arrogant way that he treats them."[63] At the close of the campaign, O'Rourke, one of a handful of players who refused to play under the Reserve Clause but were still offered jobs, resigned and signed with the Giants, for the then-unheard-of sum of $5,000.

The penny-pinching Buffalo owners named Jimmy Galvin manager in 1885 and brought back Billy Serad to spell him in the box. The team lost its first eight contests, and Galvin lost his first six starts. In early June he was replaced as skipper by Jack Chapman, a former National Association outfielder, whose dubious credentials as a manager included leading Louisville to a last-place finish and Detroit to seventh- and eighth-place finishes. As the team continued to lose, they were labeled the "Hapless" or "Inglorious" Bisons by the local press, which in mid–July predicted that there were changes coming:

> There will be shaking up of some of the dry bones in the Buffalo Club before long. Manager Chapman goes west this morning, and a new pitcher is the object of the trip. Other players are being looked for and their engagement at an early date is more than probable. It was stated on good authority in Pittsburgh last evening that the Alleghenies of that city had bought Galvin's release from the Buffalos. Some changes in that line are certainly contemplated here, but inquiries last night failed to confirm the rumor. [64]

Jack Rowe, Hardy Richardson and Deacon White, three Buffalo players who, along with Dan Brouthers, were described by the press as "The Big Four" after being sold by the Buffalo Bisons to the Detroit Wolverines in mid–September, 1885 (Library of Congress).

Two. *The Champion Batsman of the Country: 1881–1885*

Two days later Jim Galvin was sold to the American Association's Pittsburgh team, and rumors circulated that the Bisons would not finish the season. *Sporting Life* reported that Buffalo's directors had announced that there would be no club the following year for financial reasons, and had "sent out notices to other League club presidents that the best part of their team was open for bids."[65] Meanwhile, Bisons players expressed the fear that "There will be a systematic attempt to reduce their salaries by a system of fines."[66] Management confirmed this concern, stating that "hereafter the men must play ball, and if they don't play they [management] will make them play.... There is no doubt that some men on the team have a large case of the big head."[67] Three weeks after Jim Galvin's departure, overworked Billy Serad developed arm trouble, and two questionable rookies were brought in to take up the slack in the box: Pete Wood, a 28-year-old Canadian, and Pete Conway, just 19, who had been pitching for a Pennsylvania semi-pro team when the Bisons called him into service during a series they were playing at Philadelphia. The pair won 18 and lost 32 over the last weeks of the season, surrendering an average of seven runs per game.

In a move described by the press as "a stunner,"[68] Buffalo in mid–September sold its entire club to the Detroit franchise for $7,000, with the new owners agreeing that the team would finish the season in Buffalo. It was clear that Detroit did not want the entire Buffalo franchise — their only real interest lay in the four stars, Dan Brouthers, Deacon White, Jack Rowe and Hardy Richardson. Their plan was to transfer the four to Detroit immediately and use substitutes to fill their positions on the Bisons for the rest of the season.

Owners of other National League and American Association teams, who wanted an equal opportunity to sign the four Buffalo stars upon the team's demise, immediately questioned the legality of the sale. While they agreed that Buffalo could sell its stock to whomever it wanted, there were no provisions in inter-league agreements for the sale of an entire franchise. However, the owners noted an existing rule that prohibited released players from being approached by representatives from other teams until October 20. Detroit appeared to have violated this regulation by assuming it could sign Buffalo players immediately after the Buffalo franchise was purchased in September.

The New York Giants were particularly incensed by the sale. Locked in a tight pennant race with Chicago, the Giants were scheduled to play four games with Detroit and five with Buffalo during the last two weeks of September. If Buffalo's four star players were allowed to transfer immediately to Detroit, the Wolverines, who were then in sixth place, might prove to be much more formidable adversaries at a critical moment in the season. If, however, these players were required to remain with the weaker Buffalo team, the Giants stood a better chance of victory against them.

In his *Baseball: The Early Years,* historian Harold Seymour provides the standard view of how this dilemma was resolved: National League President Nick Young declared that the Bisons stars

> were still members of the Buffalo Club, so without having played an inning for Detroit they returned to Buffalo. Later in the fall, one of the Detroit Directors invited them to his Michigan hunting lodge, and in that atmosphere of good fellowship persuaded them to come back to Detroit for 1886. The quartet refused to return to Buffalo, saying they had their releases and could sign where they pleased. They won their point and remained with their new club.[69]

This summary suggests that players had some options, but in reality, according to league policy, they had no power to negotiate freely with anyone other than Buffalo or Detroit.

A week after the sale was announced, *Sporting Life* provided a more detailed account of the back-room negotiations between the two clubs, a version of events in which Dan Brouthers played a major role. Secret talks between the clubs started in July, two months before the sale, with Bisons Secretary Bob Leadley representing Buffalo, and Detroit team captain Ned Hanlon representing Detroit. "It was difficult to make any open agreement, as the league rules forbid any offer or negotiation with a player while he is a member of a League club.... Hanlon, however, was a particularly good friend of Brouthers, the latter having given Hanlon the tip that he would jump at the chance to come to Detroit. This induced some of the Detroit directors to try and secure a contract, notwithstanding League rules."[70]

Then, when Detroit was in Buffalo for a series in mid–September, a secret meeting at a local hotel was held between Brouthers, White, Rowe, Richardson, Secretary Leadley, and Wolverines captain Hanlon and other Detroit representatives. Leadley, clearly anxious to dispose of his high-salary stars, "drew up a contract in writing binding the four men to play with Detroit next season, *in case* they were released from Buffalo"[71] [emphasis added]. The four Bisons infielders signed the contract.

The biggest losers in the sale of the Buffalo club and the subsequent arbitration were Brouthers, White, Rowe and Richardson, who were twice victimized by the process. They were forced to sit out the last weeks of the 1885 season without pay, and even though the contracts they signed with Buffalo were null and void after the team's sale, were also denied the right to negotiate with other clubs for the best possible salary. All four players received good salary increases with Detroit in 1886 (Brouthers' rose from $2,500 to $4,000[72]) but given the amount that 35-year-old Jim O'Rourke had received

Two. *The Champion Batsman of the Country: 1881–1885* 47

from New York the previous year ($5,000), there is no telling what sum 28-year-old Brouthers, a two-time batting champ and five-time slugging leader, might have received.

There can be little doubt that the treatment he received from Buffalo and the league in 1885, and earlier from Horace Phillips, convinced Brouthers of the need for change in a management-controlled enterprise that had no real interest in the financial well-being of its players. He would be one of the first to join the new Brotherhood of Professional Baseball Players, and five years later would serve as Vice President of the Players' League.

Despite being caught up in Buffalo's turmoil during the 1885 season, Dan Brouthers held on to his slugging title for a fifth consecutive year and finished second in hitting (.359) behind Roger Connor of the Giants. Although required to sit out the last three weeks of the season, he still finished fourth in home runs (7) and second in doubles (32). His 44 multiple-hit games included 15 three-hit outings. Despite this record, the Buffalo press, so supportive of him in the past, criticized him in late July simply for going hitless in a 10–7 loss to New York. The irony of this position would soon become apparent. "Brouthers was showed up in the batting order yesterday and was the only one of the Bisons that failed to make a hit. The ex-champion seems to have rather lost his grip in that direction. Wonder if someone don't [*sic*] want him!"[73]

In five years with the Buffalo Bisons, Dennis Bruthers became Dan Brouthers, his salary increased from $40 a month to $2,500 a year, and he led the league in fielding percentage and home runs once, in batting twice, and in slugging five times. Although he would celebrate many similar achievements over the next decade, he would become a true journeyman during those years, never again staying with one club for so long a time. For a variety of reasons, including disbanded franchises, inter-league wars for control of the game, and his loyalty to the Brotherhood of Professional Baseball Players, in ensuing years he would play for six different teams in three distinct leagues. Whenever and wherever he took to the diamond, however, he would never forget to bring along his bat.

THREE

Big Dan: 1886–1888

> Never give him a low ball.... He'll kill it. — John Clarkson, future Hall of Fame pitcher, *Saint Louis Globe Democrat*, June 14, 1887.

As he began his sixth National League season in 1886, 28-year-old Dan Brouthers was in the prime of his career. Period photos of the Wappingers Falls slugger reveal a tall, powerfully built man whose handsome face, anchored by strong, regular features, is punctuated by the obligatory Victorian moustache. A deep widow's peak of dark hair, portent of his future baldness, defines his forehead. Though occasionally pictured in formal photos with longer, curled locks, his usual preference was for the close-cropped "buzz cut" look of Irish-American boxers John L. Sullivan and Jim Corbett, a style that communicated a dual message of practicality and rough manliness.

Although he acquired a degree of sophistication and worldly experience traveling the country for decades with his teammates, Brouthers at heart remained a devoted family man who liked nothing better than to be home in the village where he grew up. "Always 'Big Dan's' heart was in Wappingers Falls."[1] On occasion throughout his career he would exasperate his managers and teammates by heading home whenever word of a sick child or ailing wife reached him. At times he would do the same to celebrate a family birthday. Once, the ruse he used to try to get out of playing a ball game and go home failed, to humorous effect:

> The day was Saturday, and a double header was on. Brouthers had been planning for two weeks to catch a train at 5:30 o'clock that afternoon for his home ... where he intended to spend the evening as guest of honor at a birthday party that was to be given him by his family. He asked permission of ... Charles H. Byrne, president of the [Brooklyn] club to leave early, but that official ... refused

THREE. *Big Dan: 1886–1888*

to allow the first baseman to get away. Brouthers, suppressing a look of disappointment, said nothing, but began to think a great deal.... For a while nothing happened. Brouthers played out the first game and started the second. Byrne heaved a sigh of relief. Then came Brouthers' coup d'etat. In the last half of the second inning a ball was knocked back of first base. Brouthers stepped back quickly, lifted up his hands, and slyly allowed the ball to slip down between his outstretched arms and hit him on the head. He then fell prostrate to the ground, apparently severely injured. He was hurriedly carried to the dressing room.... Byrne scented a trick, however, and watched the door to the dressing room from the back of the grandstand. Presently he had the satisfaction of beholding Brouthers, suitcase in hand, make a crafty exit and start on the run for the depot and his birthday party. Byrne was after him in a flash ... and soon the glum first baseman was back in the game again.... He missed the train, but at the end of the game was presented with a candle-laden birthday cake by a bleacherite, who had procured it at a nearby bakery shop.[2]

Never a self-promoter, Brouthers was admired as an honest, good-natured player[3] whose word was "his bond."[4] Described by future Hall of Famer John Ward as an "amiable, easy dispositioned sort of chap,"[5] he was quiet by nature and "seldom said a word."[6] Accordingly, his name rarely appeared outside of the box scores in local or national sports pages, whose columnists instead preferred to write about the off-the-field exploits of charming extroverts like Mike Kelly, the clowning antics of Arlie Latham, known for his risqué language as "the Freshest Man on Earth," or juicy scandals, like the sensational divorce proceedings between John Ward and his wife, actress Helen Dauvray.

After hours, Brouthers let down his guard infrequently, and then only among trusted veteran teammates. On such occasions he could prove to be an engaging storyteller. This side of the slugger was best captured in an 1893 report of a road trip by the Brooklyn Bridegrooms (of which he was then a member), which contrasts the lively antics of younger players with those of the old veterans, including Brouthers:

> Life on the road is one round of good natured jollity among the players, who pass the time between games and on board the trains in jokes, songs, and whist ... there is a first class quartet on the team, which makes things pleasant.... Brouthers, Stovey, [and] Richardson ... are the quiet ones. Being old stagers it is worth the price of admission to listen to them talking over their old time journeys and successes on the ball field. Brouthers tells some funny things about his career and all of which are actual occurrences. One of them, which relates to Joe Farrell's riding into a saloon on horseback while down south one spring, and taking a drink in true Jesse James style, is very amusing.[7]

Brouthers rarely spoke during games, except when asked to coach or serve as substitute captain. On those infrequent occasions, his personality changed completely in the service of his team. In captain Ned Hanlon's absence during the Detroit Wolverines' 1888 season, for example, Brouthers' "voice rang out continuously, just at the right time, steadying the colts [rookies] and keeping the vets moving."[8] Thanks to an umpire, however, such rare behavior on the part of Brouthers ended for good a few years later, while Brouthers was playing for Ned Hanlon's Baltimore Orioles.

> During the Louisville games Dan Brouthers, who is always lifeless enough in a ball game, showed sufficient interest to get out on the coaching line and occasionally issue some directions in a mild tone of voice. Now was that not a commendable thing? Anyway, Baltimore people thought so, and applauded the old man.... As stated before, Dan's voice was of the mildest, and his whole action was unobjectionable to even the strictest moralist. Imagine the surprise on the stand [in the stands] then, when the umpire was observed to be gesticulating in his direction, ninety feet away, and the words, "twenty-five dollars," were heard issuing from his lips. From what could be seen and heard by spectators there was no cause whatsoever for disciplining the man.[9]

Before and after games, Brouthers' natural reticence disappeared around children, who flocked around him in the same manner in which they would a generation later with another great slugger. "Babe Ruth is very popular with the kids [in 1932] and in many ways 'Big Dan' was the same style, for 'Big Dan' would go out of his way to talk with these kids. Any time he said 'hullo [sic] boys,' these kids were happy to think that 'Big Dan' Brouthers had spoken to them."[10]

The Wappingers Falls slugger grew considerably more expansive near the end of his career, particularly, as we shall see, when asked by the press to comment on his longest home runs and other topics. During his twilight years he gave a series of interviews and wrote several columns, primarily for the *Washington Post*, full of details about the game during his era and expressing his views on how it had changed in the twentieth century.

Brouthers playing weight is often listed at a curiously specific 207 pounds[11] — his "official" weight for the 1886 campaign — the greater portion of which was concentrated in his chest and arms: "He was a Hercules above the belt."[12] Frequently much heavier, he was able to trim down somewhat each spring, apparently even in the latter stages of his career. At the start of his 13th major league season (1893), *Sporting Life* reported that "Brouthers was a bit heavy when he started practice, but my, you should have seen him scamper in the first hot game of the season that [was] played with the Troys yesterday."[13] The following April, the *Baltimore Sun* gave Brouthers weight at a highly improbable 195 pounds, after "having worked off considerable superfluous flesh."[14] Based on photographic evidence, a more realistic estimate of the slugger's weight, particularly in the latter half of his career, would be closer to 220 pounds — or more.

Brouthers height and weight, both exceptional for the era, occasionally earned him unfortunate nicknames, like "the Jumbo first baseman,"[15] which stereotyped him as a player lacking speed and mobility, even though his actions on the field often proved otherwise. The original *Jumbo*, standing 13 feet tall and weighing over six tons, was an African Bush Elephant purchased in 1881 by P. T. Barnum from the London Zoo for Barnum's circus. Thanks to Barnum, the giant pachyderm's name and image soon became well known across the country.

Despite ample evidence to the contrary, sportswriters routinely portrayed Brouthers as a baseball *Jumbo*: a ponderous, slow-moving player, a poor runner and a clumsy first baseman. A few years after he retired from the major leagues, this version of his abilities in these areas was already being set in stone: "As a first baseman, Brouthers was only fair, and he was no use whatever as a baserunner."[16]

The *Boston Globe* was particularly harsh in its criticism of Brouthers' running and sliding abilities during the three years he spent with Boston clubs (1889–1891), even though he averaged 27 steals a season over this period. After he stole a base during an August 1889 game, the *Globe* ridiculed the effort: "'Twas no earthquake.... Brouthers slid to second, that's all. Strong men turned pale and ladies fainted at the sight."[17] At the conclusion of the previous season (1888), in contrast, *Sporting Life* had praised his base-running and scoring ability. "Big Dan Brouthers is not an extraordinary base-runner, yet he is the leading run getter in the League, topping the record with 118."[18] The following spring, the Philadelphia-based weekly sports magazine reiterated that opinion: "Dan Brouthers is not only hitting the ball every time, but he is fast developing as a baserunner."[19]

Eschewing the facts, the *Globe*'s mocking August 1889, commentary about Brouthers base stealing was simply reasserting the Jumbo stereotype for comic effect. A month later, the same newspaper did an about-face, praising the big first baseman's craftiness as a runner. "Dan Brouthers used great judgment when he went all the way to second on a little fly just back of the pitcher."[20] A Milwaukee paper praised his speed in rounding the bases: "Dan Brouthers the other day performed the wonderful feat ... of coming home from first on a single."[21]

The following season, Brouthers 11th, *Sporting Life* once again complimented him on his slides, asserting that they were "features of the Boston games."[22] Three years later, the Brooklyn press praised the then 36-year-old's running abilities as a member of the local team: "big Dan Brouthers put some of Brooklyn's fastest runners to shame by his speed."[23] New Orleans sportswriters that year agreed with their Brooklyn counterparts: "Think of it, big Dan Brouthers is sliding to first base on infield hits and is stealing bases with the same ease and grace as the youngsters."[24]

Brouthers was imbibing no secret elixir of youth in his late 30s in order to garner such praise as a runner. Never a true speedster, his 21 career inside-the-park home runs and 205 triples (second among nineteenth-century players and eighth all-time) are a tribute to his hustle. After the steal became an official statistic in 1886, he averaged 25 per season by relying on his knowledge of pitchers' motions, catchers' weaknesses and game situations. In doing so, he established himself as a baserunner of considerable skill and success, in contradiction to what was often reported about him in the press.

Early in Brouthers' career, the *Jumbo* stereotype was also applied to his fielding. On joining the Troy Trojans in 1879, the *Troy Daily Times* concluded that "As a fielder he is fair, but he does not handle himself as gracefully as he might."[25] The anonymous author of his 1880 *New York Clipper* biography paid him a left-handed compliment on his fielding: "Although not the most graceful in style, he is still an uncommonly useful man to have in that position."[26] A decade after his last full major league season, this view of his defense became the standard version that continues to be accepted today: "As a first baseman he was only fair."[27]

A game-by-game review of Brouthers' defensive performance does not support such evaluations. As we have seen, in his first full major league season (1882) Brouthers was the best defensive first baseman in the league. Five years later, *Sporting Life* described him as still "lithe and agile as a cat, notwithstanding his great physique."[28] Throughout the 1880s he was regularly praised for his strong and accurate throwing arm,[29] his expertise at chasing down foul fly balls[30] and his proficiency at picking low throws out of the dirt.[31]

Late in his career, like many veterans, Brouthers was criticized for a lack of range at his position. In his case, however, it was not due just to the natural effects of aging, since a new approach to playing the position was beginning to supplant the traditional method that he had learned early in his career.

Until 1877, a ball hit on the ground in fair territory that then went foul was considered in play (the Fair-Foul rule). Many of the game's early stars, like Brooklyn's Dicky Pearce in the 1860s and Boston's Ross Barnes in the 1870s, became expert practitioners of the fair-foul hitting technique. Jim O'Rourke described Barnes' method as "hitting the ball so it would smash on the ground near the plate just inside the third base line, and would then mow the grass over the [foul] line."[32]

Additionally, until 1883, ground ball fouls caught on the first bounce were counted as outs (the Foul Bound Rule). The Fair-Foul rule and the Foul Bound rule forced "first and third basemen to regard their respective bases as the *midpoint* of the territory they were expected to cover [emphasis added]."[33] The traditional position for first basemen like Brouthers, therefore, was close to the bag, thus enabling him to gather in both grounders hit fair that went foul, and to record outs by catching foul grounders before they bounced a second time.

There were other significant reasons why early first basemen played close to the bag in the early years of the professional game:

> The nonroutine [*sic*] nature of outs in early baseball made it helpful for the first baseman to be stationed on the base to await throws. The bases were not always visible from afar, so the first baseman could naturally elicit more accurate throws by providing a stationary target. Being on the base beforehand made it easier for a first baseman to adjust to wild throws, an important and difficult feat in the days before trapping mitts were introduced.[34]

After both the Fair-Foul and Foul Bound rules were abolished, a new style of first base play, popularized by the St. Louis Browns' Charley Comiskey, gradually gained favor. It emphasized "playing a considerable distance off the bag, stretching to receive wide or high throws, and having the pitcher cover first on ground balls to the right side of the infield."[35]

In the middle of his tenth major league season (1890), Dan Brouthers began to be criticized for not fielding his position in this new fashion. "Dan Brouthers ... fails to cover his position properly, that is, judging by such men as Comiskey.... He must learn to play the bag as the advancement in the position points out daily or be criticized. It is the ground ball that goes spinning by [the first baseman] just out of the second baseman's reach that Dan turns his back on. A first baseman should go for every ball he can get, depending on the pitcher to cover the base."[36]

Earlier in the same season, however, the *Globe*—the same newspaper that subsequently criticized Brouthers for his outmoded play—praised him for playing first base the new way by going to his right on ground balls while his pitcher covered the bag: "Dan Brouthers made two fine assists on hard hit ground balls, [pitcher] Gumbert covering the base."[37] A few months later, the *Globe* was regularly praising his defense: "Dan Brouthers got around in lively style and made two fine stops of ugly balls"[38]; "Dan Brouthers is playing that first bag out of sight."[39] At the conclusion of the following season, the Boston paper appeared to have forgotten its earlier criticism when it pronounced Brouthers' defense to be superlative: "this season he excelled.... In fact, he has this year played the best first base of his career."[40]

Given the disparity between long-established notions of Brouthers' defensive skills and the reality of his playing abilities, franchises, fans and teammates often found themselves pleasantly surprised when he joined their team after a trade. In 1889, the *Boston Globe*, demonstrably schizophrenic with regard to its evaluation of Brouthers' defensive skills, now commented that "Bostoners say Brouthers' reputation as a fielder did him gross injustice. To the Boston mind, Big Dan can cover first base equal to the best."[41] This re-assessment was repeated even in the twilight of Brouthers' career in Baltimore in 1894, as he began his 14th season: "Big Dan is fast winning his way into the hearts of the Baltimore enthusiasts.... His fielding [is] much better than thought."[42]

In sum, despite Brouthers being type-cast early on as a poor fielder, the actual record reveals that while "not a phenomenon,"[43] at first base, he was a steady and reliable defensive player. Sam Crane, an early Buffalo teammate, described him as "up to the average"[44] at the position, and Orioles teammate John McGraw declared that "Big Dan, though he had passed his peak when he reached Baltimore [1894] still was a good first baseman, although he had been playing big league ball since the early 80s."[45]

Among historians today, Chicago White Stockings star Adrian "Cap" Anson is generally regarded as the premier first baseman of the nineteenth century. Anson's lifetime batting average was .334; his fielding average at first base was .972 . Dan Brouthers, who never figures in discussions on the best fielding first basemen of the era, had a lifetime batting average of .342, and a lifetime fielding average at first base of .971.

There may have been some disparity between the manner in which critics described Brouthers' defense and running skills and actual game accounts of his performance, but there was never a dispute about his ability to hit a baseball for average and power. He did his offensive damage using "a bat made specifically for himself, it being somewhat larger than the others,"[46] and he was very particular about bat selection and care. "Brouthers spends many of his leisure hours oiling up his bats. Dan thinks almost as much of his 'timber' as he does of his children."[47]

Two of Brouthers' bats have found a home in the Collections Department of the Baseball Hall of Fame in Cooperstown, New York. The first, dating from his days with the Actives and the Stottsvilles in the late 1870s, is 36 inches long and weighs 39 ounces. The second, used during his years with Buffalo in the early 1880s, measures 41.5 inches in length and weighs 38 ounces.[48] Since all wood dries out over time, it is probable that 130 years ago, each of these bats weighed at least an ounce or two more when in the powerful hands of Dan Brouthers.

Brouthers routinely carried a "big stick" to the plate, but he did not

Three. *Big Dan: 1886–1888*

advocate taking an extremely powerful swing. In a 1918 interview, he placed emphasis on timing and hitting the ball squarely.

> Don't try to kill the ball. You can shoot it just as far, probably farther, with an easy, well-timed swing as you can with a vicious swipe that carries all the weight of your body with it. The man who strikes out often is the fellow who tries to murder the ball. That's because he's so intent upon trying to put all the power of his body into the swing that his timing is poor and his marksmanship poorer. Don't use a light bat. There's too much temptation to kill the ball when you've got an easy swinging club. Use a heavy club. With it your swing will be slower, but it will be better timed and you won't be trying to smash the ball out of the lot every time and you will be able to retain your balance after the swing — something that's not possible using a "feather stick."[49]

While his preference for a heavy bat would not resonate with modern hitters, Brouthers' emphasis on balance, timing and "marksmanship" (which he defined as "hitting them square on the nose"[50]) would still find favor today.

Reviewing the Wappingers Falls slugger's career in 1904, the *Boston Globe*, once again making use of the Jumbo stereotype, declared that his "position at the bat was very awkward."[51] Former first-baseman-turned-sportswriter Tim Murnane, writing when Brouthers was in his prime (1889), provided a more comprehensive and objective analysis of the slugger's hitting technique:

> Dan goes up to the bat to hit the ball, and few men can size up a pitcher as he can.... Dan gets close to the plate with his feet well apart, and set firm.... Dan keeps swinging his bat back and forth. It's a rare thing to see him let go and miss a ball, and as for striking out, it's something a pitcher is always proud of if he can accomplish it during a season. This man can hit a high or low ball, and will seldom let go at one out of his reach. Pitchers never know how to play for him, as he is just as likely to hit to right as he is to left field.... He swings his body, and when he does catch the ball square, no man can drive one farther.[52]

In 1912, John Montgomery Ward, future Hall of Famer and Brouthers' Brooklyn manager (1892–1893) offered an insightful description of Brouthers' batting technique. In doing so, he made a passing, dismissive reference to yet another aspect of the Jumbo stereotype — that a large body meant diminished intelligence.

> They used to think that ... Dan Brouthers ... wasn't a fast thinker, and that some of his batting prowess was due to the fact that he swung a long and heavy bat.... I watched him for two months, and the longer I watched him the more admiration I had. With all the height and long reach, nobody ever saw him take a swing at the ball until the ball was right on him. He wasn't reaching for them. He waited until the ball got up to him and then he decided like a flash whether he would go after it or leave it alone.[53]

Two decades later, legendary player and manager John McGraw offered his thoughts on Brouthers' hitting prowess:

> The first time I ever ran across Brouthers was with the Red Sox in Boston. He had a great reputation as a slugger and our pitchers did their best to keep from feeding him a low ball. He not only hit low balls hard, but he hit them where nobody could get them. That was one of the real tipoffs of what a hitter Brouthers was — the efforts that were made to keep from giving him a low ball. We didn't attempt to pitch to his weakness, because, like all good hitters, past and present, Big Dan had no weakness. Instead, the pitchers pitched away from his strength — a low ball. Although a standout slugger, Brouthers was not a hit-or-miss swinger. He wouldn't bite at bad balls.[54]

Proof of McGraw's assertion that Brouthers could not be tempted by bad pitches is found in his remarkably low strike-out per at-bat ratio, one per 28.2 at-bats (238 strikeouts in 6711 at-bats). Only thirty players have ratios lower than Brouthers in this category. His season low was six strikeouts in 485 at-bats in 1889, or one strikeout every 81 at-bats. No player who struck out less often can compare with Brouthers in terms of batting and slugging averages.

As discussed in the first chapter, as an amateur, Brouthers first developed his batting skills by paying young boys to pitch to him and retrieve balls. This habit of frequent extra hitting practice remained a hallmark of his training schedule long after he became a major league star. "Brouthers would remain on the field all day hitting if he could get someone to toss him the ball."[55] "Dan Brouthers loves to bat, and will remain on the ground as long as any one will stay to chase the ball. You will generally find some ambitious amateur throwing the ball over the plate to the League's greatest slugger."[56]

Because of his success at the plate, pitchers routinely tried to bypass Brouthers in the lineup by issuing him a free pass to first base — a practice, as we have seen, that was rare in the nineteenth century. While he was playing for Brooklyn in 1893, for example, the *Brooklyn Daily Eagle* noted with disdain the efforts of Philadelphia pitcher Tim Keefe to keep their star slugger off the base paths.

> Keefe did a peculiar thing — something which would not be tolerated by any fair minded crowd, and which, if repeated, would cause trouble. As Dan Brouthers came to bat, Keefe motioned [Philadelphia's catcher, Jack] Clement[s] to one side and tossed in four wide balls, giving Brouthers his base. Brouthers looked disgusted and the crowd showed its displeasure by hooting and groaning. It was evident that Keefe was afraid of Big Dan.[57]

Keefe wasn't the only future Hall of Fame pitcher who was unwilling to give Brouthers a chance to hit. In an 1892 contest against Cleveland, Spiders starter Cy Young had a similar game plan.

> Brouthers got only a scratch hit yesterday. Twirler Cy Young had evidently studied the batting abilities of the league batters in his log cabin home in the backwoods

during the winter, and decided that Dan was a bad man with the bat. So Cy put Dan on his list and yesterday brought it out and found Brouthers at the top. When, therefore, Brooklyn's big first baseman came to bat, Mr. Young threw several bad balls over the plate and made him a present of first base on two different occasions. In fact his endeavors to treat Dan kindly were so evident that a bleacher [a fan] was forced to ask, in a voice that was full of sarcasm and contempt, "Are you afraid of him, Mr. Young?" Mr. Young was, but he did not say so.[58]

Some teams went to extreme lengths to keep the great slugger off the base paths by means of intentional walks. During a 14-inning, 1891 American Association game against Mike Kelly's Cincinnati team, for example, "Dan Brouthers was repeatedly called on for a home run by the 'bleachers' [fans], but the King [a nickname for Mike Kelly] is aware of Dan's hitting powers better than anyone else, and wouldn't let him hit. The look of anguish on Dan's face was inexpressible, and sadly he jogged to first base five times on balls."[59] Later that season against Columbus, he was issued five walks in a nine-inning game: "[Pitcher Hank] Gastright was wild, giving Dan Brouthers his base on balls five times in succession."[60]

Barry Bonds owns the official major league record for intentional walks in a nine-inning game (four in 2004). Although Columbus Colts pitcher Hank Gastright's five walks issued to Brouthers in nine innings in 1891 were alleged to be due to wildness, there is little doubt that some of these passes, if not all of them, were intentional. Currently, Andre Dawson is considered the holder of the record for most intentional walks received in an extra-inning game (five in 16 innings in 1990). In reality, this record should be shared by Dan Brouthers, given his five intentional walks during the previously mentioned 14-inning game with Cincinnati in 1891. These examples, and others that will be noted later, provide clear indication that Dan Brouthers was the first player to be walked intentionally on a regular basis.

Over the course of his 16-year career, Dan Brouthers led his league in batting five times and in slugging seven times. No other nineteenth-century player ranked at the top of either of these categories for more than three seasons. Only two nineteenth-century players led their league five times in on-base percentage: speedster Billy Hamilton and slugger Dan Brouthers. Brouthers also was a league leader three times in hits and doubles, twice in runs, home runs and RBI, and once in triples. Though ranked fourth in his era in home runs (106) behind Roger Connor (138), Sam Thompson (127) and Harry Stovey (122), many of his legitimate four-baggers, as we shall see, were declared ground rule doubles. No nineteenth-century player consistently hit the ball harder or longer than the slugger from Wappingers Falls.

There is no more telling indication of the respect which Brouthers was given as a hitter than the repeated references to aspiring young sluggers of the era either as players who offensively appeared to be "a second Brouthers"[61] or who were thought to be "hitting the ball like a Brouthers."[62] Simply put, Brouthers name was synonymous with the highest hitting standards of his era.

The sale by Buffalo of Dan Brouthers, "Hardy" Richardson, Jack Rowe and Jim "Deacon" White to Detroit in 1885 was the first mass-player transfer in major league baseball history. Two years later, the transaction helped lead the Wolverines to their first and only pennant, but ironically, it also helped lead to the demise of the franchise at the end of the 1888 season. The purchase of Buffalo's slugging infielders was a calculated risk on the part of Frederick Kimball Stearns, a wealthy heir to a pharmaceutical fortune. Stearns, who played second base and captained the University of Michigan baseball team in 1877, came aboard as a principal investor for the financially troubled Detroit Wolverines in 1885. He had a personal hand in the shady dealings that led to the transfer of the Buffalo players to Detroit, and in doing so, "he outmaneuvered [potential] buyers from New York, Chicago and Boston, who also sought the Buffalo foursome."[63]

Well aware of the Detroit team's poor attendance record and the city's preference for horse racing rather than baseball, Stearns planned to recoup the money spent on purchasing Brouthers, White, Rowe and Richardson by relying on an existing league policy that required that visiting teams receive a share of admission receipts while on the road. He reasoned that fans in other cities would flock to their own parks to see the revitalized, visiting Wolverines when the Detroit nine came to town. Rival owners, however, still smarting from being excluded from bidding on the Buffalo Bisons quartet, soon devised a scheme to dash Stearns' plans. "In the fall of 1886 ... they abolished the old policy of splitting gate receipts on a percentage basis and substituted a fixed guarantee plan. Under the new plan, visiting teams received a fixed sum of only $125 a game; all receipts above this went to the home team.... An immediate effect, of course, was to seal the economic fate of the Detroit Wolverines at the very moment when its championship hopes were highest."[64] The new "fixed sum" rule for visiting teams lasted for two years. The Detroit franchise was gone in three.

The press coined the phrase "Big Four" to refer to the quartet of talented players sold to Detroit. It was an apt nickname. In their five previous seasons, Buffalo infielders Brouthers (first base), Richardson (second base), Rowe (shortstop) and White (third base) hit for a combined .311, easily the best average among all major league infield combinations of the day.

James Laurie White, known as "the Deacon," was tall and gangly, bald and bug-eyed, and sported an enormous, unkempt walrus moustache. Out of uniform, "no one who saw him ... ever imagined him to be a pro ballplayer,"[65] but he could play the game "like a man possessed and could be counted on to lead his team to the pennant or at least keep them in contention."[66] After spending his first major-league decade as a catcher — he had the distinction of catching the first game in major league history in 1871— he switched positions to third base, a move that probably prolonged his career several years. He spent another decade at the hot corner before retiring with a lifetime batting average of .312. Thanks in large part to the efforts of baseball historian Peter Morris and the Nineteenth-Century Committee of the Society for American Baseball Research, Deacon White was recently elected to the Baseball Hall of Fame, 123 years after he retired from the game.

New Jersey-born Abram Harding "Hardy" Richardson spent most of his four minor league seasons in the outfield, but moved to the infield when signed by Buffalo in 1879, and in his rookie year led the team in every major hitting department except home runs. A disciplined hitter (.299 lifetime average) and a quick and agile second baseman who ranks second all-time in range at the position, Richardson saw his career was cut short by two sliding accidents, one in 1888 when he fractured an ankle, and a second in 1891, when he broke a leg "sliding into home to complete an inside-the-park home run."[67]

Jack Rowe, who hailed from the hamlet of Hamburg, Pennsylvania, played his minor league ball in the Midwest before signing with Buffalo in 1879. Like Deacon White, he switched from catcher to an infield position — in his case, shortstop — in order to save wear and tear on his hands. The smallest in stature (5'8") of the Big Four, Rowe was a steady infielder and a decent hitter with the Bisons and the Wolverines. After he was traded to Pittsburgh after the 1888 season, his last years in major league baseball were marred by contract disputes and a financially disastrous venture as a team owner.[68]

With the acquisition of the Big Four, Wolverines fans seriously began to dream about wresting the pennant from Chicago, Boston and Providence, who had dominated the National League since 1876. Like Buffalo, Detroit was a relative newcomer to baseball. The first recorded game played there, an intra-squad contest, took place on August 15, 1857, between members of the city's Franklin Baseball Club. A record of the game has been preserved, largely due to the fact that some of the team members were employed by the *Detroit Free Press*.[69]

In 1879, local entrepreneurs hired a team of Eastern professionals to represent the city as an independent team at the recently constructed Recreation Park, Detroit's first enclosed baseball field. The Detroit squad, dubbed the Hollingers' Nine, was defeated in their first game, an exhibition match with the fledgling National League Troy Trojans, on May 12, 1879.

Two years later, a new professional Detroit team, christened the Wolverines, made its debut in the National League, surprising everyone by finishing in fourth place, thanks largely to the hitting of first baseman Martin Powell (.338) and catcher Charlie Bennett (.478 slugging average). Powell would never again hit as well in his brief, four-year major league career. Bennett, in contrast, became recognized as one of game's premier catchers over the next dozen seasons until a horrific accident ended his career. Rushing to catch a train to begin a hunting trip in January 1894, he slipped while boarding, fell under the train's wheels, and lost both his legs.

Detroit's on-field leader was team captain Edward "Ned" Hanlon, who, we recall, brokered the back-room deal that brought the Big Four to Detroit. A speedy (69 stolen bases in 1887), light-hitting outfielder, Hanlon later managed for 19 years, winning five pennants, three of them as skipper of the Baltimore Orioles of the 1890s.

The Wolverines' fourth-place success in their 1881 debut season was short-lived. Over the next four years the team finished no higher than sixth, and in 1884 placed eighth, winning only 28 games and finishing 56 games behind league-leading Providence. In 1885, seeking new talent to help pull the team up in the standings, Detroit signed Danville, Indiana, native Sam Thompson, then a 24-year-old carpenter, who began his career playing for an Indianapolis team that subsequently disbanded. Legend has it that a year earlier, baseball promoter Dan O'Leary had brought his Indianapolis nine to Danville to play the local team, and while there he was scouting prospects. The best of them was Thompson.

> The mayor of Danville had bragged that if they had Sam [Thompson], the Browns would beat O'Leary's team. When O'Leary found him, Sam was working on the roof of a neighbor. Sam refused to play since he needed the $2.50 he was getting for the roof work. O'Leary agreed to pay him the $2.50 so he could see him play. Sam proceeded to lose two balls in a cornfield and lead his Danville team to a 9–0 victory over Indianapolis. If the roof was ever finished, it probably wasn't Sam who did it, since he was signed on the spot.[70]

Over the next 15 years, the left-handed hitting Thompson hit .331, smacked 126 home runs (second among all nineteenth-century players) and became the first man to reach the 200-hit plateau (203) in one season. Incredibly, he did so in a 127-game season (1887). Along the way, he helped the "Big Four" power the Wolverines to their only pennant.

Dan Brouthers' stay in Detroit was a three-year roller-coaster ride with a team that finished in last place two years before his arrival, won the pennant in his second year there (1887), and was out of business at the end of the following season. In 1886, the Detroit nine, advertised as "the Big Four and five more,"[71] or, simply, "the Sluggers,"[72] succeeded in putting a real scare in the White Stockings before finishing second in the standings, just 2½ games behind them. The Big Four, with three of its members hitting over .300, provided Detroit with the expected offensive boost, and they were ably assisted by the pitching of Charlie "Pretzels" Getzein and Charley "Lady" Baldwin, who combined for 72 wins.

The left-handed Baldwin, who acquired his unusual nickname as a result of his adamant refusal to drink and carouse with teammates after hours, signed with Detroit in 1885 after a brief stint in the ill-fated Union League. In addition to an excellent fastball, he possessed a repertoire of breaking-ball pitches. His unremarkable 11–9 debut-year record for the sixth-place 1885 Wolverines is misleading, since it was accompanied by an impressive 1.86 ERA. Baldwin followed this effort with a career-best campaign in 1886, posting a 42–13 mark that included seven shutouts and a league-leading 323 strikeouts. As with many southpaws of the era, his curves mystified left-handed hitters, but he also featured "a nasty in-shoot and drop that made him just as tough on right-handers."[73]

Off to a slow start due to sickness during spring training, Brouthers, now described as "the good natured giant"[74] by the *Detroit Free Press*, was, by opening day, reported to be entirely recovered from the illness that attacked him just before the start of the exhibition season. He proved the report correct by hammering out a dozen doubles in his first 14 games. At Kansas City in early May he stroked three two-baggers in a game, and a week later when Detroit opened at home against New York, he added a pair. He finished the year with 40, best in the league. The first of his league-leading 11 home runs, a total matched by teammate Hardy Richardson, came against Washington on May 21. "Big Brouthers caught an out-curve squarely, and the ball started on an astronomical investigating tour. It sailed clear over the right field fence, and the big fellow trotted around the bases amid the deafening roar of the spectators."[75]

That blow earned him a prize from two local haberdashers. "Do you observe that tall gentleman strolling down the avenue with the shiny silk hat on? It is Brouthers, and he acquired the tile [hat] thusly: Lochbihler and Dennis, the hatters, offered a silk hat to the Detroit batter who could knock a ball against or over their sign on the right field fence. Dennis put the ball over it yesterday."[76] In an era before lucrative endorsement contracts, such rewards were a ballplayer's only bonuses during the season.

Three weeks later, Brouthers hit a blast off Charlie Sweeney during a 14–7 blowout of the St. Louis Maroons that so impressed his Detroit teammate, Sam Crane, that a quarter-century later, Crane, now a sportswriter, could still recall it with awe, and in crystal clear detail:

> I think that Dan Brouthers could hit the ball harder and further than any player I had the pleasure of playing with or against.... About the longest drive I ever saw Dan make was in Detroit, when he hit a ball through the branches of a tree in deep centrefield. The ground was hard as flint at the time and the leather [ball] shot through the tree like a rifle ball and never did stop until it struck a fence that separated the ball field from a cricket grounds, a half mile away, if I remember correctly. It was a tremendous lick ... made against the St. Louis Maroons on June 12, 1886.[77]

By June 19, the Wolverines were 30–7 and leading the league, followed closely by Chicago at 26–7, and the arrival of the White Stockings in Detroit for a three-game series was the talk of baseball. Detroit had lost two of three games with the reigning champions in Chicago in early May, and now was out to even the score. The Windy City team brought along its own cheering section — a delegation of 200 Chicago fans.

After winning the first three pennants of the decade, Chicago had conceded a year each at the top of the standings to Boston and to Providence before regaining the championship in 1885, on the strength of pitcher John Clarkson's league-leading 53 wins, 308 strikeouts and 1.85 ERA. Their ranks included the two most well-known players in baseball: team Captain and Manager, Cap Anson, and Mike "King" Kelly, a multi-talented, multi-position player who was "baseball's first superstar."[78] Before home crowds that exceeded 12,000 for each contest, Detroit won two of the three closely contested games.

Close-up of Dan Brouthers from the 1886 Detroit team photograph (National Baseball Hall of Fame Library, Cooperstown, New York).

In order to take full advantage of the great interest in the series, Detroit allowed standing-room admission on the field in far left, right and center — a common practice in the era of parks with enormous outfields. This alteration required a change in ground rules: "Owing to the great crowd present, a rule was made allowing only two bases on a hit into the crowd."[79] Brouthers collected five singles during the series, and thus on this occasion was not affected by the rule change. However, this and similar ground-rule regulation changes at other parks, as we shall see, would reduce many of the Wappingers Falls slugger's potential triples and home runs to doubles over the course of his career.

Aware that the new ground rule could have a serious negative effect on the Wolverines' offense, the *Detroit Free Press* in July pleaded for an end to the practice. "This is a very good time to respectfully request that the gentlemen who run the Recreation Park base-ball grounds to kindly abstain from fencing in our three-baggers and home runs.... Let not the long hits that scrape the rear fence be born to blush unseen behind a rope fence. Give the boys [the Detroit players] a fair field and they ask no other favor."[80]

The special Detroit ground rule was not in effect when the Wolverines met Boston on July 3, and Brouthers hit an inside-the-park home run (which in the earlier Chicago series would have been a double) off Hoss Radbourn. "Big Dan Brouthers picked out a good ball and banged it on a line to the left field track. When Brouthers tore across the plate, Sutton was preparing to throw the ball in from extreme left field. It was a tremendous hit, and spectators waved their hats and shouted themselves hoarse."[81]

The "track" referred to here was a 50-foot-wide "trotting track" (for harness racing) that began 230 feet from home plate. Beyond the outer edge of the track (280 feet from home plate), was another 120-foot stretch of grass that ended at the outfield fence 400 feet away. Thus Brouthers opposite-field hit arrived at the track area as a line drive, and then bounded to the outer swatch of grass.[82]

The *Detroit Free Press* report of this hit was doubly significant, for in addition to noting another of Brouthers' inside-the-park four-baggers, it also was the first known instance in which he was referred to in the press as "Big Dan," the nickname by which he would be most commonly referred to thereafter. Fascinated with Brouthers during his first Wolverines season, the Detroit press, in addition to referring to him, as we have previously seen, as "the good natured giant" "big Brouthers" and "Big Dan," added the nicknames "gigantic Brouthers,"[83] "massive Brouthers,"[84] and "the redoubtable Brouthers"[85] in their game accounts over the course of the season.

Defensively, Brouthers was up to his old tricks at first base. In a contest against Philadelphia in June, Phillies centerfielder Ed Andrews became a Brouthers victim. With a man on second in the last of the ninth, "Andrews made a scratch hit and got to first. Big Brouthers held on to the ball, and when Andrews stepped off the plate [base] touched him, putting out the third man [and ending the game]."[86]

Despite their fine first half, the Wolverines stumbled in August, going 10–13, and after losing to Philadelphia on August 26, fell to second place in the standings and never regained the league lead. The heavy-hitting White Stockings finished the season in first place in 1886, not only in the standings but in almost every offensive category (runs, doubles, triples, home runs, runs batted in, and slugging).

Big Dan, who finished the season hitting .370 and slugging at a League-leading percentage of .581, put on a hitting display in a mid–September loss to the rival White Stockings in Chicago that earned him the respect of the Windy City's team and fans. Playing before a crowd of 10,000, he went five-for-five, including a single, a double (and subsequent steal of third), and three home runs, all off Chicago starter Jim McCormick. The first four-bagger was smashed "over to Congress Street for four bases."[87] The latter two were inside-the-park home runs, similar low liners that went "clear to the Chicago dressing room,"[88] the first in the seventh inning and the second in the ninth. With these blows, the supposedly slow-footed Brouthers became one of the few players in baseball history to hit two inside-the-park home runs in a game.

Despite the disappointment of finishing second instead of first in 1886, Brouthers celebrated a special personal event in September — the birth of his first child, Anne, who would be known throughout her life by her middle name, Lillian. "Dan Brouthers got a telegram from Wappinger's Falls yesterday that put him in a flutter. It was brief, but full of importance. It read: 'Girl. Both doing well.' Dan says he never felt more like making a home run."[89]

Half a dozen years earlier, Brouthers was bouncing from the independent New Yorks to the Brooklyn Atlantics, earning $40 a month. Now he was recognized as the greatest hitter in major league baseball, and was earning $4,000 a year on a team that was a serious contender for a pennant. His financial future secure, he had married his hometown sweetheart and was the father of a new baby girl. At age 28, Big Dan was sitting on top of the world.

Although Detroit's 1886 pitching hero, Lady Baldwin, faltered in 1887, dropping to 13–10 because of a sore arm, the team's second starter, Charley Getzein, came close (29–13) to equaling his record of the previous year (30–11), and his two backups, Stump Weidman and Larry Twitchell, combined for 24 wins. All members of the Big Four hit over .300 but they were outpaced by third-year man Sam Thompson, who, in a 127-game season, led the league in hits (203), RBI (166), triples (23) and batting and slugging averages (.372 and .565 respectively). With Thompson now hitting his stride, the Big Four could have legitimately been called "the Big Five." Although Dan Brouthers ceded the slugging title to Thompson by .003 points, he led the league in runs (153) and doubles (36), stole 34 bases, and placed fifth in home runs

THREE. *Big Dan: 1886–1888*　　　　　　　65

Team photograph of the World Champion 1887 Detroit Wolverines. Dan Brouthers stands in the back row, second left, between catcher Charlie Bennett, first from left, and outfielder Sam Thompson third from left. In 1887, Thompson became the first player to collect 200 hits in a season (203 total), accomplishing the feat in just 127 games (National Baseball Hall of Fame Library, Cooperstown, New York).

with 12. Thanks to the firepower of the Wolverines offense, Detroit was shut out only twice and never fell out of first place on the way to the league championship in 1887.

Three of Brouthers' 1887 home runs were the subject of special interest by the press, each for a different reason. His first four-bagger of the year, hit off Dan Casey at Philadelphia on May 17, broke the distance record at the Quaker City nine's new park, the Huntingdon Street Grounds. "The home run made by Brouthers was the longest ever made on the grounds." [90]

The second, an inside-the-park blast hit at home off Boston's ace, Hoss Radbourn, on August 4, was noteworthy because it provoked a rare comment from the normally laconic Brouthers. With a man on in the fifth inning, Brouthers "suddenly lit on the sphere, driving it on a line to left center for a beautifully clean home run. Johnston ran after the ball, and a good long chase he had. 'There,' remarked Dan as he took his seat. 'That little rooster has been catching me out all season, and I guess I'm even with him.'"[91]

The third, hit at Chicago off John Clarkson on August 16, captured well the dramatic, descriptive reporting style of the *Detroit Free Press*'s sports editor, who managed to include the hitter, the fans and the umpire in his account. "Not a hit had been made for Detroit when Brouthers went to bat in the fourth inning. He hitched up his trousers, waited for a good ball, then knocked a hole in the fringe of men and boys on top [of] the fence and sauntered home while Umpire Powers was opening a fresh ball."92

With the pennant nearly secured in late September, Detroit fans expressed their appreciation for Brouthers' efforts in an unusual fashion — once again making reference to the Jumbo stereotype:

> Brouthers was presented a gold-beaded can and a horseshoe by his Detroit friends [on] September 24. The horseshoe is a unique affair. It fell from the hoof of a mammoth truck horse in Detroit and is a Jumbo shoe, handsomely gilded. Inclosed [*sic*] in it is a miniature nickel shoe, containing a likeness of Brouthers. Underneath the smaller shoe are two nickel bats and the letters D.B.C.C. Around the rim of the smaller shoe are the words, "One of the Big Four."93

At the close of the season, the *Detroit Free Press*, perhaps echoing the frustration of many less successful league clubs, could not help but gloat over the Wolverines' victory over traditional Eastern powerhouse teams. "It is of course somewhat exasperating to New York, Boston, Philadelphia and other ancient landmarks of base ball to have a stripling like Detroit walk in and carry off the chief honors in the foremost base ball organization in the country."94

An 1887 Goodwin and Company Old Judge Tobacco card featuring Dan Brouthers in stylized batting pose. Small cards such as this were placed in tobacco packages to stiffen them and increase sales (Library of Congress).

THREE. *Big Dan: 1886–1888* 67

A 15-game version of a post-season "World's Series" between National League champion Detroit and American Association champion Saint Louis was soon organized by the Browns' flamboyant owner, Chris Von der Ahe, and Wolverines owner Frederick Stearns. Both men viewed the Series as much an opportunity to increase profits as a struggle for the claim to be the best team in baseball. Accordingly, the schedule required the teams to play at eight other League and Association venues in addition to Detroit and St. Louis. The winning franchise would be awarded 75 percent of the receipts. Detroit clinched the series after 11 games (although all 15 were played). Dan Brouthers, who had suffered an ankle injury (first described as a sprain, but later determined to be "badly wrenched"[95]) in the season's last series at Indianapolis, was unable to play. *Sporting Life* reported that "Dan would like to play, and gets out and hits a little before each game, but can't bear his weight on the ankle."[96] Clearly disgusted, Dan "bore his forced retirement during most of the World's [Series] games with poor grace."[97]

Despite the Wolverines' successful 1887 season, trouble was brewing in Detroit. After two years under the new league policy that eliminated visiting teams' shares of admission receipts, the franchise was close to bankruptcy. Before the joy and excitement of winning the pennant had subsided, principal owner Frederick Stearns, seeing the handwriting on the wall, resigned and returned to his pharmaceutical company.

Manager Watkins had earned the enmity of his players by fining them for making errors and for "indifference" on the field. At mid-season, he suspended back-up catcher Fatty Briody and pitcher Stump Wiedman without pay for drunkenness. Lady Baldwin, the previous year's star hurler, cried foul, claimed the suspension was unjustified, and asked to be suspended also. Watkins gladly complied.

Life-like sketch of Dan Brouthers, described as the "Great Batsman" of the League (National Baseball Hall of Fame Library, Cooperstown, New York).

The Detroit press and fans soon took up the cause, criticizing Watkins' dictatorial ways and claiming that the team was "over managed." After the post-season series against St. Louis was announced, the Detroit players, well aware of the financial windfall it represented to the franchise, demanded greater compensation than what had previously been offered them. They asked for $400 per man and an extra $100 each if the championship were won. Management agreed to the demand, but added a stipulation that required players to extend their contract through November 1. They were thus bound for another week of exhibition games after the World's Series.

In the midst of the team's financial crisis, the departure of its principal financer, and the bitter feuds between players and manager Watkins, concern arose that the franchise might be dissolved. Significantly, the press sought reassurance on the matter, not from Watkins, team captain Hanlon, or the club's Directors, but rather from Big Dan Brouthers. In an interview with the *St. Louis Globe Democrat* just prior to the start of the World's Series, Brouthers tried to quell the rumors of trades and club dissolution while suggesting a way out of the team's financial woes.

Dan Brouthers, Tobin Caricature, circa 1887. In Brouthers' era, *soak* was a slang term for *hit* (Transcendental Graphics/www.theruckerarchive.com).

THREE. *Big Dan: 1886–1888*

I feel confident Detroit will have a club here next season [1888], and as the city would not stand any but a winner, I think it will be the same team as is now here. There seems to be every prospect of the percentage system [the allotment of a percentage of gate receipts to visiting teams] again coming to the front, and under it Detroit will do well. I think the only fair system is one based on the drawing ability of a club. It makes me weary to think of the money we have drawn for some of those Eastern clubs and received nothing for it.[98]

Brouthers' prediction of a return to a shared revenue system for visiting teams came true, but the change in policy occurred too late to save the Wolverines.

Detroit's simmering pot of debt, discord and discontent boiled over in 1888, and the result was a fall from first to fifth place in the standings, the resignation of manager Bill Watkins,

Stylized die-cut portrait of Brouthers, 1887. Die-cutting, or embossing, uses a steel plate pressed against the object or material to raise its surface (Transcendental Graphics/www.theruckerarchive.com).

the sale of the club's star players, and the demise of the franchise. Through it all, Big Dan played on.

Although Brouthers' offensive numbers dropped off in all categories in his third year with Detroit, he remained among the league's top hitters, placing first in runs (118) and doubles (33) second in on-base percentage (.399), and fourth in batting average (.307) and hits (160). In contrast, none of the other members of the Big Four reached the .300 mark or figured among the league leaders either in offense or defense. Back-up pitcher Pete Conway, a Burmont, Pennsylvania, native, who was a combined 14–15 for the Wolverines in 1886 and 1887, picked up the slack for the fading Charlie Getzein (19–25), but former ace Lady Baldwin pitched in only six games and was released in August.

Injuries and controversy plagued the team from the start of its spring training sessions in New Orleans. Deacon White and team captain Hanlon were

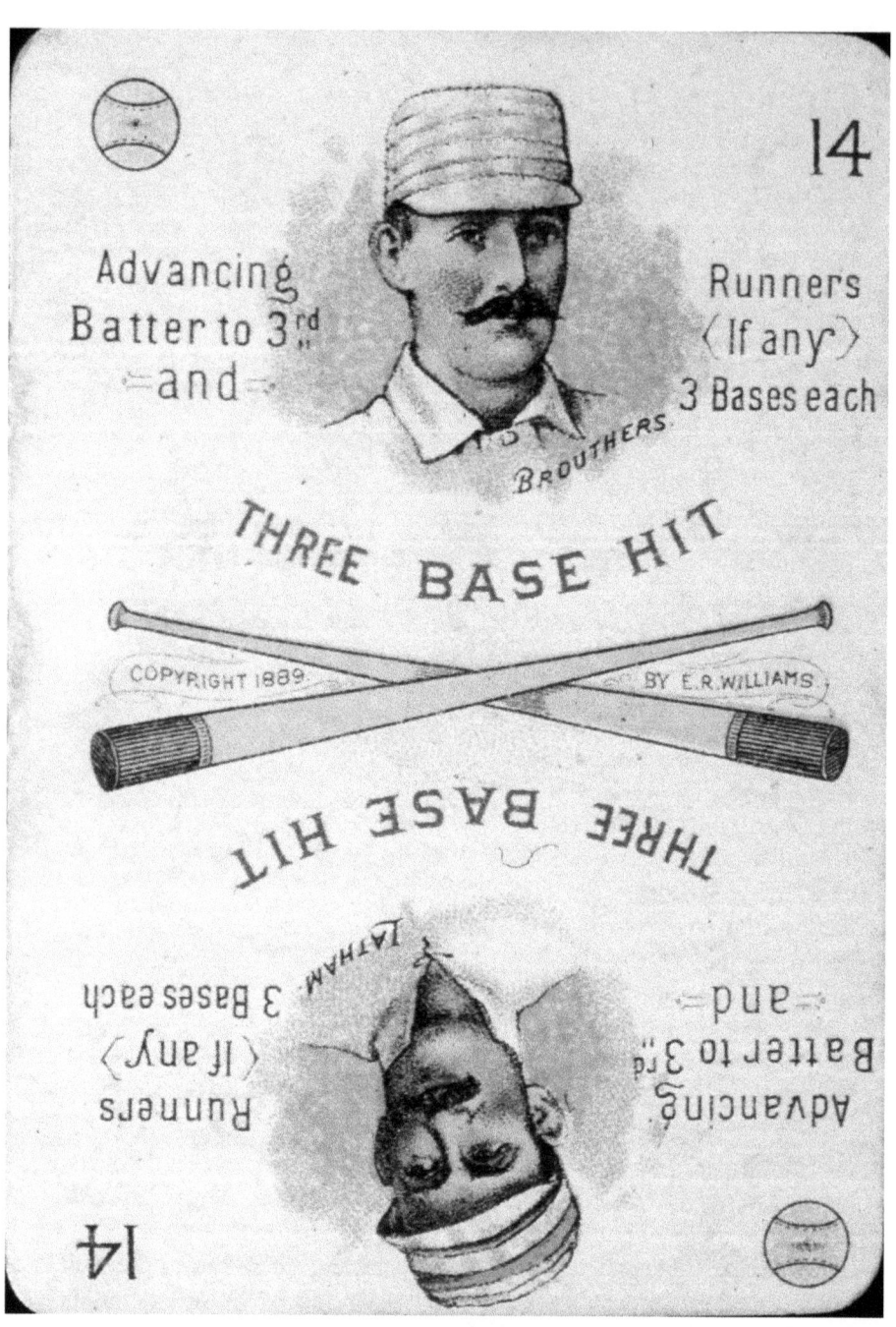

Dan Brouthers/Arlie Latham Williams Baseball Game card, 1888. Drawing the Brouthers/Latham card rewarded the game player with a triple. Brouthers ranks eighth all-time in triples, with 205, while Latham hit just 85 lifetime three-baggers (Transcendental Graphics/www.theruckerarchive.com).

holdouts, and rumors that the club's owners were contemplating trading Hanlon prompted an uncharacteristic personal response from the normally reticent Dan Brouthers: "It would be a great mistake to let Hanlon go. It would seriously affect our chances for the pennant. I don't know where a man as good could be secured."[99]

By the end of the first week in New Orleans, backup catcher Charlie Ganzel and starter Charley Bennett were both hurt, the former from being hit on the hand with a ball, and the latter with a sore arm. "If he [Bennett] tried to make a quick throw to catch a runner, he would hurt his arm, no doubt."[100] Worse still, Sam Thompson, the league's offensive leader in 1887, was reported to have an arm so lame that he could not throw across the diamond.

After an embarrassing 9–6 loss to a local team in Birmingham on April 6, the *Detroit Free Press*, under the headline "They Need to Brace Up," criticized the team for "playing with a listlessness that was very reprehensible."[101] Near the end of April, Ned Hanlon and Jim White re-signed, but White did so "only on condition that he was not to be disciplined by [Manager] Watkins."[102]

The press now took management's side in its disputes with the players, asserting that "a condition of growing insubordination exists in the team."[103] In response, the Detroit directors requested that manager Watkins return to sitting on the bench

Stylized Dan Brouthers full-figure etching, circa 1888 (Transcendental Graphics/ www.theruckerarchive.com).

with the team during games (it was common for non-playing managers to direct the team from the stands). "As some of the players had objected to his presence on the bench, he was loath to return, but he felt that better ball would be played if he was there to watch the men."[104]

Leaving Louisville after a rainout there on April 9, Dan Brouthers, while en route with the team to Cincinnati by train, joined the list of sick and injured players. "Complaining all morning of feeling badly, he said the symptoms were exactly like those of ... a case of malaria, and long before Cincinnati was reached, the big fellow had his head tied up and was struggling with alternate chills and fever. He was given medical treatment immediately on arrival and it is hoped he will come up well."[105] Weak and still ill, he returned to the lineup a few days later, but was ineffective in exhibition contests over the next week in Cincinnati, St. Louis, and Kansas City.

Detroit began the 1888 season inauspiciously in Pittsburgh on April 20 with a 5–2 loss to the Alleghenys. After dropping the next two games, the Wolverines managed a win in the final game of the series and then split four games with Indianapolis before returning to Detroit for the home opener, once again against the Alleghenys. Thanks to Brouthers' hot bat (11 hits, including three triples), the "Big Four plus Five" took four straight from the Smoky City nine. Despite injuries and dissention on the team, things were looking up. With Brouthers hitting at a .369 clip over the season's first 28 games, Detroit climbed to third place.

Brouthers celebrated the arrival of June with a terrific home run blast in Philadelphia that prompted immediate accolades. "What a hit it was! The ball went sailing a hundred feet over the fence and must have dropped a square block beyond the right field fence of the local grounds. There is no doubt about it being the largest hit ever made on the new grounds."[106] After Brouthers collected three singles in addition to the home run, Philadelphia pitcher Dan Casey had seen enough of the slugger that afternoon. "In the ninth inning when he [Brouthers] came to bat with two hands out and a man on second, Casey kept the ball a foot away from the plate and sent him to first on called balls."[107]

The controversies that plagued the Detroit team took a back seat to diplomacy during their next series at Washington, when the league champions were invited to visit President Grover Cleveland at the White House. Cleveland's meteoric rise to the Presidency began in Buffalo, where he briefly served as mayor before being elected Governor of New York in 1883. His years in public office in the city corresponded exactly to the era of Brouthers, White, Rowe and Richardson on the Bisons. Their meeting with the leader of the country was therefore charged with special meaning.

Three. *Big Dan: 1886–1888*

"How's Jimmy Galvin?" said President Cleveland during the Detroit Club's visit to the White house last Wednesday. "He is all right," said Dan Brouthers. "I am glad to hear it," continued the President. "Galvin was a great favorite of mine in Buffalo." The President recognized Brouthers, Rowe, Conway, and "Deacon" White as old acquaintances. After the formalities of introduction were over the players stood in a semicircle in front of the President while he commended their fine athletic appearance and congratulated them upon having won the title of "World Beaters." He expressed his regret that public business has prevented him going out to see them play, and alluded to the fact that the Washington team was not making a very creditable showing.

"Do you keep up your hard hitting?" he enquired of Brouthers. "I try to," said Dan with a smile.... After wishing them success in their efforts to retain the pennant for a second term the champions withdrew, highly delighted with the pleasant and jovial reception at the White House.[108]

This was the last pleasant moment the team would share in the season. At Boston a week later, "Brouthers' hand was split," and it was announced that "he will do well if he plays in ten days."[109] During the same game, starting pitcher Getzein and manager Watkins got into a shouting match after Watkins criticized his pitcher's performance. On getting some back talk from his pitcher, Watkins fined Getzein $10. The enraged Getzein continued his verbal harangue until his fines reached $100, and then went silent. A few days later, the *Detroit Free Press* published this review of the crisis in Detroit that was allegedly penned by a writer for an unnamed Boston paper: "There is more than one man in the Detroit nine who would jump at the chance to play in this city (Boston). The men themselves are the authority for this statement. They get no credit for their splendid work and at each victory they are hauled over the coals by dyspeptic writers."[110]

Meanwhile, injuries continued to decimate the team. Deacon White injured his side and Hardy Richardson was seriously hurt when his foot caught on second base while sliding, "If Hardy is seen at [playing] second base again this year he will be doing well."[111] A few days later, Sam Thompson, who had been trying to stay in the lineup even though he couldn't throw, was "laid off without pay until he can play."[112]

Recovered from his injury, Brouthers, despite a brief slump in late July, was carrying the team offensively. His inside-the-park home run off Philadelphia's Charley Buffinton on July 13 won a close 3–2 game for Detroit. Eight days later, his home run and three runs scored helped beat Chicago, 9–6. The four-bagger, hit off George Van Haltren, was one of the most unusual of his career. "The ball went with a bang against the right field fence, flew up behind the Mobley sign [an advertisement] and stuck there, Dan trotting around home."[113] Three days later, in a double-header against Pittsburgh, he collected four hits, including two doubles and a triple in the first game and a home run in the second game.

This mid–July sweep of the Alleghenys enabled the Wolverines, despite all their problems, to move into first place over Chicago. Then disaster struck. Jack Rowe contracted malaria. Sam Thompson attempted a comeback, only to have to return to the bench, his arm reinjured, prompting the opinion that it was "considered doubtful if this great fielder and mighty batsman will ever be in condition to play ball again."[114] The pitching failed, the runs dried up, and the team lost 16 straight games, remaining in the losing column for almost a month (July 28 to August 21). The Detroit sports pages echoed the question on the minds of the fans: "Will the Wolverines ever again win a game?"[115] There were, of course, more victories eventually, but not enough to prevent the Wolverines from falling out of pennant contention. In the midst of the great slump, manager Bob Watkins resigned. His place was taken by Bob Leadley, Secretary/Treasurer of the Detroit franchise, who had served as Detroit's point man in the 1885 negotiations with Buffalo that brought the Big Four to Detroit. In a few weeks, Leadley would be selling the famous infield quartet along with the rest of the team.

The final ignominy of the 1888 season came when the reigning league champions dropped two of three games to last-place Washington, leaving the Wolverines in fifth place. Amid the gloom, *Sporting Life* reminded its national audience that one Detroit player continued to hustle on the base paths until the last day of the season. "Big Dan Brouthers is not an extraordinary base-runner, yet he is the leading run-getter in the league, topping the record with 118. Ryan comes next with 115, Johnson has 102, and Anson 101. These are the only league players who have made over 100 runs each."[116]

Despite his disappointment over Detroit's 1888 finish, Brouthers soon celebrated another happy family event. His second child, Daniel Leo, was born a month after the season ended.

On Sunday, October 14, the *Detroit Free Press* confirmed the news that most in the city had feared was coming: "Detroit has lost its splendid base ball club. The Directors sell it because of lack of support, while Cleveland takes the franchise.... It was the natural consequence of non-support of a grand base ball organization, and it serves the people of this city exactly right.... Ta, ta, baseball."[117] In reality, Cleveland got little from the deal, since the highest-salaried players were sold off to Boston (Charlie Bennett, Dan Brouthers, and Deacon White), Philadelphia (Sam Thompson) and Pittsburgh (Ned Hanlon and Jack Rowe).

The Big Four was no more. Two years later, Jack Rowe and Deacon White retired from major league competition. Hardy Richardson played four

Three. *Big Dan: 1886–1888*

more seasons, the last two as a part-timer. Big Dan Brouthers outlasted them all, playing in the big leagues until mid-season, 1896. Leaving Detroit, his seventh professional team in eight years, at the end of 1888, he was forced to keep his suitcase handy, since he covered first base for another seven major league teams before heading for a second career in the minor leagues and then in semi-pro ball. He wouldn't hang up his spikes for good for another 22 years. By the end of the 1888 season, however, some critics, noting a decline in his offensive numbers, had written him off as a "back number" (a "has-been"). There was still a lot of spring left in his step, however, and a lot of thunder left in his big bat.

Four
Old Jed: 1889–1891

> Dan Brouthers, as a hitter, has always been acknowledged as being second to none.—Bill Sharsig, Manager, Philadelphia Athletics, *Sporting Life*, March 25, 1891.

Unlike the cities that hosted Dan Brouthers' two previous National League teams, Boston had a long and distinguished baseball pedigree. For a time in the 1840s and 1850s, boys in the Hub City and across Massachusetts played a unique form of early baseball, appropriately called the Massachusetts Game, whose rules included the practice of "soaking," or retrieving a batted ball, throwing it at an advancing runner, and hitting him for an out.

By the 1860s, however, New York's Knickerbocker Rules had supplanted the local playing regulations, and in 1871 a Boston team, the Red Stockings, joined the new National Association, switching to the Association's successor, the National League, in 1876. Thanks to stars like George and Harry Wright, Jim O'Rourke, Ross Barnes and young Deacon White, Boston won an unprecedented six pennants in the 1870s, four in the Association, and after changing the team name to the Boston Reds, two more in the National League.

In 1883 the club again made a nickname change, this time to the Beaneaters (its prosaic symbol was a pot of baked beans) and won another pennant. Hard times followed in the mid-1880s, when Boston fell from the ranks of the top teams, finishing fifth for three consecutive years (1885–1887). The club's owners then undertook a two-year rebuilding plan that cost them $50,000 (approximately two million dollars today), but their efforts failed to net them a championship.

In February 1887, Boston acquired the game's greatest star, Mike "King" Kelly, from Chicago. The sale cost the Beaneaters $10,000, at the time the largest sum ever paid for a player. A remarkably talented, five-skill player who was comfortable at any position on the field, Kelly won two batting titles during his

FOUR. *Old Jed: 1889–1891* 77

eight years with the White Stockings, but his penchant for raucous escapades off the field and for showing up drunk at the ball park eventually drove Chicago owner Al Spalding and manager Cap Anson to distraction. Although in general he performed well for Boston over the next three years, one of his classic drinking binges at a crucial stage of the 1889 season contributed to Boston's loss of the pennant to the New York Giants.

One year after acquiring Kelly, Boston again raided Chicago's well-stocked roster, purchasing the White Stockings' ace pitcher, John Clarkson. Born in Cambridge, Massachusetts, the 27-year-old Clarkson was returning to his native state after four seasons with the White Stockings, and was considered one of the game's top pitchers. Between 1885 and 1887, he averaged 42 wins, including 53 in 1885, and over 500 innings of work in the pitcher's

Boston Beaneaters 1889. A stout Dan Brouthers stands, third from the right, behind bowler-hatted Manager Jim Hart. To Hart's left is pitcher John Clarkson, who led the league with 49 wins. Seated to Clarkson's left is pitcher Hoss Radbourn. Mike Kelly sits to Hart's immediate right. Kelly, Radbourn and Clarkson, like Brouthers, were all subsequently elected to the Hall of Fame (National Baseball Hall of Fame Library, Cooperstown, New York).

box per season. Never an overpowering pitcher, Clarkson, a tall and slender right-hander, possessed a good fastball, better curve, and excellent change-up, but relied on pinpoint control and an encyclopedic knowledge of opposing hitters' weaknesses for his success. His on-field brilliance masked a darker side. A decade after retiring from baseball, he was hospitalized with "a nervous breakdown, combined with depression, certainly exacerbated by his excessive drinking. He was said to live in the past more than the present, often recalling his baseball days as if they were yesterday."[1] John Clarkson never fully recovered from his mental illness, and in 1905, at age 47, he died of pneumonia at McLean Psychiatric Hospital in Belmont, Massachusetts.

Besides Kelly and Clarkson, Boston's returning players included team captain and slick-fielding third baseman Billy Nash, who would lead the Beaneaters to three consecutive championships in the 1890s, and light-hitting second baseman Joe Quinn, baseball's first Australian-born player, who lasted 17 seasons in the major leagues and kept busy in the off-season working as an embalmer at a St. Louis funeral parlor. John Clarkson was assisted in the pitching box by Hoss Radbourn, the underhand-style hurler who had won a record 59 games for Providence in 1884, and who was now near the end of his career.

The anticipation with which players and fans awaited the start of the 1889 season was tempered by an accompanying sense of unease caused by continuing conflicts between players and team owners. Over the winter, the owners unanimously voted to implement a new policy, the Classification Plan, which lowered all player salaries across the board. It also based a player's remuneration not just on his skill on the diamond, but on his personal habits and attitude. Attempts to overturn this rule, as we shall see, were rebuffed.

After purchasing Dan Brouthers' contract, several of Boston's directors made the trip to Poughkeepsie in November 1888, for salary negotiations with the Wappingers Falls slugger. Clearly aware now of his status as the best hitter in baseball, Brouthers drove a hard bargain. "The Boston men never let money stand in the way when they want to seek a player, and after a long interview, said to have taken up nearly a whole day and raising the salary figure to $5,000, the big first baseman was induced to become a Bostonian.... This signing of Brouthers ... makes him a higher salaried man than the great [Mike] Kelly, who has agreed to play for $4,200."[2]

In addition to his customary battles with National League pitchers on his arrival in Boston, Dan Brouthers initially had to contend with upset fans who were staunch supporters of his predecessor at first base, John Morrill. A Boston native and the city's first homegrown star, Morrill had been with the club since 1876, and had captained and managed the team for all or part of seven seasons. Upon Mike Kelly's arrival in 1887, the team's owners chose the

Four. *Old Jed: 1889–1891*

wildly popular Kelly as captain, thus setting up an inevitable power struggle between Kelly and manager Morrill over the next two seasons.

Sold to Washington after Dan Brouthers signed with Boston, Morrill nevertheless still had many supporters among hometown fans and the press. His replacement as manager, Jim Hart, had never played professional baseball and had an undistinguished managerial career that included two losing seasons with the Louisville Colonels of the American Association. Hart's hire made it clear that Boston's directors wanted team captain Mike Kelly to make the major on-field decisions for the club.

The 1889 pennant race proved to be the closest and most exciting in the National League's 14-year history, with a champion not determined until the final day of the campaign. It soon became evident that only two teams were in serious contention: New York, the reigning champion, and the reconstituted Boston nine. New York's and Boston's closest rival, Chicago, would finish the season 19 games behind the league champion.

The Giants and the Beaneaters were perfectly balanced adversaries. Each featured a tall, left-handed, power-hitting first baseman — Boston's Brouthers and New York's Roger Connor. Both teams matched speedsters on the base paths — Mike Kelly stole 68 bases, the Giants' John Ward 62. Catchers Charley Bennett and Buck Ewing were unquestionably the best men in the league behind the plate. In the pitcher's box, Boston's John Clarkson and Hoss Radbourn's combined 69 victories would be matched by New York's trio of Tim Keefe (27), Mickey Welch (28) and Cannonball Crane (14). When the dust settled, New York had taken the championship for a second consecutive year, but only by the slimmest of margins.

Statistically, the Giants and the Boston nine were so evenly matched that in most areas the difference between them was a few thousandths of a percentage point. Boston's pitchers registered a 3.36 ERA; New York's was 3.47. The Giants' fielding average was .920; the Beaneaters' was .926. However, the scales were tipped in favor of New York in two significant offensive categories: team batting and runs scored. The Giants hit at a .282 pace, compared to Boston's .270 mark. New York also pushed more than a hundred more runs across the plate than did Boston over the course of the season (New York, 935; Boston, 826).

Brouthers' extra-base hits declined slightly in 1889, but he reached his highest career RBI total thus far (118 in 126 games) and upped his batting average 66 points over his 1888 mark to a league-leading .373. Although his home run total slipped to seven, several of them broke distance records, and another one was not counted due to a frustrating ground rule. Worse still, that blow, strangely enough, ended a game in a loss for Boston.

On May 1 at Philadelphia, Brouthers had already collected a single, a double and a walk when he came to bat in the ninth inning with Boston down two runs and a man on base with two outs. Then he met the ball

> with a whunk that rang out like the crack of a whip, and the crowd saw the ball go straight toward the centrefield fence, and fully 15 feet higher than the top [of the fence]. [Philadelphia center fielder] Fogarty stood looking. It was dollars to cents that the game was tied. But a high wire screen some 20 feet high, that is fastened to the top of the fence to keep the ball from going out on the rail road tracks, prevented the sphere from going over.[3]

Brouthers was robbed of a home run, but things then got even worse. Boston's baserunner, Tom Brown, assuming that the blast was a round-tripper, began a leisurely jog around the bases. Meanwhile, Phillies center fielder Jimmy Fogarty picked up the ball, which had fallen back onto the field, and fired it to shortstop Art Irwin. Irwin threw home to catcher Pop Shriver in time for him to tag the unsuspecting Brown out at the plate, ending the game.

Fortunately for Brouthers, other parks had not gone to the lengths that Philadelphia had to keep balls from leaving the park. In a blowout 23–3 win against Washington on the Nationals' home grounds on May 6, he went 3-for-5, including a double, triple and home run, and scored five runs. The four-bagger, hit off "Egyptian Healy" in the first inning, was crushed over the center field fence. "It was the first time a ball had ever been hit over the fence. The same hit would have cleared the centre field fence at the Boston grounds. It never raised over 25 feet high at any time."[4]

A month later, playing at home against Philadelphia, Brouthers demonstrated that he was not just a pull hitter by belting another first-inning home run, this time to the opposite field, hitting it far enough over the left-field fence to reach the roof of a passing train outside Boston's South End Grounds. "Dan didn't get into it square: [it] just had enough to clear the left field fence and dance a few steps on top of a passenger car."[5] At Indianapolis on August 7, he hit another opposite-field four-bagger for an even greater distance. "Dan lifted the leather far out over the left field fence for three runs [Mike Kelly and Tom Brown were on base at the time]."[6]

The tall first baseman also hit a tape-measure four-bagger against the rival Giants in a game played at an unusual location. Prior to the start of the 1889 season, New York City had evicted the Giants from their home grounds on the north end of Central Park in Manhattan to make room for 111th Street, which soon was cut through the heart of the old Polo Grounds. Consequently, the Giants played 25 of their early-season games at the St. George Cricket Grounds on Staten Island, home field of the American Association New York Metropolitans during the 1886–1887 seasons. In a 2–1 loss to New York on

June 11 at the St. George Grounds, Brouthers scored Boston's only run, connecting in the seventh inning off future Hall of Famer Mickey Welch. "Welch shot one at him with a spin. Dan met it square on the trademark, and away she went on a bee line, straight for the centre field fence. [Center fielder George] Gore stood up against the fence as the ball went sailing over his head for a home run, and the longest hit ever made on the grounds."[7]

Years later, an anonymous letter writer who had seen Brouthers' blast on Staten Island provided more details to the *New York Times*:

> There has been mention from time to time of long hits in baseball, and Dan Brouthers was given credit for hitting one over Babylon. I'll tell you how that came about.... It happened during the season [1889] when the Giants had to move from the old Polo Grounds, 110th Street and Fifth Avenue, to the St. George Grounds on Staten Island. This was a handsome amusement park ground built by Mr. Winan. While the Giants were playing there he presented a very beautiful and imposing spectacle called "The Fall of Babylon," the set of buildings for that spectacle being erected far back of centre field. In a game between Detroit [actually, the Boston Beaneaters] and the Giants one afternoon, Brouthers hit the ball over the highest turrets of "Babylon," the longest hit ever seen in those days and one that became famous in baseball history.[8]

In addition to news items about Brouthers' mighty drives over league fences, some sportswriters were also taking notice of how difficult Brouthers was to strikeout. Three months into the 1889 season, for example, a West Coast paper reported that "It was a big feather in the cap of young pitcher [Amos] Rusie, of Indianapolis, to strikeout big Dan Brouthers. It was the third time the big fellow has struck out all year."[9] At season's end, after 565 plate appearances, Brouthers' had struck out just six times. Rusie, the fireballing Indianapolis rookie, would spend the remainder of his career with the Giants except for three games with Cincinnati in 1901. In 1977 he was elected to the Baseball Hall of Fame.

Brouthers' exploits, and those of all players in baseball, took a back seat to sports news of a different nature on July 9, 1889, when accounts of a boxing match that had taken place the day before appeared in newspapers across the country. On July 8, the most famous prize fight of the nineteenth century, and the sport's last significant bare-knuckle bout, took place in Richburg, Mississippi, between reigning champion John L. Sullivan and challenger Jake Kilrain.

Born in Roxbury, Massachusetts, Sullivan, known as the "Boston Strong Boy," was the nation's first sports celebrity. A good ballplayer, he reportedly declined a contract offer from the Cincinnati Reds in order to dedicate himself to the ring. During his long boxing career, Sullivan frequently served as a guest umpire or substitute player in exhibition games in New York and Boston, and was reported to have accepted an invitation to fight an exhibition boxing match in 1887 against Giants slugger Roger Connor, considered at the time to be the best boxer in baseball, at Madison Square Garden. At the last minute, however, illness forced the champion to cancel the match, and it was never rescheduled.[10]

Sullivan's opponent in Mississippi on July 8, 1889, was John Joseph "Jake" Kilrain, who hailed from Long Island. Standing 5'10" tall and weighing 190 pounds, Kilrain equaled the champion in weight and height.

Since at the time bare-knuckle boxing was prohibited in the United States, the bout's location was kept secret until a few days before the event. In the early morning hours of July 8, 3,000 spectators who had gotten word of the fight made the 104-mile journey by train from New Orleans to the bout's location, a secluded wooded area three miles from Hattiesburg. The fight began at 10 A.M. and continued for over two hours in 100-degree heat, until Kilrain, his nose broken, his lips split, and with one eye swollen shut, conceded after 75 rounds.

In later life, Sullivan and Kilrain became good friends and often relived their epic battle over drinks at Kilrain's bar in Baltimore. At the champion's funeral in 1918, his old adversary served as an usher.

As the 1889 baseball season progressed, the stress of the pennant race affected Boston players, their manager, and their field captain in different ways. After an 8–2 loss at Chicago on June 29, the Beaneaters and the press tried unsuccessfully to discover the whereabouts of team captain Mike Kelly, who had not shown up for the contest. Kelly had complained of a charley horse during morning practice and by game time had disappeared. Many suspected that the former White Stocking had spent the afternoon gambling at one of his favorite old haunts — the Chicago race track.

With pitcher Hoss Radbourn "laid up"[11] and ace John Clarkson exhausted from over-work as the Independence Day holiday approached, the players expressed their displeasure to club owners over a schedule that required them to play a game each on a Monday and Tuesday at Chicago and then an exhibition game in Toledo on Wednesday, before taking the field for a July 4 double header at Cleveland. Team directors did not respond to the players' complaint, but Mother Nature took pity on the weary Beaneaters, sending rain to wash out the exhibition game.

After a disappointing loss at Chicago in mid–August, some of the team's directors criticized Jim Hart's lax team management. *Boston Globe* writer Tim Murnane soon provided specific details that explained the rationale for the criticism.[12] Two utility men who also served as back-up pitchers, Kid Madden and Bill Daley, had been drinking and carousing until 1:00 A.M. after the humiliating 9–0 loss to Chicago. Daley was scheduled to pitch the following afternoon. Murnane reported that upon returning to their hotel in an inebriated state, the pair continued to indulge and had four whiskey sours delivered to their room. Although Boston won the Saturday game, 9–7, a hung-over Daley pitched poorly, and Hart made no attempt to discipline either him or Madden.

Despite such problems, thanks to John Clarkson's arm and Dan Brouthers' bat, Boston found itself comfortably in first place as late as the second week in July, with a 40–20 record, followed by the champion Giants in second place and a surprising Cleveland team in third. Soon, Cleveland had cooled off and New York was breathing down Boston's neck.

Thanks in part to a thirteen-game stretch blemished only by a tie, the Giants had been neck-in-neck with Boston for much of September, and were within a few percentage points of the Beaneaters on October 1. On October 2, "things fell apart"[13] for Boston, thanks to the conduct of captain Kelly, who reported to the Cleveland ball grounds too drunk to play and sat on the bench in an overcoat during the contest. After Hardy Richardson was called out on a close play at home, Kelly, still incapacitated, began arguing vociferously with umpire John McQuaid, who soon summoned police and had Kelly thrown out of the park. Boston was held to four hits in a 7–1 defeat, "and Kelly, the captain and inspiration, was on the outside looking in as the game ended."[14]

New York took its next two games from Cleveland, and Boston rallied and did the same in Pittsburgh. The teams battled the same opponents for the decisive final game of the season — Boston played away at Pittsburgh while New York took on Cleveland at Cleveland. An exhausted John Clarkson lost 6–1 in Pittsburgh while the Giants were beating Cleveland 5–3 to take the pennant. Kelly's excuse was that the Beaneaters "were outplayed off the field, not on it."[15] As the future Hall of Famer's biographer, Marty Appel, observed, Kelly "ought to have known the irony of his comments."[16]

Overlooked in the gloom in Boston was the splendid performance of John Clarkson in quest of the pennant. He started 72 games, completed 68, and led the league in wins (49), innings pitched (620), strikeouts (284), shutouts (8), and earned run average (2.73). In doing so, "Clarkson compiled 21 more wins, 22 more complete games, and 200 more innings than any other League pitcher. All are major league records for the greatest margin of difference between a leader and a runner-up."[17]

While players' hits, runs and errors (on and off the field) were the sources of most baseball reports in the mid-to-late 1880s, the daily newspapers and weekly sports journals gradually began to make mention of the formation of a ballplayers' union. The first such notice appeared in June 1885, innocuously announcing that "the ball playing profession is gradually swelling in dignity and importance. A protective union has been proposed.... Each player will be assessed $5 a month."[18] This "proposed" union became a reality in October 1885, when nine members of the New York Giants established the Brotherhood of Professional Base Ball Players. A year later, the Brotherhood could claim "107 members and autonomous chapters in each [National] league city. Later, a successful mission also planted chapters in most [American] association towns, thereby adding some 30 more recruits. Soon the union would challenge the existing structure of Major League baseball by creating its own league."[19]

The architect of both the Brotherhood movement and the Players' League, John Montgomery Ward, was uniquely suited to his task. Unlike the majority of his teammates and opponents, most of whom by age 14 were working six days a week in mills, foundries, mines, or on the farm, Ward at that age was taking courses in Latin, Greek, Algebra and Geometry at Pennsylvania State College (now Penn State University). Dismissed near the end of his third year of studies for disciplinary reasons, he caught on as a pitcher with a nearby semi-pro baseball team, the Renovo Resolutes, earning ten dollars a month and board. Two years later, at age 18, he was a starter for the Providence Grays and the youngest player in the National League.

Released by Providence after the 1882 season due to arm trouble, Ward signed with the Giants, taught himself to throw left-handed and to switch-hit, and played the outfield until his injured right arm healed. After it did, he spent a decade in the infield until he retired in 1894. Ward's on-field records are a tribute to his versatility. He led the league in stolen bases (111 in 1887) and in assists (450 in 1890) and fielding (.919 in 1887) as a shortstop. As a pitcher, he led the league in strikeouts (239 in 1879), shutouts (8 in 1880) and fielding (.993 in 1880), and threw the second perfect game in major league history (1880).

During his years with the Giants, Ward returned to his studies, earning two degrees (Law and Political Science) in the off-season at Columbia College. Handsome, articulate and intelligent, he was the ideal man to lead the Brotherhood, and proved a serious, determined adversary in the struggle for the control of baseball that took place during the 1890 season.

The players of the 1880s had a long list of grievances against team owners, including salary limits, broken promises for bonus pay, salary suspension while they were recovering from injury, and blacklisting, which "could be applied to many offences, from drinking and training violations to jumping to a rival league."[20] The most hated restriction was the Reserve Rule, which by 1885 had been expanded to include 12 players per club, thus effectively covering almost the entire team.

To address these issues, John Ward and some New York teammates secretly formed the Brotherhood of Professional Base Ball Players and recruited more members in clandestine meetings with players from all other league teams. Dan Brouthers and other Detroit Wolverines were the first men outside of the New York club to sign up. Brouthers' early alignment with the Brotherhood, even after having just signed a lucrative contract with Detroit, confirms that while he had done well in his negotiations with the Wolverines' owners, he was well aware that if he had had the right to offer his services to all other clubs, his salary would have been considerably higher.

In November 1886, with the union membership now over 100, John Ward went public with the announcement of the Brotherhood's existence and introduced the organization's leadership. Ward himself was elected President, Dan Brouthers Vice President, and New York pitcher Tim Keefe Secretary. Ward then took his campaign to the press, first sending a July 1887 letter to the *New York Times* that succinctly criticized the Reserve Clause. A month later he published a 4,000-word article expanding on the topic in *Lippincott's Magazine*, a popular literary journal of the day.

In November 1887, Nick Young, President of the National League, and Al Spalding, informal head of the club owners, agreed to meet with a three-man Brotherhood delegation consisting of John Ward, Dan Brouthers and Ned Hanlon, to discuss the Brotherhood's grievances. Ward's selection of Hanlon and Brouthers to accompany him is noteworthy. As captain of the Wolverines, Hanlon had served as the club's representative in the 1885 negotiations for the transfer of the Big Four to Detroit, a role that had proven his ability as a player to negotiate both with, and on behalf of, club owners. Brouthers had no equivalent experience, but the mere presence of the game's greatest hitter, who now was serving as the Brotherhood's Vice President, sent a powerful signal to Young and Spalding of the Brotherhood's ability to gain support from the top players in the league. Although the league agreed to make a few changes to players' contracts at the meeting, these promises were subsequently broken. Ward, Brouthers and Hanlon's efforts did succeed, however, in gaining formal recognition of the Brotherhood by the league.

The tipping point in the League/Brotherhood struggle came at the end of the 1888 season. With John Ward out of the country, league owners unanimously passed a new salary limitation plan, based not only on a player's on-field ability, but also on his "personal habits and attitude."[21]

Shortly before the opening of the 1889 season, a Brotherhood committee consisting of Ward, Brouthers and three others met at the Fifth Avenue Hotel in New York and voted to consider calling a player strike if the new classification plan was not rescinded. Ward subsequently met privately with Spalding in Chicago on June 24, only to be told to wait until the end of the season to express the Brotherhood's concerns at the league's annual meeting.

On July 14, convinced of the league's intransigence, Ward revealed to Brotherhood representatives from all league teams his plan to form a new league. Four months later, on November 4, the Brotherhood went public with the plan. In the short span of five months, Ward found financial support for eight teams and organized an entirely new baseball league, the Players' National League of Base Ball Clubs, which would compete against National League and American Association teams in 1890. Players were asked to invest in their new clubs by buying at least $500 worth of stock at $100 per share. Blacklisting and the Classification and Reserve systems were abolished. A new day in major league baseball had arrived.

Six Players' League franchises were placed in cities with existing National League teams (Chicago, Philadelphia, Boston, New York, Cleveland and Pittsburgh). Two others (Buffalo and Brooklyn) were located in non-league towns. Playing fields were leased, baseball diamonds laid out, grandstands constructed and players signed to contracts. Over the course of just a year, the players' dream of a league of their own had gone from an idea to a fully functioning organization.

John Ward, architect of the Brotherhood and the Players' League, was elected to the Hall of Fame in 1964. His Cooperstown plaque makes no mention of his remarkable leadership role in both the Brotherhood and the Players' League.

All players who sided with the Brotherhood or who jumped their contracts and signed with the Players' League did so at considerable risk. Dan Brouthers' high-profile role in the organization and the new league made him potentially more vulnerable than most. A new addition to the Brouthers clan, son Daniel Leo, arrived in November 1888, and the slugger's family responsibilities now included his widowed father as well as his wife and two children. It is likewise probable that he also was providing financial assistance to some of his siblings. Had the Brotherhood failed, Brouthers, as a "prime force"[22] in recruiting his teammates and players from other teams, could have faced penalties that included banishment from the National League and blacklisting should he try to play elsewhere. If the Players' League failed, Brouthers would lose his obligatory stock investment in it, and could expect no mercy from triumphant National League owners. Despite such risks to his future livelihood, Brouthers remained a loyal soldier in the Brotherhood and the Players' League wars.

With the exception of John Clarkson and Charley Bennett, the Boston Players' League team, known as the Reds, looked very similar to the 1889 National League Beaneaters squad. Newcomers from Philadelphia's American

FOUR. *Old Jed: 1889–1891* 87

1890 Players' League Boston Reds. Dan Brouthers stands third from left. Pitcher Addison Gumbert stands, far right. Seated, center: player/manager Mike Kelly; Hoss Radbourn is third from right. The Reds won the only Players' League pennant behind Radbourn and Gumberts' combined 50 wins and Brouthers' team-leading .330 batting average. Brouthers named his second son, Addison, after pitcher Gumbert (National Baseball Hall of Fame Library, Cooperstown, New York).

Association team included Art Irwin, a light-hitting shortstop, and fleet-footed outfielder Harry Stovey. Irwin, who is credited with having invented the fielder's mitt, would manage four different major league teams in the 1890s. Stovey, who led the American Association in 1889 in runs (152), home runs (19) and RBI (119), is one of three players in major league baseball history (the others are George Gore and Billy Hamilton) to record more runs scored than games played in his career. A third new man, Rhode Island-born rookie, Morgan Murphy, took Charley Bennett's place behind the plate.

John Clarkson, hero of the 1889 Beaneaters campaign, ruined his reputation among most players and many fans when he deserted the Brotherhood to play for the Beaneaters, taking Charley Bennett with him. Clarkson's reward was a guaranteed two-year deal at $6,500 per year. In his absence, the pitching box for the Players' League Bostons was occupied in part by the returning Hoss Radbourn and by Ad Gumbert, a Pittsburgh native and former member of Chicago's White Stockings. The duo performed well for the Reds in 1890, compiling a combined 50–24 mark.

Although challenged early in the season by Chicago and Brooklyn, the Reds easily took the first (and only) Players' League pennant, posting an 81–48 mark, 6½ games ahead of second-place Brooklyn. Dan Brouthers hit a healthy .330 and led the league in on-base-percentage, and most of his other offensive statistics were at the same level as they had been in 1888. Defensively, 1890 was his poorest season, as he led the league in errors at his position with 49, a career high.

Brouthers hit only two official home runs in the Players' League (most sources today incorrectly state that he hit just one[23]), but several other blasts that he hit over league fences in regulation games were officially scored either as doubles or triples. In a home game early in the season at the Congress Street Grounds against New York, for example, a ball he drove into the seats was recorded as a double. "The champion batsman of the world was not going to be outdone, and the crowd saw a ball go on a line to the seats in centre field that left a trail after it, and [Billy] Nash crossed the plate with the ... last run of the game."[24] The game's box score credits Brouthers with two bases for this hit. As baseball historian David Nemec explains, before 1920 "the rule was firm that a team batting last could not win by more than one run when it won the game in the ninth or an extra inning."[25] A month later, in the second game of a Decoration Day doubleheader against Buffalo, Brouthers again "drove the ball to the top of the centre field seats," [26] but he earned only a double for his effort.

On July 10 against Pittsburgh, Brouthers hit his first official home run of the campaign with two outs in the eighth inning. "Dan Brouthers put the ball over the left field fence for a homer."[27] The following day against the same team, however, he hit "one of the hardest drives ever seen on the grounds,"[28] but was awarded only a triple for the effort:

> Dan Brouthers was next up. Dan is recognized as the greatest living batsman, and has struck his old gait.... Dan walked up to the plate much as a man would face a jury, and to prove that he is still the scientific slugger of old, let his trusty club go at the ball, much the same as a man would hurl a stone at a black snake in huckleberry time.... A sound followed like the cracking of a hickory nut with a flat iron, and the ball was seen cutting a pigeon wing over [Ned] Hanlon's head as he went on a dead run for the bleachers in centre field.... There was never a ball hit harder. It hit the seats about half way up and came bounding back nearly to second base, while [Harry] Stovey scored and Dan anchored at third, covered with a smile of satisfaction.[29]

A few days later against Chicago, he was credited with another double for a blast hit into the outfield bleachers. "Brouthers hit the leather over [center-fielder Jimmy] Ryan's head on to the seats. Kelly was on third and Brouthers on second when the ball came back."[30] The following day, this scene was repeated, with Dan ending up on third base this time rather than on second. "Brouthers started the second inning by driving the ball over Ryan's head on to the seats for three bases."[31]

The five blows over the center field fence at the Congress Street Grounds that were not counted as home runs were tremendous blasts by 1890 standards. According to data provided in the *Boston Daily Globe* in February 1890,[32] and in December 1889,[33] the center field fence at the park measured 385 feet from home plate. All of the above-mentioned hits cleared the fence, one of them hit "about half way up"[34] in the seats, and another, as previously mentioned, reached the top of the center field bleachers. Brouthers' last official home run of 1890 came in August at New York, an inside-the-park shot in the cavernous new Players' League Polo Grounds. "Brouthers hit one over [center fielder Dick] Johnston's head for a home run."[35] This park later served as the National League's New York Giants' home for more than six decades.

Despite ground rules that cost Brouthers at least five home runs in 1890, fans still found ways to celebrate and commemorate some of his many long hits that stayed inside the fences. After he went 4-for-5, including a single, two doubles and a triple in a 10–2 win at Pittsburgh on July 25, an anonymous admirer penned the following ode to the slugger's hitting and fielding efforts:

> Oh! he hit the ball awful hard.
> It was like this:
> Bing to the right field
> Bing to the left field
> Bing to centre field.
> Then bing-bang up against the fence between the fielders.
> Big Dan not only hit the ball like
> a man doing a steal, but he made
> pickups that were great and
> covered first in grand style.
> Oh! Big Dan was much in today's game.[36]

Brouthers himself had a personal reason to celebrate at the end of the season — the birth of his third child, Dennis Addison Brouthers, in October. Like his sister (Anna) Lillian and brother (Daniel) Leo, Dennis junior preferred to be known by his middle name, Addison, in later life. Brouthers' third child was named "after [pitcher] Ad[dison] Gumbert, whom Dan admired for his honest endeavors"[37] in the pitcher's box for the Boston Players' League club.

All three leagues lost money in 1890. Despite outdrawing both the National League and the American Association, the Players' League's financial backers, who had to pay start-up costs for park rental, field preparation and grandstand construction in addition to team salaries, ended up in deeper financial trouble than the National League. At the end of the season, they capitulated, selling out to the National League and leaving their players in limbo. Historian Charles Alexander aptly summarizes the failure of this last attempt by players to control their own destinies in the nineteenth century:

> It was a unique episode in baseball history ... an experiment ... that, had it somehow managed to endure, might have changed the sport's entire structure.... In the Brotherhood and its league, the ballplayers had tried something drastic to redress what they saw as a gross imbalance in their circumstances vis-à-vis their employers. The serf's revolt didn't work, and not until the 1970s would club owners have to face a comparable threat to their power.[38]

The 1891 season found the 1890 Players' League Boston Reds players scattered to the four winds. Billy Nash and Joe Quinn rejoined Brotherhood defectors John Clarkson and Charley Bennett on the Beaneaters nine. Future Hall of Fame pitcher Hoss Radbourn moved on to the National League Cincinnati Reds for his last season in baseball. His Players' League partner in the rotation, Ad Gumbert, ended up back in Chicago with the White Stockings. Mike Kelly agreed to manage Cincinnati's new American Association team, nicknamed "Kelly's Killers," but the Queen City, as we shall see, would not be the final destination of the mercurial Kelly in 1891.

In February, Beaneaters owner Arthur Soden, still smarting from the losses he had suffered during the Players' rebellion, offered Dan Brouthers a contract for the paltry sum of $1,000, one-fifth of the slugger's earnings in 1889, and $500 beneath the lowest pay level of the Classification System passed that year. After stating, "I consider a notice like that an insult,"[39] Brouthers signed to play for the new Boston American Association team. Hardy Richardson, speedster Tom Brown and catcher Morgan Murphy followed suit, and Art Irwin joined the team as its manager.

Slugging catcher/utility man Duke Farrell and outfielder Hugh Duffy, orphans of the now defunct Chicago Players' League nine, were other newcomers on the team. In 1894, the diminutive (5'7") Duffy would hit a sizzling .440 for the National League Beaneaters — the highest batting mark in major league history. Two refugees from other Players' League clubs — George Haddock (Philadelphia) and Charley Buffinton (Buffalo), formed the new pitching staff.

The American Association, in business since 1882, was fighting for its life in 1891. All three leagues lost money during the 1890 baseball war, but the Association's losses "were almost as much as the others combined."[40] It would limp through the 1891 season before throwing in the towel.

Seeking to get a jump on the National League, the American Association opened its 1891 season two weeks before its rival did. Dan Brouthers himself got a jump on the race for the Association batting title in the Reds' first game against the Orioles by smacking a home run off Sadie McMahon in the first inning, "the ball going high over the right field fence, one of the longest [home runs] ever made by this slugger."[41] After Brouthers collected two more hits in an 8–7 win the next day, the *Globe* felt confident enough to predict that "Dan Brouthers will lead the American Association men on a lively dance to keep up with him on the batting average. He certainly has his eye on the ball and is hitting like a battering ram."[42] A few days later, Brouthers was called home to attend a sick child in Wappingers Falls. Returning to the lineup after missing four games, he went 4-for-4, including two doubles, and scored four runs in a 23–6 romp over the first-place Orioles.

The extra-base-hit king also found other methods of helping the Reds offensively. On May 9 against Cincinnati he stole three bases, including a steal of third in the sixth inning. On May 11 he added a steal to a four-hit performance against the Columbus Solons that included a triple and a double. Two days later, again against the Solons, he repeated the double/triple combination and stole another base.

By mid-season, Brouthers was leading the Association with a .365 average, and while his slugging numbers were down from his mid–1880s marks, he had accumulated 16 sacrifices and 20 steals through early July.[43] He finished the year with 37 sacrifices and 31 steals. As has been previously detailed, sacrifice hits (bunts, ground balls and flies which advanced a runner) counted as at-bats from 1889, when the sacrifice was originally recognized, to 1893. Brouthers' official 1891 batting average was a league-leading .350. If his sacrifices were not charged as times-at-bat, as they would not be after the 1893 season, his average would have been .379.

Although challenged by St. Louis and Baltimore in the first half of the season, Dan Brouthers' bat and George Haddock's and Charley Buffinton's combined 63 wins were enough to give the Reds the pennant over the Browns by a comfortable 8½ games. Two roster changes on the team after the season started added a bit of controversy to an otherwise uneventful pennant drive. After Hardy Richardson broke his ankle in late April, manager Art Irwin aroused the ire of the press and many of his players by signing his brother John to take Richardson's place. The *Globe* complained that John was "not capable of keeping up with the fast men he is playing with."[44] On this occasion, the *Globe* was correct in its evaluation. John Irwin hit .222, committed eight errors on 49 chances in the field, and was released after 19 games.

In mid–July, the financially-troubled Cincinnati Association franchise was transferred to Milwaukee, and Boston Reds President Charles Prince offered Cincinnati's now former manager, Mike Kelly, the position of Captain on the Reds team. While the move rumpled some feathers among the players, Kelly's drawing power could not be disputed. A crowd of 10,067, the largest of the season, was on hand in Boston on Kelly's return.[45] After only four games with the Reds, however, the erratic Kelly jumped across town to the National League Beaneaters, where he spent the rest of the season.

Almost forgotten amid the controversy over John Irwin's hire and the Mike Kelly saga was the late-season signing of pitcher Clark Griffith, a rookie who had been released by Saint Louis. Griffith logged a 3–1 record with the Reds in the last weeks of the season, and would spend the next six decades in the major leagues. On retiring from the game as a player, he purchased the Washington Nationals, a team that he owned for 35 years until his death in 1955.

Dan Brouthers hit just five home runs in 1891, but three of them hit in August figured among his longest. In a 10–0 whitewash of the Columbus Solons on August 9, he stroked a four-bagger off Jack Dolan. "His home run in the sixth was a record breaker, and was without a doubt the longest hit ever witnessed on the home [Columbus] grounds. It cleared the center field fence, and this feat has never before been performed."[46]

In 1894 Brouthers reminisced about this Columbus home run, although his recollection of where the four-bagger landed and the game situation were different from the 1891 press accounts:

> I guess the longest hit I ever made was at Columbus, when I was a member of the Boston Association team. Columbus was in the Association then. They had a deep right field fence, so deep that it looked a mile away, and no one had ever put a ball over it. Jack Dolan was pitching for Columbus, and they had held us to no runs, while they had two, if I remember right. On the earlier trip, Columbus had wiped up the earth with us, and we were naturally anxious to give it to them hard. Well, there were two men on bases when I went to bat. Dolan gave me a nice one, and I put the ball not only over the right field fence, but way out into the commons outside. That killed Dolan. We had him easy the rest of the game. I think that was the longest hit I ever made. I know it was the only ball ever put over that fence.[47]

In a 13–9 win over Baltimore on August 18, "Scarcely had the game started when a wild cheer went out from the ground that lasted fully two minutes. Dan Brouthers caused this wild outbreak by driving the ball over the right field fence for a home run with two men on bases.... Big Dan is now hitting the ball hard, but it is doubtful if he ever hit a ball with more force than the first one yesterday."[48] Back home in Boston three days later, the Wappingers Falls slugger connected for another record-breaker. "Dan Brouthers opened the eighth with the longest hit ever seen on these grounds, the ball going over the right field fence within fifty feet of the corner."[49]

The press, both local and national, christened Brouthers with an unusual nickname in 1891. In June, a *Sporting Life* article reported that "Dan Brouthers now leads Association batsmen. 'Old Jed' is hitting the ball safe nearly 40 times out of every 100 that pitchers allow him to hit."[50] A month later, after he had pulled one of his disappearing acts, the *Boston Daily Globe* used a version of the same nickname when it asked, "Where was Dan yesterday ... he ... was on the grounds at 1:30 practice, but when the time for the game came he was not to be found. It was suspected that 'Jed' had gone on the stage."[51]

The explanation for the "Jed" and "Old Jed" nicknames is linked to the popular culture of the era. On May 14, 1889, a musical comedy, entitled *Old Jed Prouty*, premiered at Union Square Theater in New York City. Co-authored by actors William Gill and Richard Golden, the work was described in the *New York Dramatic Mirror*[52] as a pastoral comedy depicting life in rural New England. The play's protagonist, interpreted onstage by the work's co-author, Richard Golden, was Old Jed Prouty, a Maine tavern owner who dispensed practical advice laced with wit and humor to his customers. After its debut in New York, *Old Jed Prouty* toured nationally to rave reviews, and with Richard Golden in the lead role had a run of over 3,000 performances from Maine to California.

Old Jed Prouty helped popularize Down East humor, a type of comedy featuring rural characters dispensing advice accompanied by doses of folksy humor. Though lacking formal education, Old Jed relied on common sense, traditional values and practical experience in making his way in life. *The Bangor Daily News* described him as "a rugged and loveable old man whose good heart and quaint humor ... made a happy impression."[53]

Old Jed's creator, author/actor Richard Golden, became so indentified with the character that he portrayed, that while reporting his death and burial in 1909, his home town newspaper automatically linked him with his theatrical creation: "Old Jed Prouty buried at Mount Hope Cemetery."[54] The press's association of Dan Brouthers with Old Jed Prouty demonstrated that at age 33, having overcome most of the negative elements associated with the Jumbo stereotype of his youth, the great slugger was now viewed with respect and appreciation as a venerable veteran player.

Beloved, wise, and older he may have been, but Brouthers' record during his three years in Boston while playing for three different teams and in three different leagues demonstrated that he also was still a potent offensive force. Playing in an average of 126 games a year from 1889 to 1891, he hit at a .351 pace, scored an average of 113 runs, averaged 144 hits, 29 doubles, 12 triples, and 5 home runs, knocked in 107 runs, and slugged at a .466 clip. Completing his 12 major league season, Big Dan was still considered "the greatest slugger in the country."[55]

At the conclusion of the 1891 campaign, Brouthers was feted with a banquet in his home town that was attended by 40 village dignitaries: "the businessman, the lawyer, doctor, athlete and 'man about town' were represented."[56] The event was whimsically described in *Sporting Life*'s alliterative headline: "Bread Bountifully Broken on Behalf of Bostons Big Batter and Baseman."[57] The banquet was "designed as a little testimonial of appreciation to Big Dan for the excellent work which he did for his club this year, and for the manner in which he kept the reputation of Wappingerian ballplayers to the front."[58]

The evening's program included speeches, a boxing demonstration, and the performance of a well-known Irish-American popular song, "My Dad's Dinner-Pail," popularized in the mid–1880s by Irish tenor Edward Harrigan. The song's lyrics, which served as a reminder of the Irish labor responsible for Wappingers Falls' economic development, struck a chord in the hearts of many in attendance, especially Dan Brouthers:

> Preserve the old kettle, so blackened and worn;
> It belonged to my father before I was born;
> It hung in a corner beyond on a nail
> 'Twas an emblem of labor, my dad's dinner-pail.
>
> For it glistened like silver, so sparkly and bright;
> I am fond of the trifle that held his wee bite;
> In summer or winter, in rain or in hail,
> I've carried that kettle, my dad's dinner-pail."[59]

Deeply touched by his hometown's tribute, the first ever afforded a Wappingers Falls citizen, Brouthers affirmed that "The remembrance of this evening will be regarded by me as even more precious than any of the valuable souvenirs I have previously received in recognition of my work as a ball player."[60]

As the evening concluded, all "were proud to shake the hand of Dan ... and wish him success for the coming season, which, if possible, would surpass that of the one just closed."[61] However, the question on many minds — including Dan's — that evening, was "Where would the great slugger play in 1892?"

A month after the banquet, the American Association merged with the National League, forming a new league of 12 teams that would prove to be as cumbersome as its official name: The National League and American Association of Professional Base Ball Clubs. For a while the name was shortened to the League-Association. Soon it would be known in the press simply as "the Big League."

Four of the eight Association teams — St. Louis, Washington, Baltimore

Four. *Old Jed: 1889–1891*

and Louisville — found a home in the new league. The remaining Association nines — Philadelphia, Columbus, Milwaukee and Brouthers' Boston Reds — were disbanded. Despite his excellent offensive record in his three years with Boston clubs, Brouthers would be 34 years old at the start of the 1892 season — an age at which many players of his era were retired. Nearly half the 128 players who had joined the Brotherhood in 1890 were no longer active. Where would the aging veteran Brouthers find a place in the new, consolidated league?

The answer came in mid–February 1892, when the *Inter-Ocean*[62] reported that he had signed with the Brooklyn Bridegrooms, so nicknamed because several of the team's players had recently married. As his opponent on the field for many years, the Bridegrooms' player/manager was thoroughly familiar with Brouthers' record, and from close personal experience during the recent Players' League wars knew the ex–Vice President of the Brotherhood to be reliable under pressure, both on and off the field.

Brooklyn's manager was Brotherhood and Players' League leader John Montgomery Ward. Dan Brouthers was the first man he signed for the 1892 season.

FIVE

Big Brother with the Stick: 1892–1895

> The Orioles are the center of much attention in all the cities they visit. Brouthers is pointed out as the best batter in the world.—*Baltimore Sun*, April 5, 1894

The 1892 season marked the beginning of a tumultuous half-decade in Dan Brouthers' personal and professional life. On the field, he maintained a .337 batting average and recorded career highs in hits (197) in 1892, and in RBI (128), triples (23), and stolen bases (38) in 1894. Although he could still occasionally astound fans and the press with tremendous home run drives, his overall power numbers decreased. Contrastively, his first base play during these years was the best of his career. His continued hitting prowess, accomplished at what was considered a venerable age, drew praise from the press. "Dan Brouthers is in his usual place among the leading batters. Few of the old timers keep on their batting togs like Dan."[1]

A long illness and the emotional effect of a family tragedy would limit Brouthers' playing time in 1893. Equally troubling were his increasingly frequent unexcused and unexplained absences from his team, and subtle suggestions in the press that the great slugger had a drinking problem. Brouthers' longtime sensitivity to criticism of his play became more acute in this period, causing conflicts with some of his managers and teammates and alienating some fans. Reduced to playing for Louisville, the doormat of the National League in 1895, he chose to resign from major league play in mid-season of that year. Although the press announced that his major league career was over, the great slugger still had one more scene to play on the national stage before his exit.

The new consolidated league, the League-Association, reigned supreme in 1892, marking the first time in more than a decade that baseball was controlled by a single organization. The league's monopoly was achieved at a heavy price. Each team was saddled with the responsibility of paying part of the debt accrued from buying out the four disbanded American Association teams. Accordingly, in 1892, a portion of each game's receipts — first ten, then 12, then 16 percent — was surrendered for the purpose of wiping this slate clean.

With their power once again centralized, team owners quickly moved to recoup their losses and return to profitability by imposing draconian cost-cutting measures. In June, team rosters were cut to 13 players and payrolls reduced by 30 to 40 percent. By 1894, a $2,400 ceiling[2] was in place for the league's top players, with virtually no exceptions. Another cost-savings ploy was the practice of releasing all players just before the end of the season to avoid having to pay the final installment of their salaries. "In October, nearly all clubs gave their players ten days' notice that they would be 'released' at the end of the playing season. Since the contracts ran to November 1, the players would lose two weeks' pay. But the men were not really free agents, because clubs acted in collusion by agreeing not to lure each other's men."[3]

The cutthroat tactics of management in the 1890s found a parallel in the evolution of a dog-eat-dog playing style on the field. With the number of major league teams halved from 24 to 12 between 1890 and 1892, and the number of roster places on each team reduced to 13, players were desperate to keep their jobs, and many were willing to do almost anything to stay in the lineup. Accordingly, team playing strategies became meaner and more brutal than ever before. "The tactics of the eighties were aggressive; the tactics of the nineties were violent. The game of the eighties was crude; the game of the nineties was criminal. The baseball of the eighties had ugly elements; the game of the nineties was just ugly."[4]

Brooklyn, "The City of Churches," fielded an American Association team from 1886 until the Association's 1891 demise, and also supported a Players' League team in 1890 that was managed by John Ward. Upon the dissolution of the Players' League, Ward took command of Brooklyn's Association entry and continued in the same capacity for the city's National League team in 1892.

Ward signed many of his 1891 American Association players for the following year's National League Brooklyn squad, including outfielders Mike Griffin and Darby O'Brien, catchers Con Daily and Tom Kinslow, and utility men Hub Collins and Dave Foutz. He needed to recruit a completely new pitching staff, however, including George Haddock, Dan Brouthers' teammate on the 1891 Boston Reds, Ed Stein, late of the Chicago White Stockings, and journeyman Bill Hart, who earned his living in the off-season as a typesetter for the *Cincinnati Star.*

John Ward's signing of Dan Brouthers planted the seeds of potential conflict in Brooklyn between the Wappingers Falls slugger and his new teammate, Dave Foutz, a conflict that would take root the following year after Ward left the club to manage the New York Giants. The tall, gangly Foutz — he stood 6'2" and weighed just 165 pounds — was a talented utility man who had been a starter on Brooklyn teams since 1888, when he played 78 games in right field, 42 at first base, and 23 in the pitcher's box, where he was 12–7. From 1889 to 1891 he pitched infrequently, spending most of his time at first base and compiling respective batting averages of .275, .303, and .257.

With the arrival of Dan Brouthers, manager Ward switched Foutz's role on the team to backup pitcher and utility outfielder. He did a serviceable job in the box, compiling a 13–8 record, but hit just .186 in 61 games while playing the outfield. The following year, 1893, Foutz was named Brooklyn's manager upon John Ward's transfer to New York. The stage was set for a possible confrontation between the new manager and the man who had taken his place the year before at first base — Dan Brouthers.

The Bridegrooms wintered in the south in 1892, using Ocala, Florida, as their home base in March, and then gradually moving north, finishing with exhibition series in Atlanta and Charleston. Ward's 1891 Association Bridegrooms had paid the city of Ocala $350 for use of the city ball grounds. In return for agreeing to locate in Ocala again the following spring,

> "Ward announced that not only would Ocala give Brooklyn free use of their field, but the city fathers would furnish the team with various free railroad tickets around Florida. The plan was for the major leaguers to play games against Florida State League teams. This modest inducement was, effectively, the beginning of a century-long bidding war among communities in Florida and later Arizona to host major league teams during spring training."[5]

A few days before the 1892 opener, the Bridegrooms' hometown *Brooklyn Daily Eagle,* in an article entitled "Play Ball," celebrated the arrival of the baseball season by waxing poetic on the healthful benefits of the sport that had become the National Pastime:

> "Play ball" is the order of the day. In the green fields, on the vacant lots, and even on the side streets ... ball playing is the feature of the spring recreative exercises.... How our boys revel in base ball on a warm, bright spring Saturday, when they are free from school restraints and full of youthful enthusiasm in their enjoyment of "a day off" in the ball fields. By all means, let us say to our boys, "Play ball".... It is the game of games, it is America's national field sport, and one well worth of the great popularity it has achieved.[6]

FIVE. Big Brother with the Stick: 1892–1895

Brooklyn opened the season at Baltimore before a small crowd of 5,329. John Ward's lineup featured six Brooklyn veterans: Hub Collins, Oyster Burns and Mike Griffin in the outfield, Ward himself at second base, and battery mates Con Daily and Dave Foutz. Ward's choice of Foutz as starting pitcher on opening day instead of George Haddock, who had won 34 games for the Boston Reds the previous year, was a clear attempt to compensate Foutz for losing his starting role as the team's first baseman to Dan Brouthers. Foutz won the season opener, 13–3, with Brouthers contributing a double and two sacrifices. Commenting on the victory, Brooklyn's President, Charles Byrne, affirmed that "The work of Dan Brouthers at first base was up to the highest mark, besides which his batting was of the best."[7]

Byrne's evaluation would ring true for Brouthers for the entire season. Playing in 152 games, the most in his career, he led the league in batting (.335, 90 points higher than the league average), RBI (124), hits (197) and total bases (282), and finished second in on-base percentage (.432) and slugging (.480). He also stole 31 bases and contributed a career-high 37 sacrifices. Defensively, he recorded the highest mark to date of his career—.982, behind Giant Roger Connor's league-leading .985.

By the end of the first week of May, Brooklyn was in second place when two players, Dan Brouthers and Hub Collins, fell ill. Dan's ailment, a severe cold, was treated humorously by a *Sporting Life* reporter:

> Dan Brouthers, otherwise known as Big-Brother-With-the-Stick — began to yearn for quinine, mustard baths, plasters and such things, just when the big club got fairly started on its journey. Big-Brother-of-the-Stick-with-the-Sunny-Upper-Lip gathered in the nucleus of a cold on the opening day at Eastern Park, but steeled himself against it until he reached Louisville, when his condition became a matter of concern to all in the club. President Byrne realized that the gentleman with the yellow molasses moustache was in a bit of danger and soon had a bluegrass sawbones shooting a rare assortment of drugs into his six-foot-twoship. Mr. Brouthers is still working the wheezes out of himself, and it is no secret that every game he has played since his illness has entailed more of less pain unto him. He is now in fairly good trim, but not first class shape.[8]

Collins' malady was more of a concern. During a series in Boston, the speedy utility man fell ill with what was initially diagnosed as a mild case of typhoid fever. Ten days later he was dead. The demise of the 28-year-old Louisville native shocked his teammates. A stunned John Ward remarked, "only two weeks ago he played his usual position on the Brooklyn team. Now his is only a memory."[9] Collins was a six-year major league veteran who had spent the previous four years on Brooklyn teams. In his brief career he averaged .284 at the plate and stole 335 bases, including 85 thefts in 1890. The Hub City was a typhoid haven in the early 1890s. A year after Collins' death,

Philadelphia's Billy Hamilton was leading the league in hitting (.380) when he contracted the same disease in Boston. Unlike Collins, Hamilton survived the attack and went on to hit .403 the following year.

Dan Brouthers may have suffered from a cold in the early going in 1892, but his bat was hot, banging out 14 hits in his first eight games. During a Memorial Day doubleheader against Cincinnati he was given "a bad shaking up" on the field. "He was catching a wide throw [thrown] ball from [shortstop] Corcoran when Holliday ran plump [right] into him. Brouthers swung all the way round and fell, dropping the ball."[10] Two days later against Louisville, he gave clear indication that the blow had done him no permanent harm. In a 12–4 Brooklyn win, he connected off Jouett Meekin in the second inning, lining the ball to deep center field and circling the bases for an inside-the-park home run — his first four-bagger of the season. In the fifth inning,

> A little life was imparted to the game ... for, greatly to the delight of the bleaching board occupants, Meekin gave Brouthers a chance for a fungo [long fly] hit to the outfield for a home run, and Denis [*sic*] on reaching home received the plaudits of the boys in their shirt sleeves for his splendid Prospect Park hit. Previously two men had been given bases on battery errors and Brouthers had sent them and himself home."[11]

In mid–June Brouthers experienced a rare hitting slump (5 for 21), which the *Eagle* attributed to "a new bat he was using."[12] He responded with three hits and a sacrifice in a loss to Philadelphia, nine hits in a three-game series against Washington, and five hits in a double-header against New York. There was no more talk about problems with new bats in the *Eagle*. When Pittsburgh's Ad Gumbert was asked how he pitched to the streaking Brouthers, he responded, "I put the ball straight and high over the plate and trust to luck he doesn't smash it through me."[13]

To try to create a sense of excitement for fans during what would be the longest campaign on record due to the cumbersome 12-team structure, team owners established a split season, "with the winners from each half meeting in a championship series"[14] at the end of the year. The Bridegrooms captured second place behind Boston in the season's first half, and Dan Brouthers, in 296 at-bats, had already collected 101 hits. The team dropped to third in the second half of the season, overtaken in second place by Boston. Cleveland took first place, thanks to the strong right arm of third-year man Cy Young, who collected 36 wins, hurled nine shutouts, and registered a 1.93 earned run average.

Brouthers' hustle on the bases and his base stealing were club highlights after mid-season. Brooklyn fans, unfamiliar with the big slugger's work on the base paths, originally found his efforts there to be humorous. "Big Dan

Brouthers caused a big laugh in the sixth inning by running home from first on O'Brien's two bagger."[15] "Brouthers did an unusual thing yesterday — he stole second in record time."[16] Gradually, the fans' initial amusement turned to admiration. "In the fifth inning ... Brouthers hit a daisy cutter between center and right field and ... had the extreme pleasure of making a 120 yard sprint run with the thermometer at 95."[17]

On another occasion, in an early August game against Philadelphia, he seemed determined to make it to home plate after a sharp single to left field, and his aggressive running provoked errors that allowed him to achieve his goal. "Brouthers made the round of the bases in the second inning owing to a peculiar combination of circumstances. He sent a rattling single to left, on which he ran to second, and on Hamilton's wide throw Dan continued to third. He did not stop running, however, as Cross let the ball go by, thus completing the circuit on a base hit."[18] In mid–August against New York, he banged out four hits in a 12–2 win, but his running garnered as much praise as his hitting. "Besides setting the Brooklynites by the ears by his hitting, Mr. Denis [*sic*] Brouthers made an addition to his collection of haloes by stealing second base. He did it in the sixth inning, after making a single, and he did it without sliding, too."[19]

By September, Brouthers' hustling running, once viewed with humor, was recognized by Brooklyn fans as yet another reliable aspect of his overall offensive attack. "Brouthers proved himself to be an active participant in the contest at Cincinnati. He whacked out a couple of three baggers, scored two runs, and, most wonderful of all, stole a base. Brouthers' work on the bases this season is a radical departure from his former style, and the way he steals them is a source of intense delight to all his admirers."[20]

Although Brouthers played in 152 of the Bridegrooms' 158 contests in 1892, the few games he missed became controversial in the press. At the start of the season's second half he missed a game when called home to Wappingers Falls. "Dan Brouthers had to let yesterday slip. He received word that his wife was ill and ran up home. He was back to-day with better news."[21]

In late July he disappeared from Eastern Park again, this time without leaving notice why, and missed three consecutive games, one with New York and two with Washington. The *Brooklyn Eagle*, its interest peeked, reported that "Dennis Brouthers has not been heard from"[22]; "Brouthers had simply gone and stayed and [that] was all anybody could tell. The strangest thing about his going away is that he skipped only a few days before pay day."[23] Asked what he had heard from Brouthers, Brooklyn President Byrne responded, "Absolutely nothing."[24] On his return, the slugger added to the mystery by offering no explanation for his absence. "Dennis Brouthers got back, but is silent as to his mission or doings while away. He picked up some ginger [energy] during his wanderings, which is a comfort."[25]

Brouthers' mysterious, unexplained disappearance soon set tongues wagging in the press. *Sporting Life* suggested that he might have escaped to Canarsie, "a little two-cent Coney Island"[26] in southeast Brooklyn on Jamaica Bay. Originally a fishing village, by the 1890s Canarsie boasted amusement rides, hotels, and gambling and beer halls. While no reason was given for the press's conjecture, clearly the implication was that if Brouthers had been in Canarsie, he was up to no good there. After he missed another game in September without excuse, news reports revealed that despite his superior on-field production, he was now receiving criticism from the fans and his teammates for his mysterious absences. "Brouthers is reaching the point in his play where the shriekers of the bleachers rise and jeer. He was absent from his post again yesterday, and as the boys had to go up against Cleveland [the league leader at this point in the season] ... there was no little comment on his non-appearance."[27]

Once Brooklyn fell out of contention for the pennant, game news was neglected by the local press and attendance at Eastern Park fell off precipitously. An October 5 contest against New York was attended by only 200 spectators. John Ward's decision-making as manager, particularly his preference for batting first while at home [home teams would not be required to bat last until 1950], was roundly criticized for not allowing the team "to rally in the last inning"[28] due to this practice.

Worse still, President Byrne began shifting the dates of final games in order to accommodate more profitable contests in other sports at Eastern Park. "There will be no game tomorrow [Saturday] at Eastern Park, the scheduled game with Washingtion having been deferred until Monday to allow the Crescent and Yale football clubs to play their match. President Byrne thinks that foot ball [*sic*] in cold weather is more profitable than baseball."[29]

At season's end, a disappointed fan penned an ungracious poetic farewell to the team that was published in the *Eagle*:

> Farewell, ye Brooklyn wonders,
> 'Tis not hard to say farewell.
> Ye have made full many blunders,
> Ignobly ye fought and fell.[30]

Under such conditions, Dan Brouthers' status on the Bridegrooms was in jeopardy, despite the fact that he had led the team in all offensive categories except home runs. In early October the *Eagle* reported that "The Boston Herald says that President Byrne of the Brooklyns will undoubtedly give some other club a chance to sign Dan Brouthers for next season. On more than one occasion the big fellow has not turned up when he was wanted and has been away without proper excuse. Dave Foutz is slated to play the bag in 1893. He is a reliable player and can fill the bill. President Byrne refused to talk on the subject."[31]

A week later, after news broke that the club had lost $15,000 over the season, it was suggested that "Brouthers, who drew $4,500 on the strength of his batting, is likely to be replaced by a cheaper man although he is willing to stand a reduction."[32] These stories proved false when Brouthers again signed with Brooklyn for the 1893 campaign.

All attention in America in 1893 was directed to Chicago, site of the Colombian Exposition, or World's Fair. Here visitors could experience first-hand the latest technological advances and try new products, from processed foods like Shredded wheat, to Morris chairs and a "clasp locker and unlocker for shoes,"[33] an early version of what we now call a zipper.

Baseball also introduced something new in 1893. In hopes of bringing more offensive excitement to the game — league hitting in 1892 was an anemic .242 — the pitching distance was increased to 60'6", and the pitcher was required to keep one foot in contact with a four-inch-wide, 12-inch-long, rubber slab while delivering the ball. The change achieved its desired effect — batting averages jumped 35 points and attendance rose around the league.

Controversy, disease and death stalked both Dan Brouthers and the Brooklyn Bridegrooms in 1893. As spring training began, a hopeful Brooklyn fan penned a poem to team owner Charles Byrne:

> With Daly, Brouthers and Stein
> To back invincible O'Brien
> All other folks will have to crawl
> Or on the ground supinely sprawl —
> Play Ball.[34]

The "invincible" O'Brien mentioned in the poem was Darby O'Brien, a speedy (91 steals in 1889) stalwart in the Brooklyn outfield for five seasons, who was soon reported "sick at his home in Peoria, Ill."[35] Ten days later, news arrived that stunned his teammates. "The Brooklyn team have [sic] ascertained the fact that their old companion, good natured Darby O'Brien, is physically disabled from lung disease from taking the field again this season, if, in fact, he ever does again."[36] Two months later, the 29-year-old outfielder was dead of consumption (tuberculosis).

The departure of John Ward to New York left a gaping hole in the Bridegrooms' middle infield that the team sought to fill by acquiring Danny Richardson from Washington. Richardson had helped the Giants gain their first two pennants in the late 1880s, but proved to be of little use to Brooklyn. Lambasted by the press for drinking heavily and then claiming sickness when not able to play, he was suspended for the season without pay at the end of July.

Chided for arriving late and out of shape to spring training, Dan Brouthers explained that "he would have toed the mark at Eastern Park earlier in the season, but sickness at home made it imperative that he should linger. One of the boys was quite bad with a juvenile complaint."[37] The sick child was Dan's third son, Paul, born the previous October. A week later, the *Eagle* reported that "Brouthers got back to the city the other day after being absent on a sad errand. His little boy, whose illness detained him at home prior to reporting here [for spring training] died last week and the big fellow had to go home and comfort his grief stricken ones."[38]

Burying his grief in furious training, Brouthers slimmed down and appeared to be in excellent shape by the start of the season. "Dan seems to have entirely lost that dead weight sag that formerly distinguished his gait, and goes about like a 2-year-old with ginger in his pockets."[39] Brooklyn opened the 1893 campaign in the rain at Philadelphia. Brouthers collected three hits and scored twice in the short two-game series, and then promptly was laid low with what was initially thought to be a bad cold, but which soon was diagnosed as the "grip" (influenza). "Dan Brouthers is quite a sick man. Grip has taken quite a hold on him and it was necessary to send him to his house down East to recuperate."[40]

He did not return to the diamond for six weeks. In his absence, player/manager Dave Foutz took over at first base, and at the end of May was leading the league in fielding his position with an average of .989.[41]

After Brouthers' recovery, news of his imminent return was met with mixed emotions. "A big howl is expected when Brouthers takes Foutz's place at first and Dave goes to the bench, if such is the intention. The general impression ... is that while Brouthers is a heavy hitter, Foutz is no stripling with the ash [bat] while in fielding and base running he can play all around Dan. Dan is still weak from his long illness and Dr. McClean has cautioned the big fellow not to play ball just yet. He will have to practice some before he can go into harness again."[42] Brouthers' 25 hits (including ten doubles) over a 13-game period shortly after his return soon silenced his critics.

Despite the salutary effects of the belated return of Dan Brouthers' bat to the Brooklyn lineup, by August 1, the team was in deep trouble. Tied for first place at the end of June, they now found themselves mired in fifth, thanks to a terrible extended road trip in July (15 losses, one win and one tie from July 1 to July 20). Part of that collapse can be attributed to the rigors of the road schedule, which often left them too tired to play. "The Brooklyn base ball club arrived here [Baltimore] this morning [July 17] after a straight run

Five. Big Brother with the Stick: 1892–1895

[by train] of thirty-six hours from St. Louis, and put up in the Eutaw House."[43] Roster issues, however, were the main cause of the problem. Pitching ace George Haddock, who had collected 63 victories over the prior two seasons, injured first a knee, then an elbow, and then a thumb. He was released in August. Aging veterans Danny Richardson, Harry Stovey and Ed "Cannonball" Crane were brought in to fill vacancies in the infield, outfield and the pitcher's box respectively, but all three proved ineffective and subsequently were let go, followed by back-up catcher Tom Kinslow, who was fired for drunkenness. Given Brooklyn's steep slide in the standings and miserable recruiting record, manager Dave Foutz found himself under enormous pressure to turn the club's trajectory around.

On July 27, Brooklyn purchased the contract of a diminutive (5' 4") left-handed third baseman from the New York Giants. His name was Willie Keeler, he looked more like a mascot than a player, and his size and youthful appearance would soon earn him the nickname "Wee Willie." A 21-year-old Brooklyn native, three years earlier Keeler was just another local teenager selling scorecards at Eastern Park. He debuted with the Giants in the last weeks of the 1892 season, but early in 1893 he was sidelined for eight weeks after breaking an ankle sliding into second base.

Although common in the early years of professional baseball, left-handed infielders had largely disappeared from the game by the 1890s. A southpaw's need to pivot his upper body in order to throw to first base after fielding ground balls gave a decided advantage to a hitter or runners when hustling toward bases.

Keeler had demonstrated the weakness of being a southpaw infielder in his first game in the major leagues against Philadelphia in September 1892. "The Phillies wasted no time testing him. 'Sliding Billy' Hamilton, the leadoff batter ... was fast as a telegraph. He laid down a bunt [to third base] and arrived before the ball [thrown by Keeler] did. Three batters later he scored."[44] Although Keeler hit well for the Giants (17 hits in 14 games), his poor reputation as a lefty at third base followed him to Brooklyn. A few days after his arrival, visiting Boston tested him again, with disastrous results.

> Brooklyn was leading, 1 to 0, in the seventh inning when one of the Beaneaters laid down a bunt. Willie rushed in and scooped it and pivoted fiercely to his left and sent the ball curving and cavorting across the diamond. Big Dan Brouthers, the Brooklyn first baseman, threw up his hands in horror. By the time the ball was retrieved at the edge of the fifty-cent stands, runners hugged second and third. Brooklyn's shaken twirler served up a fat pitch and the Beaneaters led. One out later, another Beaneater bunted. Willie was determined not to repeat his mistake. He pounced on the ball and flung it so high that Big Dan would have needed a net. Willie had given the game away.[45]

Unaccountably, manager Foutz's response to Keeler's play was to leave him at third, bench Dan Brouthers, and install himself at first base, where he fared just as poorly as Brouthers had in corralling Keeler's errant throws. "Foutz took a try at first and managed to let a few go by."[46] Keeler was soon sent to the outfield, and a short time later was benched. The *Eagle* reported that "Brouthers was laid off for not fielding properly on Thursday,"[47] even though the paper acknowledged that Keeler's throws had been wide and that he had been assigned throwing errors on the plays. After the team lost five of the next six games, *Sporting Life* encouraged Brooklyn to re-instate Big Dan. "While Brouthers has not been moving as fast as the law allows whether on the bases or at the bat, still the general idea is that his failure to gather in the wild winged throws of Keeler at third had something to do with his layoff.... Probably in a few days he [Foutz] will realize that a Brouthers at first is much better than a Keeler at third."[48]

Sporting Life's assessment was faulty in two areas. First, Dan Brouthers could not be construed of as being "slow" at the bat, since in the "second season," which began in mid–July, he was hitting .390.[49] Additionally, Foutz refused to realize that "a Brouthers at first is much better than a Keeler at third," since he did not return Brouthers to the lineup until three weeks later, after the Bridegrooms had fallen to seventh place.

There was no logic to Foutz's decision to bench a veteran star hitting at a near .400 clip for three weeks simply because he failed to gather in two wild throws from the club's inexperienced new third baseman. The *Eagle* concluded, therefore, that "There must have been bad blood between Dan Brouthers and Foutz."[50]

The laconic Brouthers said nothing to the press, but clearly was humiliated by Foutz's action. In late August, after the Bridegrooms had slipped into seventh place, the Brooklyn manager finally relented. "A noteworthy incident of the contest was the recognition given to Brouthers, who resumed his old position on the team, and played it finely, although he was rusty at the bat.... He was received with an outburst of cheers.... His presence there undoubtedly strengthens the team and he will remain there to the close of the season."[51]

Willie Keeler never returned to the infield, and even as an outfielder never excelled defensively, compiling a .960 fielding record in 18 major league seasons. His lifetime .341 batting average, however, was more than sufficient to earn him a plaque at Cooperstown in 1939.

At the conclusion of the season, sixth-place Brooklyn competed in a six-game exhibition series against fifth-place New York which, although billed as the "Metropolitan Championship," was in reality nothing more than a plan to provide a few extra dollars for the players and a considerable sum for each franchise. After playing in the first game of the series, Brouthers finally made a silent statement about being benched earlier in the season by Foutz. He packed his bags and went home to Wappingers Falls. "Dan Brouthers did not show up for the [second] game [of the series] today, and it was said that he had concluded to fade away from the series."[52]

Despite his continued success on the field, 1893 was a difficult year for Brouthers. He had buried an infant son, battled a serious illness, and suffered the humiliation of being benched for the first time since his days with the Troy Trojans. In late October he let it be known that under no circumstances would he play in a Brooklyn uniform in 1894. Just before the annual league meeting in November, *Sporting Life* insisted that "the Brooklyn Club is not at all anxious to unload Brouthers, as is being constantly stated.... Brouthers is a valuable man at any stage of the game, his stick work alone sufficient to keep up his stock, but it is only his little whims that nag him occasionally and lead to the stories of his not being wanted here [in Brooklyn]."[53] Despite such assurances, on January 1, 1894, Dan Brouthers and Willie Keeler were traded to the Baltimore Orioles for infielder Billy Shindle and outfielder George Treadway.

The Orioles manager who brokered the trade that brought Brouthers and Keeler to Baltimore was Brouthers' old friend, Ned Hanlon, the man who had negotiated the sale to Detroit of Brouthers and the other Big Four members in 1886, and who had participated with Brouthers and John Ward in difficult negotiations with the National League during the Brotherhood war. "Determined, meticulous, assiduous,"[54] and a man of few words, Hanlon had taken the reins in Baltimore in the latter part of the Orioles' disastrous 12th place 1892 campaign and promptly started a rebuilding program, releasing or trading 14 of the team's 17 players at the end of the season.

Prior to the merger that returned major league ball to a single league operation, "players customarily changed teams during periods of interleague war ... or when they were released, sold, or otherwise wore out their welcome."[55] After rules about player exchanges became more flexible upon the consolidation of the leagues, Hanlon became the first manager to make extensive use of player trades, typically for untried rookies, castoffs or aged veterans. His skill in this regard helped move the Orioles from last to first place in the league in less than two years.

Starting with his retained team nucleus of infielder John McGraw, catcher Wilbert Robinson and pitcher Sadie McMahon, Hanlon first traded with Pittsburgh for outfielder Joe Kelley, then with St. Louis for shortstop Hughie Jennings, and then with Brooklyn for Keeler and Brouthers. He dropped down to the minor-league level to acquire rookie second baseman Heinie

Peitz. Finally, he acquired outfielder Steve Brodie and pitchers Bill Hawke and Kid Gleason from St. Louis, and pitcher Duke Esper from Washington.

Hanlon's four pitchers, McMahon, Hawke, Gleason and Esper, were responsible for 66 of Baltimore's 89 victories in 1894. Brodie, McGraw, Robinson, Kelley, Jennings, Keeler and Brouthers all hit over .300 for the 1894 team. How good was Hanlon's judgment? McGraw, Robinson, Kelley, Jennings, Keeler and Brouthers were eventually elected to the Baseball Hall of Fame. Eventually, so was Hanlon.

Ned Hanlon's brand of baseball combined hustle with strategy. The steal, the sacrifice and the hit-and-run play were its basic weapons. These approaches were not what Dan Brouthers was known for, but, as we have seen, he had been adding some of these elements to his game for years. To everyone's surprise

April 1894 photograph of the Baltimore Orioles team accompanied by thirteen boosters. Future Hall of Fame inductees pictured here include Brouthers, second row, fourth from left; Joe Kelley, second row, far right; John McGraw, first row, center; Hughie Jennings, and Willie Keeler, respectively, seated to the right of McGraw (National Baseball Hall of Fame Library, Cooperstown, New York).

FIVE. *Big Brother with the Stick: 1892–1895* 109

except his and Ned Hanlon's, he fit in perfectly in Baltimore, enjoying his last great major league season and helping lead Baltimore to its first pennant. To be sure, the old "Jumbo" stereotype occasionally resurfaced, particularly early in the season. "Big Dan Brouthers cannot be expected to work into shape as soon as some others, for when he has an ache, it must certainly by an immense one. Just think of an elephant having a pain."[56]

Manager Hanlon knew better. With the core of his new team in their early to mid–20s, he looked to Brouthers not only for his on-field skills, but also for his steadying influence. His team of youngsters "needed someone to look up to."[57] As the season progressed, "Dan Brouthers found himself surrounded by colts who listened with open mouths as he reminisced about the old days in the game."[58] "Jumbo" Brouthers had once again transformed into "Old Jed."

Baltimore opened the season at home against the Giants on April 19 before 15,300 Orioles fans. Having finished eighth in 1893, New York was not on Baltimore's radar as a serious pennant contender, but they would soon prove to be one. Sadie McMahon held the Giants to three runs while the home team collected eight for the win. Brouthers introduced himself to the Orioles fans by collecting three hits, sacrificing, and stealing a base. It was his last hit, however, his second double, that left the home fans in awe.

By modern standards, Union Park, the Orioles' home field, had short left and right field fences down the line (335 feet). The distance rapidly increased in the alleys, however, until arriving at dead center field, 393 feet from home plate and considered an "impossible"[59] distance to reach with a hit in the era, so much so that bleachers occupied a space on the field in front of the fence. In the eighth inning of the season opener, Brouthers came to bat against Giants starter Amos Rusie. "He let several of Rusie's pitches go by. The next pitch leapt from his heavy bat, into distant center field. It soared over the heads of the awestruck crowd. The ball struck the center field fence three feet from the top and bounced back. By the ground rules, a two-bagger. Union Park had never witnessed as long a hit."[60]

After three games, with five hits, three sacrifices and a stolen base added, Brouthers was well on his way to being considered a fan favorite. "'Big Dan' Brouthers is fast winning his way to the hearts of the Baltimore enthusiasts. His batting has been most timely and his fielding is much better than thought."[61]

Ten days after his record-setting double, another wallop from the Wappingers Falls slugger's bat, this time against his former team, Dave Foutz's Bridegrooms, surpassed the previous blast's distance by a considerable length.

> It is not stretching things to say that Mr. Brouthers made a hit. It was the longest hit ever made at Union Park. The ball went over the right field fence, fifty feet from the foul line. Tom Burns, the Brooklyn right fielder, who was the last man to see the ball, says it was at least twenty feet from [above] the top of the fence when it went over.... The point over which Mr. Brouthers' hit passed over the fence is 365 feet from home plate. The ball touched mother earth sixty feet from the fence on the outside of the grounds. Then it galloped up an alley to Calvert Street and assaulted a Blue line [railroad]car. A policeman arrested it and returned it to the Union Park box office. Secretary Herman Vanderhorst will have it gilded and hung up in base-ball headquarters with an appropriate inscription."[62]

If the estimated distance that the ball traveled from the fence to its landing point outside the park is correct (60 feet), this would have been a 425-foot home run — a long hit even today, but an astounding distance for the era.

Soon Orioles fans would witness an even mightier blast from Brouthers' bat, one that until the end of the Deadball Era was considered by many to be the longest ever hit made in a regulation game. In the sixth inning of a June 16 game against St. Louis, Brouthers crushed an offering from Ted Breitenstein to right-center field. At the time, 23rd Street (street names have subsequently been changed in Baltimore) ran roughly parallel to the outfield fences at Union Park. Another street, then named Guilford Avenue, ran perpendicular to 23rd Street and intersected it well beyond the Baltimore ball grounds. Brouthers' June 16 home run cleared Union Park's 12-foot fence, sailed over 23rd Street, and landed either in the first or second block of Guilford Avenue.

Years later, *Baltimore Sun* sportswriter S. C. Appleby, who had witnessed the home run, provided a written statement documenting the historic drive. He began his report by listing those present at the event, including Brouthers' teammates and manager, representatives from the *Baltimore American* and the *Baltimore News*, and team secretary Herman Vonderhorst. Also present was a Mr. Hassenbalg, described as "a devoted rooter of championship days" who had been the custodian of the ball Brouthers hit since the day of the home run, 19 years earlier. According to Appleby,

> As I saw this hit from the press box it appeared to go on an absolutely straight and rising line from Dan's bat to the point where it crossed the fence. The curve, or "trajectory," as gunnery engineers call it, was not observable within the grounds — at least from the high position of the press box. The ball seemed to describe a straight upward slant from bat to fence. Then the curve toward the earth became apparent and the leather reached the ground.... Two figures were seen in the distance chasing it. There were houses on the western side of Guilford avenue [*sic*], but none on the eastern side obstructing the view. The running men were the watchman and Herman Vonderhorst. They sped past the row of

FIVE. *Big Brother with the Stick: 1892–1895*

houses, which denoted the first block of Guilford avenue, and kept on, indicating that the ball was still going.[63]

Another eyewitness, Abe Marks, who sold score cards at the ball park, noted that "The day after that hit was made they painted a sign in great big, white letters. It was just one word—'Here'—and it marked the place where Brothers' hit went over. The sign stayed on the fence until the park was torn down and there isn't a rooter in Baltimore old enough to remember it who doesn't warm up every time he thinks about it."[64]

In October 1907, during celebrations in Baltimore commemorating the Orioles' league champions of 1894–1896, Brouthers was presented with the ball he knocked onto Guilford Avenue 13 years earlier by the *Baltimore Sun*'s S. C. Appelby. In his brief remarks, the old slugger stated, "This ball went so far that I never expected to see it again. Now that it has been given to me, I shall ever keep it as a memento of my connection with the champion Orioles."[65] Commenting on this Brouthers blast, his 1894 teammate John McGraw asserted, "I have never seen a hit made to equal the one made by Brouthers in Baltimore and don't think I ever will."[66] In his 2010 *Baseball's Ultimate Power*, Bill Jenkinson, contemporary expert on the all-time greatest distance home run hitters, estimates that Brouthers' June 16,

Sepia-tone Mayo Cut Plug Tobacco card image of Dan Brouthers, circa 1894. Like the Goodwin Old Judge cards, Mayo cards consisted of a photograph glued to a stiff cardboard backing (Transcendental Graphics/www.theruckerarchive .com).

1894, drive at Union Park traveled 450 feet, and describes it as "likely the longest home run of the 19th century."[67]

These memorable drives were just two of nine home runs hit by Brouthers in 1894, his highest total in seven seasons. Several others hit on the road were also noteworthy for their distance. At Boston's South End grounds in May, after Charley Ganzel of the home team Beaneaters homered to deep left field in the top of the fifth inning (Boston chose to bat first in this home contest), Brouthers followed with a longer drive to the same area. "Dan Brouthers enabled the Orioles to hold the lead in their half of the [fifth] inning by a beautiful drive over the left field fence at a point thirty feet beyond that over which Ganzel's hit has passed."[68] In the second game of a doubleheader on August 1 at Washington, Brouthers connected for another tape-measure shot off Otis Stockdale. "Brouthers' [home run] was a wonderfully long drive, the ball sailing thirty or forty feet over the right field fence, which is further from the home plate than the right field fence at [Baltimore's] Union Park."[69]

Another four-bagger that Brouthers hit at home is worth special mention, for it seemingly defied gravity. "Brouthers' home run in the fifth was somewhat unusual. The ball went over Carnavan's head on the line, struck the fence, and rolled up it and then disappeared over it."[70]

Sometimes, however, a timely Brouthers single meant as much as a long home run to the Orioles. At home against Chicago on June 5, he tied the game by singling in the ninth inning, scoring Sadie McMahon. The Orioles won the contest in the tenth, and with the victory moved into first place. A jubilant *Baltimore Sun* sportswriter reported, "It was that, and that alone which saved the Orioles from bitter defeat. It is said that when the hit was made, Mr. Brouthers' red setter, which was watching the game from the clubhouse, turned two back somersaults and gave vent to a yell of joy."[71] An ecstatic Orioles fan penned a poem about the hit in the style of the popular *Casey at the Bat*:

> Two hands were out — Three thousand hearts
> Were throbbing and sore;
> One club was just one run ahead —
> It was not Baltimore.
> But what a scream the welking split,
> Oh, what a deafening roar,
> When with a might giant's whack,
> Big Dennis tied the score.[72]

Rarely in Brouthers' career did he wield a hotter bat than in 1894. Of his 40 multiple-hit games, three were four-hit efforts, 19 were three-hit games, and in 18 contests he collected two hits. In a four-game series at Boston in mid–June he totaled 11 hits, including two triples and four doubles. At

FIVE. *Big Brother with the Stick: 1892–1895*   113

Pittsburgh on July 10 he delivered two triples and a double, and the following day his three hits were a single, double and triple. In keeping with manager Hanlon's "small ball" strategy, Brouthers contributed 18 sacrifices (eighth in the league), and stole a career-high 38 bases. His steals often occurred in bunches — he stole two sacks in a game six times, and at Washington, on May 8, stole three while also collecting three hits and scoring four runs. After a 7–1 win at Cincinnati in late May, an incredulous *Baltimore Sun* reporter noted that "Dan Brouthers surprised [Cincinnati's third baseman] Latham yesterday by stealing third base. Dan is apt to do most anything this year."[73]

An 18-game win streak from August 24 to September 16 in 1894 gave the Orioles the cushion they needed to win their first pennant. With the demise of a two-league structure after the 1891 season, the traditional "World's Series" that had been held most years between the American Association and National League champions was discontinued. In an effort to reinstate postseason play, Pittsburgh owner William Temple offered a silver trophy, the Temple Cup, to the winner of a best-of-seven series between the National League's first- and second-place teams — Baltimore and New York, respectively. Winners were to receive the trophy and 65 percent of the gate receipts, with the losers taking the remaining 35 percent.

Portraits of the tuxedo-clad National League champion 1894 Baltimore Orioles. At age 36, Dan Brouthers, featured top-right, hit .347 and stole 38 bases for the Orioles (National Baseball Hall of Fame Library, Cooperstown, New York).

Baltimore players, in particular John McGraw, tried to hold out for a 50–50 split, reasoning that since they were the champions regardless of which team won the Temple Cup, they deserved a higher cut of the proceeds. Temple refused to allow it, and the series was played, but the Orioles' hearts were not in it. The Giants' two aces, Jouett Meekin and Amos Rusie, stymied Baltimore's hitters, and New York won the series in four straight games. Although Dan Brouthers injured his leg in a late September game at Cleveland, he recovered enough to steal two bases in the third Temple Cup contest, but overall collected just three singles and scored two runs.

At season's end, Brouthers was feted with a special celebration in Wappingers Falls.

> The only man to whom the elegant village of Wappinger's Falls, N.Y. ever gave a public reception was Mr. Dennis Brouthers, the first baseman of the champion base ball club.... The village was decorated ... with Japanese lanterns and Oriole colors, and from the time that Mr. Brouthers arrived upon the train until late at night the place was brilliant with fireworks, while on every corner was an oil barrel giving out a blaze of glory.... Two fire companies with new uniforms marched in the line, for Dan was once a Wappingers fireman, and the village president with the trustees and a big reception committee welcomed the honored Wappingerian, who sat in a decorated carriage in the parade.... The people, of course, packed the streets and all the bands were out. The keynote speech, given by Mr. George Wood, related how "one of our own boys ... went from our midst to cover himself and the home of his birth with fame.... Through him Wappingers has been heard of from East to West, from North to South.[74]

Dan Brouthers was a contented man after the 1894 campaign, but he also was a practical one. He would be 37 at the start of the next season, and he knew that his time in the major leagues was growing short. Even he would be surprised, however, at how swift and difficult his departure from the big leagues would be.

For several years there had been whispers of concern or criticism in the press, often in veiled language, about his habits and approach to the game. His sudden, unexplained disappearances while with Brooklyn had raised eyebrows. He was praised for being thrifty and saving his money, but at the same time some suggested that his wealth had made him indifferent on the field. "Dan has planted his wealth in brick houses in Wappinger's Falls, and can lie back at his ease with his 30,000 'plunks' [dollars] and laugh at the magnates [owners]. It is this feeling of contentment which has made Dan almost too independent and affected his playing lately."[75] A similar sentiment was expressed after he abandoned Brooklyn during the Metropolitan Championship exhibition series with New York. "Dan Brouthers has too much real estate lying around ... which people are fighting to buy, to lose any time on a supplementary season of baseball."[76]

FIVE. *Big Brother with the Stick: 1892–1895* 115

After being dealt to Baltimore, *Sporting Life* claimed that he needed to be "'handled' and 'jollied' and 'managed'" in order to get him to work hard.[77] At first base, the journal continued, "He can be a perfect symphony if he chooses ... but it appears, from all accounts, that he must be 'handled' for it. Now really, Dan is big enough and old enough and experienced enough to put forth his best skill at all times without 'handling' ... and if he does not do it he will certainly be classed in public estimation with the back numbers [has-beens] and end his career in one of the minor leagues."[78]

There was also a troubling suggestion that Brouthers had an alcohol problem. In the middle of his fine year with Baltimore in 1894, a brief note in *Sporting Life* reported that "Dan's annual town-painting spell is still in abeyance,"[79] hinting that his temperance was partially responsible for his success on the diamond. There may also have been an indirect reference to alcohol issues when, after he disappeared for three days in Brooklyn, the press suggested that "Old Jed has gone on stage." Those familiar with *Old Jed Prouty* knew that Old Jed's "stage" was his tavern, where he dispensed alcohol and advice to his customers. In a few years such fears would be confirmed by Brouthers himself, as in March, 1896, when the *Washington Post* reported that he had sworn not to go on any "benders."[80]

Despite having just won Baltimore's first league championship, all was not well with the Orioles during their 1895 spring training and exhibition schedule. Manager Hanlon and Secretary Harry Vonderhorst had been angered — and perhaps a bit intimidated — by the players' bold threat not to participate in the Temple Cup series unless their take of the profits was greater. They subsequently were disappointed by the humiliating results when the series was finally played.

The team's core of young, previously unknown players had suddenly become well-known stars, and quickly developed healthy egos to match their newfound status. In the struggle for the 1894 pennant, four of the young Orioles — McGraw, Jennings, Kelley and Keeler — had become fast friends. "All four were Irish, and scrappy and ready to laugh. They were friends, who had played the same way. On the diamond and off, they had learned to work as one."[81] McGraw, their ringleader, had already earned an on-field reputation as a rough and tumble type who gave no quarter. "Little McGraw of the Baltimores is the most pugnacious man in the business. He admits to kicking Tommy Tucker in the face at Boston, and says he'll do it again if the big fellow tries to monkey with him."[82] He could be equally as belligerent with the Baltimore brass.

Manager Hanlon, who had invested his life savings in the club and now also served as franchise President, soon realized that in McGraw and his compatriots, he had serious rivals who could vie for control of the team. When March arrived, all the Orioles had signed contracts except the four Irish teammates, and although they eventually acceded, relations between them and Hanlon remained tense. Furthermore, the quartet's cocky intransigence was causing resentment among their teammates and the press.

Prior to reporting to the Orioles' winter camp in Macon, Georgia, 37-year-old Dan Brouthers sent word that he was working hard to get in shape: "Dan Brouthers announces that he is walking ten miles a day and will continue to do so until the time arrives for him to report."[83] His work on the field, however, was unspectacular after the team headed north on its exhibition schedule, with the exception of a towering home run hit in Raleigh, North Carolina, on April 3 against a Wake Forest College team. Years later, Hughie Jennings, Brouthers' teammate on the 1894 and 1895 Orioles, stated that in his opinion, this blow, which landed in a graveyard far outside the confines of Raleigh's Athletic Park, was longer than the famous home run hit out of Union Park in Baltimore the year before.[84]

Brouthers' mediocre performance in spring training was probably affected by the presence of a tall, agile rookie named George Carey, who had established himself as a fine fielding first baseman with the Milwaukee team of the Western League the previous year, and who was given a tryout by Hanlon. In a long essay on the team's prospects for the season, the *Baltimore Sun* made it clear that Carey was favored to replace Brouthers at first base.

> It is not possible to appreciate Carey's work until they [*sic*] see him in active service. In time he will be a wonderful first baseman. He handles his big mitt beautifully and can catch a ball in it alone as easily as he can with his bare hand. He bats naturally, uses a stick as heavy as Big Dan's and usually hits the ball squarely. He takes kindly to the delivery of a left-handed pitcher. Most of his drives go to right field and on them the runner on first base can invariably go to third. He is a fine utility man at outfield and infield work.[85]

After Brouthers started the first few games of the season, Hanlon substituted Carey for him at first base. The *Sun* immediately suggested that the rookie's style of play would fit in better than Brouthers' with the other members of the Baltimore infield. "Carey will be a first baseman of the Jennings, McGraw and Reitz class."[86] Stung by this turn of events, Dan, in typical Brouthers fashion, had words with Hanlon, packed his bags and went home to Wappingers Falls, notifying the press that he was suffering from a toothache.[87] His impetuous behavior gave Hanlon the opening he needed, and on May 8, he sold the veteran slugger's contract to the Louisville Colonels for $700.

First reports after the sale blamed the transfer on the fact that "Brouthers

FIVE. *Big Brother with the Stick: 1892–1895*

and Hanlon could not get along. They had some words ten days ago and the champion's manager removed Dan from first."⁸⁸ It was soon confirmed that Brouthers' age and the incompatibility of his defensive style with that of his infielder teammates were also factors in his release.

> Apologies for Dan Brouthers were made all winter in about this way — Dan was an old veteran (very old) who steadied the youngsters. So he did. Dan was awfully steady on first base, any player of his age would naturally be. But it is just quite possible that the hot fast game of the youngsters requires no steadying at all.... Carey by his years and temperament appears to be just in the condition to absorb the spirit of play and general style of McGraw, Jennings and Reitz, and Dan naturally could not."⁸⁹

Sporting Life's final pronouncements on the Wappingers Falls slugger left the clear impression that his departure from major league ball was imminent:

> Brouthers unquestionably did the best he could and he only succumbed in the way that is natural with all base ball flesh. All honor is due to him for his self command while a member of the Baltimore team, and he has that sympathy which all old players have who work faithfully and only bows [*sic*] to the mandate of Father Time — the inflexible arbiter of every player's base ball career. He has a life of usefulness before him in other walks and can take an honorable place alongside of Spalding, Reach, George Wright and many others whom he can emulate in their honorable and more profitable career.... So farewell to good old Dan. He will always be remembered in the annals of baseball as one of the greatest.⁹⁰

As a franchise, Louisville was a sinking ship through whose revolving doors "has-been" and "want-to-be" players passed in rapid succession in 1896. Among these major league misfits, however, was one gem, Iowa-born Fred Clarke, a fleet-footed outfielder whose debut with the team in 1894 featured a five-for-five effort. Clarke remained with the Colonels until the franchise's dissolution in 1899, and then logged 15 years with the Pittsburgh Pirates. He retired from the game with a .312 batting average, and was elected to the Hall of Fame in 1945.

Brouthers' heart clearly was not in a move from a first- to a last-place team. He stayed just a month with the Colonels, hitting .309 with 30 hits in 24 games, including ten doubles and a pair of home runs. On June 14 in Philadelphia he slammed the two four-baggers over the right field fence at the Huntingdon Street Grounds.

On the road at Brooklyn the following day, he went 3-for-4, and then, taking advantage of his proximity to home, packed his bag, caught the next train to Poughkeepsie, and upon reaching Wappingers Falls, sent a telegram to Louisville manager John McClusky that reportedly read, "Have quit baseball for good. Will go into hotel business here with my brother. Let us be friends, Mac [Manager McClusky]. Please mail me check for salary."[91]

The press had already written Brouthers' baseball obituary when he was sold by Baltimore to Louisville, and his subsequent quick decision to leave the Colonels and go home seemed to confirm that his major league playing days were now in the past. Two months after the season ended, however, he surprised everyone by obtaining his release from Louisville and signing with the Phillies. Perhaps he hoped that on a team in a town whose nickname was the City of Brotherly Love, he would fare better. He must have known that whatever happened there, Philadelphia would be the last stop in his big league career.

SIX

The Sage of Wappingers Falls: 1896–1906

The days of Big Dan are over, I guess. — Dan Brouthers, *Boston Daily Globe,* July 7, 1899

Philadelphia — Dan Brouthers' tenth major league team — was a pennant-hungry franchise. Under managers Harry Wright (1884–1893) and Art Irwin (1894–1895), the team had never captured a championship since its admission to the National League. Hoping to change the Phillies' luck, owners John Rogers and Al Reach hired a new skipper, player-manager Billy Nash, for the 1896 season. An 11-year Boston veteran who had captained the team's 1892 and 1893 pennant-winning clubs, Nash was a strong-armed third baseman and a lifetime .275 hitter.

In order to acquire Nash, Philadelphia traded outfielder Billy Hamilton to Boston. Today the Nash-Hamilton trade is regarded as one of the most lopsided in baseball history.[1] In six years with the Phillies, Hamilton stole 508 bases, hit .361 and compiled a .468 on-base percentage — statistics that remain all-time Philadelphia records 11 decades after the speedy outfielder retired. Nash, in his only year as player-manager for Philadelphia, led the Phillies to an eighth-place finish. After being beaned by Louisville pitcher Tom Smith in May, he played in just 65 games and hit .247. In his first year with Boston, Hamilton hit .365, stole 83 bases, and led the league in on-base percentage (.477).

Future Hall of Famer Hamilton's departure from the Philadelphia outfield still left two other future Cooperstown inductees running down fly balls at the team's Huntingdon Street Grounds: Sam Thompson, Dan Brouthers' teammate and Big Four member from the Detroit Wolverines, and Cleveland-born Ed Delahanty. A right-handed power hitter, Delahanty led the league in almost every offensive category during his 16 major league seasons, compiling a .346 lifetime batting average—fifth highest all-time. Like his contemporary, Mike Kelly, Delahanty's exceptional career was compromised by alcohol abuse. In his case it also played a direct role in his death. On July 2, 1903, the then 35-year slugger was thrown off a train traveling near Niagara Falls, New York, due to his drunken and abusive behavior. Walking in the dark along a trestle bridge over the Niagara River, he stumbled, fell into the river, was swept over Niagara Falls, and drowned.

Before Billy Hamilton's departure from Philadelphia, he, Delahanty and Thompson established a record that will never be broken. In 1894, all three hit over .400, earning them the undisputed title of greatest offensive outfield in baseball history.

Other veterans on the Phillies' 1896 squad included infielders Lave Cross and Bill Hallman, and catcher Jack Clements, all three having played for Philadelphia's American Association, Players' League, Union League or National League teams for a combined 33 years. Clements, a Philadelphia native, is one of 11 nineteenth-century left-handed receivers, and the only one to log more than 1,000 games behind the plate.

The Phillies were an excellent hitting team, leading the league in 1894 and 1895, but their fielding and pitching were poor. They finished either ninth or tenth in both categories during these years. On their way to an eighth-place finish in 1896, 14 different men were tried on the mound in Philadelphia, with their three "aces," Jack Taylor, Al Orth and Kid Casey barely able to stay above the .500 mark with a combined 46–43 win-loss record.

Thirty-seven-year old Dan Brouthers, who had not played since June of the previous year, showed signs of being ready for a comeback. He arrived at the Phillies' spring training camp in Norfolk, Virginia, weighing a trim 203 pounds,[2] and announced to the *Washington Post* that he had sworn off binge drinking: "Dan swears ... that he will never again in his life go on any more of those notorious 'benders.' If Dan will quit 'periodicals' [periodic drinking bouts] he may remain stationary on the Phillies first bag for several seasons to come."[3]

Spring training press reviews of Brouthers' hitting were positive. "Batting was always Dan's long suit and judging from the way in which he has started, even at this early stage of the game, he will come pretty near to equaling his own best record."[4] Initially he interacted well with his teammates, and after Ed Delahanty christened him with a new nickname, "Old Wappinger," other

Six. The Sage of Wappingers Falls: 1896–1906

Dan Brouthers, Philadelphia Phillies portrait, 1896. Although he hit .344 in 57 games for Philadelphia, Brouthers was released by the team in July. In August, he was replaced at first base by rookie Nap Lajoie, who spent another year at the position before switching to second base. A lifetime .338 hitter, Lajoie was elected to the Baseball Hall of Fame in 1937, eight years before Brouthers (Transcendental Graphics/ www.theruckerarchive.com).

positive observations were made about his potential value to the team. "even leaving his batting out of the question, where Brouthers will improve the team is his thorough knowledge of every point of the game gained from long experience on champion teams, and the fact that he is a waiter. Dan makes a pitcher put them over the pan [plate], and if there is such a thing as getting a base on balls, he will get it, despite his hitting ability."[5]

Criticized earlier in his career for lacking hustle on the field and for being unenthusiastic on the bench, the Wappingers Falls slugger was eager to demonstrate to the Phillies that he had turned over a new leaf. "Dan Brouthers is no slouch as a kicker for the rights of himself and his team."[6] After he scored five runs, stole two bases and collected four hits — including two doubles — in a 19–8 blowout victory against the Giants in New York on April 23, the *Philadelphia Inquirer* sang his praises: "Old Wappinger was positively coltish. He 'rooted' and 'chewed' all the way through and contributed four hits and a clean steal to third."[7] The reference to "chewing" here may be figurative, meaning *assertive*, or it may be literal, given his penchant for obsessive gum-chewing: "The most noticeable thing about big Dan Brouthers is the perpetual motion of his jaw, for Dan is a chronic gum chewer."[8]

After the season's first two series, against Boston and New York respectively, Brouthers was praised for his strong and accurate arm and dedicated work ethic. "In every game so far Brouthers has been doing something fine in the throwing line.... [Dan] has been an agreeable disappointment to those who thought he would not be able to play and bat as he once did. No man on the team is working harder or is in better shape than 'Old Wappinger.'"[9] His unexpectedly strong start after nearly a year's layoff even suggested to some that he had found the mythical Fountain of Youth. "Dan Brouthers must have discovered Ponce de Leon's elixir of life, for he is playing ball like a wild man in Philadelphia and all the Quakers take their hats off to him."[10]

The Phillies began the season auspiciously, winning 12 of their first 16 games and claiming first place on May 5. In Brouthers' first 15 games, he collected 18 hits, including four doubles, a triple, and a home run. The four-bagger, a blow over the right field fence hit off St. Louis Browns hurler Bill Kissinger on May 5, would be his only home run in a Philadelphia uniform, and the last of his major league career. The team's high hopes for a pennant began to fade after losing eight straight games on the road in mid–May, including consecutive losses by wide margins (11–5 and 9–3) to the Louisville Colonels, the doormats of the league, who would win just 38 games all season.

Road losses continued to plague Philadelphia over the course of the season. At home on the Huntingdon Street Grounds, the team was 42–27, outscoring their opponents by 84 runs. On the road, the Phillies logged a pitiful 20–41 mark, and were outscored by 83 runs.

Philadelphia's slide to seventh place in late May was blamed on the team's poor pitching and lack of hitting, both ostensibly caused by "dissipation,"[11] with Sam Thompson, Dan Brouthers, Lave Cross, Al Orth and Manager Nash singled out as "lushers."[12] However, Francis Richter, editor of the Philadelphia-based *Sporting News*, came to the defense of the five players, describing them all as "temperates."[13]

Internal strife plagued the club. Billy Nash's position as manager appeared in jeopardy after he was criticized for a lack of good judgment in handling the team. In July, veterans Ed Delahanty and Lave Cross asked to be traded, and rumors persisted that John Ward would replace Nash as manager. Managerial ineptitude, veteran discontent, pitching woes and constantly shifting lineups all took their toll on the team. The Phillies, who had finished third the previous year, landed in eighth place at the close of the 1896 season.

In addition to poor pitching and weak hitting, Philadelphia was carrying too many players on its roster, and constant lineup and position shifts were preventing the development of a cohesive team. Instead of trading for quality players to fill vacancies, team owners Rogers and Reach took the inexpensive route, trying out a constant stream of rookies or second-tier veterans in the hope of finding the spark to turn the team around. Aside from regular pitching starters Taylor, Orth and Casey, for example, another five former minor league pitchers and four major league veterans pitched for the 1896 Phillies, averaging five games each. Four rookie infielders were switched in and out of the lineup in a total of 26 games. Rookie catcher Phil Geier put in 17 games behind the plate and rookie Sam Mertes covered the outfield in 37 contests.

In early July, Dan Brouthers became Philadelphia's first victim of owner, fan and press discontent with the franchise. Returning to the lineup after an unspecified illness that sidelined him for a week at the end of June, he made two errors at first base and collected nine hits in seven games. Only one hit was for extra bases. A few days later he was released by the Phillies. No explanation was offered by the team for its action. *Sporting Life* offered a brief farewell to the departing slugger: "He tried hard to get into shape and succeeded as well as ever in his long career, but failed at the bat, and as that was his chief value as a player he had to make way for a new man."[14]

Based on Brouthers' on-field performance, it is difficult to understand the rationale for his release by Philadelphia. Although his extra-base hits had decreased, he hit .344 in 57 games and collected 75 hits, including 13 doubles, three triples and a home run. He walked 44 times, stole seven bases and scored 44 runs and his on-base percentage of .462 was second only to Ed Delahanty.

Defensively, his .983 fielding percentage was the second-best figure of his major league career.

Given Brouthers' solid hitting and fielding record for the Phillies, his early departure likely was due more to the franchise's financial woes and his own interpersonal conflicts with teammates than to his on-field performance. Philadelphia's 1896 strategy of employing minor-league hopefuls and over-the-hill veterans revealed the owners' reluctance to spend enough money to obtain quality starters. Brouthers' departure from the Phillies would allow a rookie to take his place at a much lower salary.

It also appears likely that Brouthers himself was caught up in internal turmoil on a team whose manager feared being fired and whose veterans requested to be traded. A month after his release, the normally good-natured Brouthers had uncharacteristically harsh words for his Philadelphia teammates. "In a letter to a Baltimore friend, Dan Brouthers accuses the Phillies of 'knocking' one another, and to that he attributes their ill success."[15] Given his well-known sensitivity to criticism, we can assume that some of the "knocking" he describes came in the form of criticism of his play by teammates, fans and the press. At the conclusion of the season, Brouthers' Detroit and Philadelphia teammate, Sam Thompson, in turn directed some harsh criticism toward him. "Sam Thompson says that knocking [criticism] is what caused Dan Brouthers to be released by Philadelphia. Almost every member of the team was down on 'Old Wappinger.'"[16] Given such a blunt assessment and knowing Brouthers' penchant for heading home when under stress or criticism, his week-long absence from the team in June for an "unspecified" illness might instead have been due more to damaged ego than an illness — a state of affairs, which, if known by his teammates, would have exacerbated any pre-existing tension between them and the Wappingers Falls slugger.

Sporting Life's "farewell" to Brouthers on his release, however, which observed that "he had to make way for a new man,"[17] suggests that manager Nash and Philadelphia owners Rogers and Reach may have had another motive for releasing the veteran. On Brouthers' departure, outfielder Ed Delahanty was moved temporarily to first base. Over four previous seasons (1890–1891, 1893–1894), Delahanty had filled in at first 42 times. Never a good fielder at any position, his poor prior fielding averages at first base (.950 in 1890; .946 in 1891; .950 in 1893; .937 in 1894) made it clear that his switch to Brouthers' former position was not permanent.

It is possible that even before Dan Brouthers was released, the Phillies management already had its eyes on a minor league player to replace him. His name was Napoleon Lajoie, a 21-year-old, 6'1", 195-pound utility player of French-Canadian heritage from Woonsocket, Rhode Island. Lajoie had been

Six. *The Sage of Wappingers Falls: 1896–1906*

catching and playing first and second base for Fall River of the New England League that year, and hitting over .400. Signed by Philadelphia in August, he spent 39 games at first base for the team over the last two months of the season, collected 57 hits, including 12 doubles, seven triples and four home runs, and hit .326. His fielding average was .995. Lajoie spent another year at first base before moving to second in 1898, a position which he played equally well. He spent 21 seasons in the big leagues, retired with a .338 batting average, and was elected to the Baseball Hall of Fame in 1937.

Although Dan Brouthers departed the major leagues without fanfare, 12 decades later his records continue to impress. He won five batting crowns, seven slugging crowns (six in consecutive years), and five on-base-percentage crowns. In the recently conceived statistical category of OPS (on-base percentage plus slugging — a measure of a player's ability both to get on base and hit for power) he was a league leader eight times. Other categories in which he was a season leader include total bases (four times), hits and doubles (three times each), runs, RBI, home runs and fewest strikeouts per at-bat (twice each) and triples, fielding percentage and put-outs (once each).

Among his peers whose careers were played entirely in the nineteenth century, Brouthers ranks first in slugging (.519) and OPS (.942), second in triples (205), third in doubles (460), fourth in batting average (.342), hits (2,296) and home runs (107), and sixth in runs scored (1,523).

In all-time records categories, Brouthers fares well in comparison with the game's greatest hitters. In slugging, all bow to Babe Ruth, who twice led the league for six consecutive seasons. Three other players led the league in slugging for six consecutive years: Ty Cobb, Rogers Hornsby and Dan Brouthers. In OPS, Babe Ruth reigns supreme, leading his league once for seven consecutive seasons and once for six. Cobb, Hornsby and Brouthers are the only other players to lead the league in this category for six consecutive seasons. Only seven men in baseball history have won more batting titles than Dan Brouthers: Ty Cobb, Honus Wagner, Rogers Hornsby, Stan Musial, Rod Carew, Wade Boggs and Tony Gwynn.

Some of Brouthers' hitting exploits can only be appreciated when they are contextualized within the framework of nineteenth-century ground rules, playing regulations and game schedules. For example, he ranks eighth all-time in triples with a career total of 205 three-baggers. While a praiseworthy achievement, this record becomes more significant within its nineteenth-century context.

All-time records in categories like hits, doubles, triples and runs scored have been achieved by talented players who enjoyed long careers that consisted of long (154 games or 162 games) seasons. Dan Brouthers had a long career, but his playing seasons averaged just 125 games, and his first three seasons were even shorter, averaging under 85 games. What he accomplished in two of those first three years, however, would have been able to be accomplished by a "modern" Dan Brouthers in a little more than a year, given the present-day 162-game schedule.

The potential statistical implications of great careers played in long seasons versus great careers played in significantly shorter seasons are self-evident: no nineteenth-century player holds any all-time marks in "quantity" categories like hits, doubles, runs, home runs, RBI or triples. Other methods of comparison, however, provide significantly different results.

The top three all-time triples leaders, for example, are Sam Crawford (309), Ty Cobb (295) and Honus Wagner (252). If triples per at-bat are used to measure performance, however, Crawford remains first all time, with an average of one three-bagger every 30.9 at-bats. Dan Brouthers moves into second place, averaging one triple every 32.7 at-bats, and Roger Connor ranks third, with one per 33.4 at-bats. Cobb and Wagner, who rank second and third respectively in career triples, move down to fifth and seventh place respectively in triples per at-bat.

If triples per game were the criterion, Dan Brouthers would tie Sam Crawford for first place all-time, each registering an average of one triple per 8.2 games. Roger Connor would rank third, with one triple per 8.6 games.

Dan Brouthers leads all nineteenth-century players in slugging, with a lifetime average of .519, but he ranks just 60th on the all-time list in this category. The 59 players who precede him on the list, however, had the distinct advantage of always facing a pitcher who threw from the same distance — 60'6" from home plate. Brouthers had to adjust four times to differing pitching distances (45', 50', 55' and 60'6") while establishing his slugging record.

The 1884–1886 seasons, when helmetless batters stood just 50 feet away from pitchers who were throwing overhand, were arguably the most dangerous and challenging years for hitters in the long history of the game. These seasons figure among the six successive seasons that Dan Brouthers lead his league in slugging.

Restrictive ground rules and the condition of the baseball in play were other significant factors in the nineteenth-century game. As we have seen previously, ground rules that allowed balls to remain in play or be limited to doubles when hit over the fence, into the seats, or into overflow crowds in the outfield, affected not only Dan Brouthers, but every nineteenth-century hitter.

The ball used in Brouthers' era was the same "dead ball" in use until the cork-centered version was introduced by Bill Shibe in 1910. Until the year of

Brouthers' retirement from major league competition, "a ball a game was the norm, and if batted out of the park, the game's continuance awaited the pleasure of some anonymous 'urchin.' If he chose to return it he was given free admission, if not, the house reluctantly put a new one into play."[18]

Softer than its modern counterpart, the nineteenth-century ball was kept in play whether it became scratched, soiled, or waterlogged, or the seams broke, prompting some managers, as we have seen, to choose to bat first when playing at home in order to get a crack at a fresh, new ball. The longer a ball was in play, the more difficult it was to hit for distance. Significantly, 34 of Dan Brouthers' 107 home runs were hit in the sixth inning or later, and 14 of them were hit in the eighth or ninth inning, when the ball was hardest to hit for distance. Hitting a heavily-used, softer ball for distance or average was never a dilemma faced by the sluggers who precede Dan Brouthers on the all-time slugging list.

Despite the significant challenges for early era hitters like Dan Brouthers, which were unknown by their successors, Brouthers' consistently high slugging and batting averages, when considered in conjunction with his extremely low strikeout rate, his excellent stolen base and sacrifice record and his intentional walk rate, fully justifies his characterization by the press of his era as "thundering, ball murdering Dan"[19] and "the greatest slugger in the country."[20]

Dan Brouthers' release by Philadelphia set off a minor league bidding war for his services that was won by the Springfield Ponies of the Eastern League, whose manager, Tom Burns, had spent a dozen years with the Chicago White Stockings as a utility infielder. "Manager Burns has been after him for a fortnight.... Other managers have also been after Brouthers, but Mr. Burns made terms which were satisfactory, and Brouthers has become a 'Pony.'"[21]

Brouthers' Springfield signing began a decade-long roller coaster ride for the veteran slugger that would commence with spectacular success in the Eastern League, but be followed by a precipitous decline in his skills and his voluntary retirement. After more than a year's layoff from Eastern League competition, Old Wappinger would once again return to the ball field, this time closer to home, in the Class D Hudson Valley League. Three years later, after being embarrassed by a drinking scandal and frustrated in his first role as a team owner, he retired from the game.

While the idea of a baseball superstar competing in the minor leagues after completing a major league career would be unthinkable today, it was commonplace in the nineteenth century. In the modern era, million-dollar contracts and lucrative commercial endorsements allow most former stars to live comfortable, even luxurious lifestyles upon their retirement from big league play.

Early era players were not as fortunate, and therefore needed new jobs to support their families when their playing days ended. Few of them had acquired professional or business skills. Most left school in their early teens to help support their families by working in the mills, mines or farms. These players' baseball abilities provided them with salaries that tripled or quadrupled those earned by their fathers, but their work on the ball field left little time to develop skills that would lead to financial success after baseball. There were a few notable exceptions to this rule, such as John Ward and Jim O'Rourke, both of whom studied law in the off-season. Unlike the great majority of their fellow ballplayers, however, they had completed high school-level studies before beginning their baseball careers.

If recently released major league players' baseball skills had not declined precipitously, many, especially those with national reputations, were able to continue their careers in the minors without immediate drastic pay reductions from their previous salaries. Former stars remained big draws in the smaller markets and were unlikely to be re-signed by raiding big league teams hunting for replacements.

Some players with limited educational backgrounds were able to develop administrative and business skills after their big league careers by serving as managers or owners of minor league teams. Cleveland outfielder Jesse Burkett, a future Hall of Famer, for example, played, managed and owned a team in the New England League. Former Giants great Roger Connor did the same in the Connecticut State League.

Nevertheless, results from two studies of the principal occupations of retired major leaguers, one based on data from the generation of players that preceded Dan Brouthers, and the other from the generation that succeeded him, illustrate well the fact that most players were not prepared for any particular occupation except baseball when they retired.

Data on ex-major league retirees who were active between 1871 and 1882 reveal that 85 percent worked in low-level white-collar (clerks, sales, small business proprietors) or blue-collar jobs, with only 15 percent employed as professionals, managers or high-level business proprietors.[22] These proportions improved slightly for retired ex-major leaguers active from 1900–1919. Almost 24 percent enjoyed high-level white-collar careers, but 76 percent were still employed in low-level, white-collar or blue collar enterprises.[23]

By all accounts, Dan Brouthers had been careful with the money he earned during his baseball career, investing primarily in real estate in and around his home town. Numerous reports published near the end of his major league career affirm that he had saved or invested nearly $20,000 to $30,000 — about one million dollars in today's currency. He was also known to be

Six. *The Sage of Wappingers Falls: 1896–1906*

exceptionally thrifty. "Dan has planted his wealth in brick houses in Wappinger's Falls, and can lie back at his case with his 30,000 'plunks' [dollars] and laugh at the magnates [team owners].... Dan is what ball players call 'hard paper' [thrifty or cheap], which was a most distinguishing characteristic of every one of the 'big four.'"[24]

His celebrated tightness with a dollar made him an easy target for practical jokers among his teammates.

> Dan was so close [cheap] that he kissed the Goddess of Liberty every time he parted with a silver dollar. He always had a suspicion of banks, and instead of depositing his money in one bank, he split it in sections and deposited it in long green institutions all over the League circuit. Mike Kelly put up a trick on Dan over in Boston during the Brotherhood year that scared the knock-kneed first bagger out of a year's growth. Mike flung himself into the dressing-room one morning after practice, and asked Dan if he had heard the news: "the Boston Savings Bank has busted, Dan." Dan let a roar out of him, and attired in nothing but a sweater and an air of virtuous indignation, scampered out of the dressing room and was half way across the ball park when he came to. When he returned, Kel [Kelly] indulged in a merry guffaw, and Dan was so tickled that he hustled on his clothes a bought a round of drinks for the gang. Kel got the dollar bill that Dan had given in payment for the drinks, framed it, and hung it in the dressing-room with the inscription: "Dan Brouthers bought a round of drinks with this."[25]

Despite his thrift and savings, retiring at age 37 with a wife and four children to support was not an option for him. Baseball was the only profession he knew, and he would continue to make his living from the national pastime in some way or another until his death at age 74.

When Brouthers began his career in the late 1870s, there were no "major" or "minor" designations applied to any of the numerous professional leagues in existence. After the founding of the National League, all other such leagues were properly designated as regional rather than national in scope, as their names frequently implied: Western League; Southern League; New England League.

The 1883 National Agreement, a pact signed by the National League, the American Association and the Northwestern League, significantly advanced the concept of two levels of professional play that would soon be designated as major and minor. By this agreement, the National League recognized the American Association as an equal league of national proportion, and each of the three signatories agreed to respect each other's reserve rules. Although the Northwestern League's participation in the pact was almost exclusively motivated by a need to protect its team rosters from being raided by the other signatories, signing the agreement, *de facto*, categorized it as a secondary organization compared to the National League and the American Association. At this juncture, major and minor leagues became a reality.

The Eastern League, established in 1884, had evolved from the original International Association (1877), and consequently retained an international flavor by including at least one Canadian club, usually Toronto, among its team franchises. After undergoing many reconfigurations, the Eastern League had achieved a measure of stability by 1896, the first year in the organization's history in which there were no franchise relocations. Its teams were located in Buffalo, Providence, Rochester, Springfield, Scranton, Syracuse, Toronto and Wilkes-Barre. Joining the Eastern League was a homecoming of sorts for Dan Brouthers, who, as we recall, apprenticed with the Rochester Hop Bitters in 1880, spent five years on Buffalo's National League team, and played for years against Providence when it was a major league franchise.

With the consolidation of the two major leagues in 1892, the new "Big League," now assured of its monopoly, abandoned all pretense of respecting minor league reserve clauses and regularly lured away the best minor league players with lucrative contracts. After winning the 1895 Eastern League pennant, Springfield was victimized in this fashion by National League raiding parties, and consequently found itself in the league basement midway through the 1896 season.

The Springfield franchise was a transition station for youngsters headed up the ladder to the majors and veterans headed down. Of the team's total roster of 44 players — many of whom stayed for just a few games — 33 either had or would have major league experience over the course of their careers. Ed Crane's story was perhaps the most somber of all. A short, stocky pitcher whose blazing speed was accompanied by intimidating wildness, his career highlight occurred during the 1889 World Series, when he won four games for the Giants against the Association's Brooklyn team. Uncontrolled weight gain and alcoholism lead to a quick decline in his skills, and by 1894 he was back in the minors. Springfield manager Tom Brown gave Crane a brief try in 1896, signing him on June 25, but released him on June 30. Three months later, Crane committed suicide in the rooming house where he lived in Rochester by drinking a bottle of chloral hydrate.

Dan Brouthers began his minor league career inauspiciously by failing to report for his first game. His excuse, while not new, was perhaps understandable, given the sad memory of having lost an infant son to illness just a few years earlier: "He found one of his children ill on his return home, and yesterday a bad turn in the disease delayed him until he could summon the physician and find out if anything serious was anticipated."[26] He finally made his debut on July 18 in a 3–2 win against Albany, and although going hitless, managed to satisfy the crowd. "Dan Brouthers did nothing phenomenal with the bat, although the small boy element kept urging him to. In fact, he didn't make a hit, but the two long flies to centre were made with apparent ease. All the fielders played very deep for him, the outside men covering nearly to the track."[27]

It did not take Brouthers long to find his hitting stroke. In 48 games with the Ponies, he collected 76 hits, including 16 doubles, nine triples and three home runs, finishing the season with a .398 average. His slugging and fine fielding helped lift the team out of the Eastern League cellar and into sixth place.

Although Brouthers officially hit three home runs for Springfield in 1896, another of his circuit shots was erased under unusual circumstances. After he hit a four-bagger early in a contest at Buffalo on August 9, the game was delayed by rain after four innings. Believing it impossible to continue play, the Springfield nine packed up their equipment and headed for the train station. Sometime later, the umpire declared the grounds playable. With the Ponies nowhere to be found, he awarded the game to Buffalo as a 9–0 forfeit, and Brouthers' home run was erased from the record book.

Most minor league ground rules of the period were similar to those of their major league counterparts with regard to balls that left the park. These hits were considered in play if the ball could be returned to the diamond. Brouthers was victimized by this rule during the second game of a doubleheader played at home against Buffalo on July 21. Having already connected for a triple in the first inning, he hit a powerful drive that cleared the fence in the fourth inning, but which yielded him just three bases. It was a "tremendous riverbound drive ... which was only saved from the water and a home run by the advertising boards beyond the track, which it struck and bounded back into the field and was fielded in time to hold Dan at third."[28]

In mid–August, he had better luck when his long hit managed to avoid the advertising signs and land in the river. "In the third, after Leahy had hit safely, Brouthers made a terrific drive out into right field. It was a line hit and the ball bounded over the dike into the river, and before it was returned 'Dan' might have circled the bases half a dozen times."[29]

Later that month against Scranton, Brouthers finally hit a ball so far that no one could retrieve it:

> "Dan" more than lived up to his reputation as a heavy hitter. In the fourth he knocked a home run and sent the ball traveling farther than it has ever traveled in the history of baseball in this city [Springfield]. Away over the treetops that fringe the riverbank it sped, and had the water in the Connecticut [River] been high the sphere would certainly have had a ducking. Meaney in left field evidently

mistook the ball for a soaring hawk—at any rate he saw that any attempt at capture would be ridiculous, and moved only to turn and follow, with sad expression, its sky-high course. Small as was the crowd in attendance at the game, it kept the grand stand reverberating for some minutes. Besides this phenomenal wield, "Dan" knocked a triple and a single. Four times at bat and once sent on ball [sent to first with a walk] he rounded the circuit four times.[30]

Brouthers consistent first base play for Springfield also drew high praise, both locally and in the national press.

"He is, as far as his record with us is concerned, a perfect man on the initial bag."[31]

"Dan did good work on first, where he handled the ball with enviable ease. It gives a team confidence to have its initial bag covered by a giant."[32]

"[Dan] ... is covering that bag to perfection. His playing is of a superior order."[33]

"That big fellow 'Dan' controls much acreage around the initial bag and captures all invading spheres."[34]

In addition to his offensive and defensive prowess, Brouthers' long years of experience and grace under fire were also appreciated by the Ponies and their fans. "By his solidity of presence and his cool deliberation and accuracy, he steadies the rest of the team."[35]

Brouthers stellar performance for the Ponies in 1896 was just a prelude to what he would accomplish in 1897, when he enjoyed his last great season in baseball. Playing in 126 games, he eclipsed his previous career highs in batting (.415), slugging (.645), hits (208), doubles (44), and home runs (15). His 60 multiple-hit games included 17 three-hit, seven four-hit, and one five-hit effort. At age 39, he remained surprisingly nimble on the base paths, stealing 21 bags. Serving as team captain and referred to respectfully by his newly-minted nickname, "Gladstone" (after British politician William Gladstone, whose career lasted 60 years), Brouthers helped move the Ponies up to third place from their 1896 sixth-place finish in the Eastern League standings.

There were numerous Brouthers highlights over the course of his exceptional 1897 season. After getting just one hit in the campaign's first two contests—both losses to Buffalo—he was getting heckled in a game against Toronto by impatient fans who apparently had forgotten his contributions to the team the previous year. As we have learned, he was famously sensitive to this type of criticism. On this occasion he was able to silence the naysayers with his bat work. In the fifth inning, "Gladstone had his revenge on the 'cranks' [fans] who have been guying [criticizing] him for the last two or three games, as he calmly put the ball over the right field fence and followed Scheffler across the plate."[36]

Two weeks later against Scranton, his double and two home runs were

Six. *The Sage of Wappingers Falls: 1896–1906*

responsible for all the Ponies' scoring in an 8–3 loss. At Toronto on June 14, he collected five hits, including a triple, scored three runs, and stole a base. In a mid–September win at Montreal, his four hits included two doubles and a triple.

At Wilkes-Barre on August 9, he hit "two of the longest hits ever seen on the grounds,"[37] first a three-bagger over the left fielder's head, and then a line drive far over the right field fence. These hits were topped by another blow against Wilkes-Barre a month later in unusually cold September weather. In the fifth inning,

> "Dan" Brouthers came to bat. The bases were full when the old man stepped to the plate, but [pitcher] Odwell's arm and his head didn't work well together in the emergency. The first ball he presented for Dan's inspection was a well-ripened peach, with which Dan was well pleased. With a gentle wave of his magic wand the old man converted that well-ripened peach into an overdone dumpling, and four runs came in. As the captain rounded up his men from the bags, the half-frozen spectators took occasion to warm themselves with enthusiastic howls of glee. It wasn't an ordinary, everyday affair of a home run. Dan didn't aim at the nearest point on the fence and hit for that. He just sighted his bat carefully on the water tank at the south end of the park, and "let'er go." She went.[38]

During the course of his long major league career, Dan Brouthers never spent more than five years with one team. His nearly constant movement from club to club or from league to league was necessitated by a variety of factors, including franchise dissolutions, inter-league wars, team financial crises, or his own Brotherhood loyalties and unbending salary requirements. Similar extenuating circumstances in the Eastern League, and the new-found luxury of remaining closer to home after years on the road, would lead to similar patterns of movement from one team to another during the slugger's minor league years.

The Eastern League's shorter season and regional focus meant that Brouthers, who turned 40 in May 1898, could spend more time at home with Mary Ellen and the four children, now aged 12, ten, eight and four. There had been many changes in Wappingers Falls since he left two decades earlier. Telephone service arrived in the early 1890s and a trolley line to Poughkeepsie was inaugurated in 1894. By 1900, most of the village's factories would convert to electricity as a power source, although it would not be available in homes until 1914.[39]

At the beginning of Brouthers career, sportswriters began attaching his hometown name to their descriptions of the big slugger, and soon, as we have seen, he became known throughout the country by nicknames like "the Wappingers Falls terror,"[40] "the Wappingers Falls boy,"[41] and "Wappinger Dan."[42]

The village's quaint, rustic character was thus, by extension, applied also to its first representative in the major leagues. Years later, Brouthers' "Old Jed" nickname would continue to suggest an image of a country hayseed of humble, rural origin.

In the 20 years that had passed since Brouthers first left Wappingers Falls to pursue his career, however, the village had grown and matured along with the rest of the country. The recent discovery and meticulous review of some of the town's hotel registries from the period by Wappingers Falls Historical Society Archivist, Rena Corey, reveal that the village was a regular stopping point for salesmen, industrialists, politicians, musicians, and artistic and theatrical groups, thus confirming that in Dan Brouthers' absence, it had become "an industrial and mercantile hub."[43] Once a sleepy hamlet, Wappingers Falls was now a busy, modern Poughkeepsie suburb.

Brouthers' pride in his community, his high status and visibility in Wappingers Falls, and his new, more flexible work schedule prompted him to take a new direction in his life. In March 1898, he made his first sally into local politics. "Dan Brouthers made his political debut this spring by being elected one of the village trustees of Wappinger Falls. Dan is intensely loyal to his home and it is related that when he discovered in a Scranton hotel last spring a large map which had Wappinger Falls located on it, he was so delighted that he at once entered into negotiations with the landlord to secure the map with a view of placing it in the archive of the town."[44]

Word of the slugger's new political position provoked a humorous response from *Sporting Life*, serving notice that despite Wappingers Falls' progress, some outsiders still considered it a backwoods hamlet inhabited by "rubes":

> Dan Brouthers, a trustee of Wappinger's Falls, eh? Well, well! Imagine big Dan presiding over a town meeting and about seven of those long whiskered rubes ... yelling for the floor. Imagine Dan: "Hee, hee, order or I'll have John Brush [owner of the Boston Beaneaters] tend to ye! Haven't you fellows got yer batting order arranged yet? Where's your scorer? Deacon Elphalet Brown [an oblique reference to Deacon White of the Big Four] is first to bat, and Abner Jones is on deck! Keep quiet, now, or I'll put you on the bench, Hezekiah Gray, and put the rest of ye out of the park!"[45]

Due to a salary dispute with the Springfield team's owners, Brouthers did not participate in spring training or the team's rain-plagued pre-season tour through Connecticut. "Brouthers wants too much money and says he won't play at all unless he gets the price asked for, which the club is not willing to give, so Dan may stay on his farm in Wapppinger Falls, NY."[46] At the last minute, an agreement was reached and contract signed, allowing him to be in lineup for the Ponies' opener against Toronto on April 30.

Trouble, however, was brewing both in the league and on the Ponies team. In what was clearly a cost-cutting measure, Springfield released manager Tom Burns and hired a 24-year-old Bridgeport, Connecticut, native, Bill Lush, to skipper the team. Lush's resume — three years as a backup utility man for the Washington Nationals — paled in comparison to Burns' extensive big league resume, and Lush's youth and inexperience would make controlling team members who were former major league players difficult. League team owners, worried about the effect the outbreak of the Spanish-American War would have on attendance, feared the prospects of a "disastrous"[47] season: "When a man is pondering about the fate of some battleship, he won't care much about a base ball game."[48] Noting that "rain has made every magnate a loser on the exhibition tour,"[49] Syracuse's owner, George Kantzsh, predicted that if regular season patronage fell 15 percent, "The Eastern League would not last the season."[50]

In order to shore up the league financially, President Pat Powers proposed condensing the season from five months to four and a half, thus eliminating the players' last two weeks' salary. Players responded with a threat to strike. The league backed down, but then substituted an alternative economizing measure — club rosters were reduced to 12 men.

Nineteen games into the season, Springfield, at 5–14, was in last place, Big Dan had gone hitless in seven of the contests, and talk of trading the great slugger surfaced. "It is rumored that big Dan Brouthers may be exchanged for a desirable player in another position. Brouthers' batting has fallen off perceptibly from previous seasons."[51] At the end of May, the rumor became reality. "The Directors of the Springfield baseball association voted tonight to release Dan Brouthers, George Bannon and pitcher Korwan. This action, it is thought, will not prove popular with the patrons of the game. The release of Brouthers is especially condemned, although Brouthers himself will not suffer, three teams in the league having wired him to send terms."[52]

As had happened twice before in his career (with John Ward in Brooklyn and with Ned Hanlon in Baltimore), Brouthers now found a benefactor in the person of another of his Brotherhood compatriots — Toronto-born Art Irwin, manager of the 1898 Toronto Canucks of the Eastern Association, who had also managed him at Boston in 1891. In Brouthers' brief 33-game stay with Irwin's Canucks, he recovered his hitting form, posting 12 multiple-hit games, including a four-hit effort against Wilkes-Barre on June 28 that included a double and a triple, and home runs hit against Wilkes-Barre on June 27 and Buffalo on July 5.

In mid–July, however, another drastic cost-cutting measure was implemented by the struggling league. Salaries were cut by 20 percent, effective immediately. Players who did not accept the cut were fired and were ineligible for playing for other league teams. Brouthers refused to accept the salary cut, played his final two games for Toronto — a doubleheader on July 9 — and went home to Wappingers Falls.

Brouthers' last Eastern League season, 1899, would be even shorter than his brief 1898 campaign. With Tom Brown back at the helm at Springfield, he signed again with the Ponies. It soon became clear that the man who showed up to play was not the old Dan Brouthers. Perhaps it was due to the fact that he had not played a full season in two years, or to a lack of proper conditioning, or simply to the inevitable aging process, but his hitting had fallen off dramatically and he was slower than usual in the field. There were flashes of the former slugger — a home run hit against Toronto on May 22 and a long triple against Hartford on the first of June. Overall, however, he was batting in the .230s instead of the customary .330s or higher.

Ultimately, it was not his slow start, but his well-known sensitivity to criticism that influenced his decision to ask to be released. "Of late ... his batting has fallen off, few of his hits going safe. For this reason there has been a good deal of 'knocking' [criticism] from the cranks [fans]. This is something Dan is not accustomed to and it has broken his spirit.... This probably means the close of a baseball career of twenty-one years."[53]

After a few days' reflection, however, Old Wappinger decided he wanted one more chance. He contacted Rochester Patriots manager Al Buckenberger, former skipper of the National League Pittsburgh Pirates, and offered his services. Buckenberger agreed, and for a brief, magical moment it seemed that the old Dan Brouthers was back. Six days after his resignation from Springfield, he stepped to the plate in his first game as a Patriot and hit the first pitch over the fence for a home run.

It proved to be a very short reprieve. Eight frustrating days later, now convinced that his great hitting skills had diminished to the point of no return, Brouthers resigned from his second team in less than three weeks. The national press took his action as his definitive farewell to the game.

> Big Dan Brouthers, for 20 years one of the greatest basemen in the country, and the last of Detroit's "big four" of 1887, has left baseball for ever. His decision was made yesterday morning, when he tendered his resignation to the Rochester team of the Eastern league. In resigning, Brouthers said: "I am satisfied that I have seen my best days on the diamond and am ready to quit. When I received manager Buckenberger's telegram ... asking me to join the Rochester team, I hesitated for four days before replying. I finally decided for Rochester, but I can't hit them square on the nose as I did once. I know that I am not satisfactory to the Rochester team and I do not want you to keep me a moment longer. I am going home to Wappingers Falls to run my little hotel. I am mayor of that little

Six. The Sage of Wappingers Falls: 1896–1906

town, and there I will spend the rest of my days reading the stories of what the younger bloods are doing on the diamond. The days of Big Dan are over, I guess. I have enough of this world's goods to keep me going until I die."[54]

The initial portion of this farewell statement appears to represent authentic, heartfelt thoughts penned by the Wappingers Falls slugger. Later portions appear to be fabrications. Dan Brouthers' name, for example, never figured on the list of his hometown's mayors[55] although, as we have seen, he did serve as a town trustee. He owned property in the area, tenements and a saloon, but never a hotel, despite the fact that in the telegram he sent to manager John McCloskey in 1895 when he resigned from the Louisville Colonels, he expressed a wish to open one with his brother. Dutchess County, New York, records[56] verify that in 1900, Dan's brother James did open a hotel in nearby Hughsonville, but Dan was not listed as a co-owner, and when the property was sold in 1924, five years after James' death, his widow and two daughters, and not Dan, were listed as the property's owners. Furthermore, it would also be highly uncharacteristic of Brouthers to suggest or advertise that he was financially well-off, as his farewell letter suggests. In his later major league years, however, the press, as we have seen, had commonly reported that he was wealthy.

There are two possible explanations for the disparity between truth and fiction in Brouthers' alleged farewell statement. One is that he himself uttered the falsehoods, exaggerating the truth in order to assuage his embarrassment over having to retire from the game due to poor performance. Such a ploy, however, is at odds with everything known about his character over his long career. A second possibility is that the press embellished information about his role in town governance, his real estate holdings, and his financial worth in order to present a sympathetic portrait of a former star upon his exit from the game.

Big Dan's sudden exit from the Eastern League was not the end of his baseball career. After a two-year leave, he donned a uniform again to inaugurate the Hudson River League. Then, after another sabbatical from the game and a change of address, he would manage, captain, and play for a Manhattan semi-pro team for yet a few more seasons. To the great joy of the graying former star, for a time one of his understudies on that team was his own son, Addison.

With his Eastern League career behind him, "Old Wappinger" settled down for a period of baseball-free domesticity that was not without its exciting moments. In early April 1900, he was acclaimed a hero due to his actions during a village tragedy. The event, a house fire that took the lives of two women, was described in the *Poughkeepsie Daily Eagle* as "a catastrophe as singular as it was sudden and terrible."⁵⁷ The two women in question, a Mrs. Hill and a Mrs. Sullivan, were drinking beer at their home in central Wappingers Falls on a Saturday afternoon. "During the excitement that attended this mode of entertainment, a kerosene lamp was knocked over by the elbow of one of the women. It fell to the floor and exploded, the oil scattering over the furniture, carpet and dresses of the two women."⁵⁸

The victims ran from the house screaming and were attended by onlookers. "It was stated by the many witnesses to the scene that as the two women rushed into the street they formed neither more nor less than two living torches illuminating the neighborhood brightly with their ghastly light."⁵⁹

Dan Brouthers, a volunteer village fireman in his youth, had been walking nearby and soon sprang into action:

> Meanwhile another scene was being enacted at the home of Mrs. Sullivan. Big Dan Brouthers, hearing the alarm, rushed to the scene, and as the two women had already been taken care of, he went into the home where everything was ablaze. A moment's inspection showed him that the carpet was not nailed down, and with all his mighty strength he gathered it up and hurled it out the door, where it continued to burn in the street. He then picked up the various articles of furniture that were blazing and sent them after the carpet. Turning to the room he found two little children who had just been awakened by the smoke and uproar. He carried these also out and into a neighbor's home.⁶⁰

Both women subsequently died from their injuries.

Eight months later, however, Brouthers' hero's reputation was badly tarnished after a brush with the law. "Dennis Brouthers, the former base ball player, known as 'Big Dan,' who conducts a saloon in Wappingers Falls, is one of six saloon keepers indicted and arrested for violating the Excise law and having slot machines in their places."⁶¹ While there is no record of the outcome for Brouthers of this embarrassing incident, given his status as a town trustee and a local sports hero, he probably was released after paying a fine.

After he spent another year at home and out of professional baseball, a series of events in early 1902 revealed how eager, or perhaps desperate he was to get back into the game he loved. In early February he contacted *The Sporting News* to report his interest in playing again and provided details about his physical condition. The Philadelphia-based weekly obligingly noted his communication and endorsed his planned comeback.

> Dan Brouthers, the retired slugger of old, one of the most famous players ever in the game, informs us that he wants to play ball again after a brief retirement of one season. Dan says he played about thirty games around Dutchess County last season with strong amateur and semi-professional teams, and found that he could field and bat — and particularly bat — as well as ever he did: also that his

Dan Brouthers in his Wappingers Falls saloon, circa 1900. Playing minor league ball closer to home allowed Brouthers to participate more fully in town life. In addition to the saloon, he owned apartment houses. In 1898 he was elected a trustee of the village. In 1900, Brouthers was arrested and fined for having illegal slot machines in his saloon (Transcendental Graphics/www.theruckerarchive.com).

throwing arm is as strong and accurate as it was fifteen years ago, when Dan was only a "kid." Dan is confident that he can play first base acceptably for several years yet, and that his long experience would make him additionally valuable as a captain. Brouthers, moreover, still takes as much keen delight in the game as a boy. Considering that Brouthers has all his facilities unimpaired, is in good health and down to weight, he ought to be able to secure a good engagement in these piping times of competition, when good players of established reputation are at a premium. We would advise minor league magnates and managers to give Brouthers a thought, and either write, or better still, take a run to Wappinger's Falls, N.Y. to size up the former veteran personally. Who knows but what some club may make an unexpected hit personally and artistically with Brouthers.[62]

The New England League's New London team soon expressed some interest in Brouthers, but the unusual contract that his agent, a friend who managed a nearby Newburgh semi-pro team, had approved on his behalf, made it clear that there were still doubts about the old veteran's readiness to play. "It was agreed that Brouthers will bat on an average of .300 or over or not make any claim to salary."[63] A month later, Brouthers himself repudiated the contract.[64]

With that option off the table, he began the process of getting back in the game on his own on two different fronts. At home in Wappingers Falls, he organized a team for his parish church, St. Mary's, and underwrote the restoration of the diamond nearby where he began his career with the Actives years before.

> St. Mary's Lyceum ball team has been organized for the season, with Dan Brouthers as manager and captain, besides which he will play first base. Dan has had the old diamond enclosed by the track at Powers Recreation Park scraped and put in excellent condition. Arrangements are underway to bring the Haverstraw team here for Decoration Day and the following Saturday half holiday. It is possible that the first game may be played on Saturday, May 24. It will revive many old memories to see Dan at the bat on the old diamond. His last game there was on July 4, 1878, nearly twenty-four years ago.[65]

Soon afterward, he also became involved in an attempt to create a new Poughkeepsie team. "Poughkeepsie has organized a base ball team composed of minor league players with Dan Brouthers at the head. They are desirous of playing Sunday games within 150 miles of Poughkeepsie."[66] While there is no indication that this effort was successful, he helped lay the groundwork for a new league organized the following year that featured a Poughkeepsie nine and teams from other mid–Hudson towns.

Late in 1902, Brouthers went to New York to offer testimony in a suit brought by infielder Fred Pfeffer against the New York Giants, an occasion that served as a reunion for some of the principal figures of the Brotherhood and Players' League movements. Pfeffer, a Brotherhood man who spent the 1890 season with Chicago's Players' League team, was an outstanding second baseman who had briefly been Brouthers' teammate at Louisville in 1895 before moving on to New York. In April 1896, he was suspended indefinitely without pay by the Giants, "until such time as he was in fit condition to play ball."[67]

Pfeffer hired lawyer John Ward, former Giant, founder of the Brotherhood union and creator of the Players' League, to represent him in his suit against New York's owners. He claimed the suspension was not justified by his physical condition at the time and that his contract permitted the club to suspend him for a definite time only. Dan Brouthers and Ned Hanlon, who along with Ward, we recall, formed a Brotherhood Committee that challenged the National League owners during the Players' League war, both testified in Pfeffer's defense, and the jury "returned a verdict in Pfeffer's favor for the full amount of $737."[68] Although the financial return to Pfeffer was not substantial, the successful suit gave Brouthers and some of the other principal Brotherhood leaders the satisfaction of winning a small victory against an old enemy.

The formation of a new league in the mid–Hudson River Valley soon gave Dan Brouthers the opportunity to return to the diamond in the region where he learned the game as a boy. The architect of the new organization was William McCabe, Poughkeepsie Chief of Police and former second baseman for the town's team in the short-lived (one year, 1886) original Hudson River League. Working closely with J. H. Farrell, President of the New York State League and Secretary of the National Association, and Henry Ramsey, a former minor league player representing the baseball interests of Kingston, New York, McCabe formed the Hudson River Baseball League on April 1, 1903. Franchises were established in Kingston, Hudson, Saugerties, Newburgh, Ossining and Poughkeepsie, and play began in late May.

Formed as a class D organization and upgraded to class C in 1904, the Hudson River League played 90-to-110-game schedules for four years before disbanding early in its fifth season (1907). In its brief lifetime, ten New York towns, Paterson, New Jersey, and Pittsfield, Massachusetts, fielded teams at one time or another.

Noted baseball historian John Thorn, himself a resident of Saugerties, has identified several unique aspects of the Hudson River League:

> The HRL [Hudson River League] of 1903–07 is notable for several oddities and firsts. Its teams and fans traveled together to distant games by riverboat, boarding the celebrated *Mary Powell* for the trip south to New York City to play the Paterson (New Jersey) Intruders, who entered the league in 1904. The Kingston and Saugerties teams defeated two of the most famous barnstorming outfits of

Steamboat *Mary Powell*. Known as the "Queen of the Hudson," the *Mary Powell* was commissioned in 1861 and ferried passengers up and down the river for 55 years. Fans of the short-lived Hudson River League (1903–1907) would accompany their teams on the *Mary Powell* or other steamships to games at opponents' grounds along the Hudson, returning with the local nine after the contest (courtesy Wappingers Falls, New York Historical Society).

the day, the All-Cubans (the genuine article, not African-American imposters like the Cuban X-Giants) and the Sioux Indians (whose real pedigree as Sioux, or even Indians, was open to question). The contest between these Sioux Indians and the Kingston Colonials the previous year [1903] had been played at night, incredible as that may seem, under arc lights at the Driving Park. The major leagues' first night game did not take place until 1935.[69]

The humble Hudson River League also organized "the first midseason all-star game in professional baseball,"[70] played on August 17, 1903, between a squad of "All-Leaguers" and the Poughkeepsie Giants. Owing to a large number of rainouts, another unique baseball record was set that season, when the Hudson Marines played a quadruple-header against Poughkeepsie, winning all four games by scores of 2–1, 6–4, 3–1 and 4–2, in what was "the longest day any professional team has endured in the twentieth century"[71]

The new Hudson River League faced many obstacles. Eastern League and New York State League teams vied with it for fan loyalty and attendance. Despite the organization's membership in the National Association, team rosters were often raided and its reserve clause frequently ignored. Clubs often folded or transferred in mid-season due to financial problems. Inexperienced umpires frequently led to rowdy crowds or poor attendance. The league's salaries were low and its long schedule of games played in a compressed time frame precluded the possibility of players holding jobs elsewhere during the season. Rosters, therefore, were primarily determined by a player's youth and lack of family or financial responsibilities rather than his baseball talent. Dan Brouthers was the exception to this rule — an established veteran playing simply for the love of the game.

Despite the league's drawbacks, Dutchess County baseball historian Joseph Poilucci paints an idyllic picture of what a Poughkeepsie fan might have experienced on a Hudson River League game day in 1903:

> You would take a trolley to the new ballpark on Buckingham Avenue to see the Poughkeepsie Giants [also known as the Colts] play a visiting team from Newburgh, Kingston, Saugerties, Hudson, or Ossining. You would probably hear fat Bill McCabe, the team manager with the ever-present cigar in his mouth, call the boys of the local club some choice names. He would call a player anything, a minute or so later he would be patting him on the back.... Maybe you took one of the riverboats to see the home team play against the club of one of the other river teams. In the early days of the league you knew most of the players.... They were all river valley boys, the pick of amateurs of a year or two before.... In addition you had a chance to see one of baseball's great players in the twilight of his career — one of the Original Big Four of baseball, Big Dan Brouthers of Wappingers Falls. Big Dan's playing career was nearly over, but he was still a big good-looking guy and the fans thought the world of him.[72]

Brouthers' sense of nostalgia must have been considerable as he prepared to don the Poughkeepsie uniform. Nearly three decades after his big league career began, he found himself playing ball again in his backyard, traveling up and down the Hudson to compete in towns whose earlier teams he faced while pitching for the Wappingers Falls Actives.

Although press accounts of Hudson River League games are incomplete, the patchwork of available and accessible information on games and standings is sufficient to provide a clear picture of the highs and lows of Big Dan's years in the organization. Despite his obvious eagerness to get back into baseball in 1903, he played only 16 games for the Colts in their debut season. While this minimal record has been explained by the fact that he "reportedly found great difficulty in "getting in condition,"[73] initial conflicts with manager McCabe's harsh leadership style may also have been contributed to his absences from the team.

After debuting in a June 4 contest against Ossining in which he collected two hits, Brouthers played intermittently through June 25, then not at all until July 24, apparently his final 1903 appearance. At precisely the time in early July when he discontinued play, *Sporting Life* reported that several Poughkeepsie players "became mutinous during the past week and stayed away without leave."⁷⁴ A week later, the same journal indicated that "It is expected that Manager McCabe will resign ... if so, [Umpire] Tom Kennedy or Dan Brouthers will succeed him. Should one of these men assume the management, they will have $300 behind them to secure a nine to carry away the pennant."⁷⁵

The Kingston Colonials took the first Hudson River League pennant, while Poughkeepsie finished fifth. Despite troubles on the Colts, the players, including Brouthers, made peace with McCabe, who held on to his managerial position. Brouthers collected 18 hits in his 16 games, including four doubles, and hit .286.

Brouthers' most notable accomplishment on the field in 1903 was one that no one expected of him. In a June 10 game against Saugerties, the Colts were behind 1–0 in the bottom of the ninth inning. Two men [Hogan at second, Walsh at first] were on base when he strode to the plate.

> Brouthers then stepped to the plate with stick in hand and everybody was yelling themselves hoarse. They all wanted to see Brouthers hit the ball out [of] the lot. Brouthers has played ball before and knew what kind of an effort would do the best work at this stage of the game. When the ball was pitched up he gave it a little bunt and it rolled toward first base. The pitcher got the ball and got Brouthers out on the baseline. This was just what he wanted as his sacrifice hit had advanced Hogan and Walsh.... The fourth man up was Downing.... The second ball pitched to him he met squarely and sent it twisting across the diamond toward the second baseman. The crack of the bat brought forth cheers and everybody arose in their seats. The hit was such a hard one that Philips could not handle it and Hogan scored. This finished the game and the crowd left cheering in a happy mood.⁷⁶

Although Brouthers' conditioning challenges, limited on-field performance, and possible conflicts with his manager in 1903 did not bode well for the future, Old Wappinger surprised everyone the following year by returning to his old form on the diamond, enjoying his last full season of play and leading the Colts to the Hudson River League pennant.

Poughkeepsie opened the 1904 season against the Paterson, New Jersey, Intruders, the newest member of the league and the club that would battle them for the pennant until September. Now team Captain, Brouthers, who had celebrated his 46th birthday four days earlier, collected two hits and demonstrated that he was in good shape by stealing a base. The following day against Newburgh, he stroked three hits, including a double, and continued his running and stealing. "Dan Brouthers had two stolen bases to his credit, which demonstrated that 'the big fellow' is improving in old age."⁷⁷

A week later, again against Newburgh, the veteran won a game with a drive over the fence in the ninth inning, but ground rules, which dictated

Six. The Sage of Wappingers Falls: 1896–1906

that in such circumstances the game was over when the winning run crossed the plate, robbed him of a home run. "The feature of the game was Dan Brouthers' hit in the ninth inning, when, with one out and two men on bases. He hit the ball over the center field fence for what would have been a home run had the runs been needed."[78]

On June 1 at Saugerties, Big Dan outdid these early season efforts with a remarkable power-hitting performance. In an 18–8 drubbing of the home team, "Dan Brouthers gave an exhibition of batting seldom seen in one game. He was at the bat six times and made a total of twelve bases, two of his hits being home runs, with the bases filled both times. He also had four single base hits."[79] In 1981, historian John Thorn interviewed a Saugerties native, Merce Farrell, 83, who attended this historic game. Although just a child of six at the time, Farrell "declared that the old man's [Brouthers'] two home runs were the longest balls anyone in the town had ever seen or would ever see."[80]

Playing in his first full season since 1897 and in only his third in a decade, the Wappingers Falls veteran was again gaining national attention due to his hitting prowess. The *Boston Globe* reported that "'Old' Dan is hitting just as hard as ever," and that the "Famous batsman has not forgotten how to line 'em out."[81] The *Los Angeles Times* marveled that "Though forty-eight years old [actually he was 46], he is still swatting out home runs as of yore along the Hudson and is said to be playing as good ball as ever."[82]

On the strength of Brouthers' bat, Poughkeepsie slipped by the Paterson Intruders by one game to win the pennant. The seemingly ageless Brouthers led the league in hitting with a .373 effort, "a mark 135 points above the league average,"[83] slugged 11 home runs and collected 44 doubles, registering a .531 slugging average. A disappointed *Paterson Guardian* sportswriter, frustrated by his Hudson River League team's loss of the pennant to the Colts, commented humorously on the age of the league champions' best hitter: "He has been playing for a long, long time. Dan was Chief Engineer on Noah's Ark and played with General Grant in the Civil War League of 1861."[84]

Unfortunately, the national press's rediscovery of Big Dan was not always accompanied by positive comments. Some of them had the effect of reinforcing the old, false stereotypes for younger readers unfamiliar with Brouthers' earlier exploits. A generally favorable biographical sketch that appeared in the *Boston Globe*, for example, affirmed, as has been previously noted, that Brouthers' batting stance was "very awkward," that his first base play was "only fair," and that as a runner he was "of no use whatsoever."[85] Such inaccurate evaluations of Brouthers' skills continue to be repeated today in summaries of his career.

News of Big Dan's heroics on the Poughkeepsie nine in 1904 briefly had to take a back seat to another baseball story from Wappingers Falls. This mid-June narrative, however, was about a set of *baseball brothers*, and not about Dan *Brouthers*:

> Today, Wappingers Falls points proudly to a baseball team of nine who, younger than "the immortal Dan," all have the same name, which is Birkenmeyer. They are all brothers, each being a son of Mr. and Mrs. Alfred Birkenmeyer of High Street, and they all live with their parents. An additional wonder is that the nine brothers, constituting the regular team, have a tenth who is a substitute. Of course the parents of the young men are confident that their boys can defeat almost anything in the shape of a baseball club.[86]

In late September, another acknowledgment of Dan Brouthers' great season came in the form of an invitation from his former Orioles teammate, John McGraw. In the decade that had transpired since the two players had shared the Baltimore bench, McGraw had jumped from the National League Orioles to their American League counterpart, and then jumped back to the Senior Circuit as player-manager of the Giants in 1903. He would skipper the Giants for 29 years, leading them to nine pennants and three World Series victories, compiling a total of 2,763 wins, second all-time to Connie Mack.

McGraw had a Jekyll/Hyde personality. On the field, both as a player and a manager, he openly cultivated a reputation as a brutal, violent thug who would do anything to win a game. Off the field he was a mild-mannered, tea-totaling gentleman with a soft spot for any ball player who was down on his luck. "He was especially generous in the spring [spring training], as the Giants traveled across the southern states. It seemed that every down-and-out old ballplayer (or his wife or offspring) came to McGraw in cities like New Orleans, Memphis, Birmingham, Louisville and Washington. Sometimes McGraw asked perfunctory questions, sometimes nothing at all, before peeling off his roll of bills."[87] For those needy ballplayers living in or near Manhattan, as we shall see, McGraw could bestow special favors.

McGraw also had a deep appreciation of the national game's history. To that end, near the conclusion of the 1904 season and with the pennant all but assured for the Giants, he sent out invitations to two retired veterans to suit up and play one more big league game in front of the home crowd at the Polo Grounds. The first of these old-timers was Orator Jim O'Rourke, who had played on the last two Giants' pennant-winning teams in 1888 and 1889. The second veteran, although born in New York State, had never previously worn a Giants uniform. He was the man who in his era was known as the greatest batsman in the country — Dan Brouthers.

As a veteran of the Giants, O'Rourke's opportunity came first. On September 22, Orator Jim caught nine innings for New York and singled in four

Six. *The Sage of Wappingers Falls: 1896–1906*

appearances at the plate, and at age 54, "became the oldest player to hit safely in a National League game."[88]

Thirteen days later, on October 3, Dan Brouthers manned first base for the Giants in a 3–1 win against Saint Louis. He went hitless but fielded perfectly at first (six putouts and an assist), although he had little work to do there, given winning pitcher Christy Mathewson's 16-strikeout effort. Called on the next day to pinch-hit, Brouthers again failed to connect, but the thrill of being back in the big leagues after eight years and the acknowledgment of the fans helped diminish his disappointment. "The veteran Dan Brouthers, who led the Hudson River League in batting, played first base for the locals and was the recipient of many reminders of his popularity with New York base ball enthusiasts."[89]

After the season ended, McGraw organized an exhibition game between the 1889 champion Giants team and their 1904 counterparts, and Brouthers again donned a Giants uniform, substituting in left field for an absent member of the 1889 squad. Within two years, the Wappingers Falls slugger would become a Giants employee, working first as a scout for McGraw for seven years, and then as a ticket-taker and night watchman at the Polo Grounds for the last two decades of his life.

The 1905 Hudson River League campaign would start auspiciously for Dan Brouthers but end abruptly and embarrassingly for the veteran slugger. It was also an unsettling season for the league. The Peekskill team, absent from the league in 1904, attempted a comeback, but was forced to disband on June 1. Yonkers, a new franchise, folded after just 18 games. The Saugerties club was moved to Pittsfield on July 4, but lasted just three weeks there before giving up the ghost.

The remaining five teams played on, but three of them experienced mid-season changes of ownership. The dissolution of the Yonkers, Peekskill and Saugerties/Pittsfield clubs left over three dozen players scrambling to earn spots on the surviving teams' rosters, and their ensuing comings and goings left fans never knowing what the next game's lineup would be. On the field, constant roster changes made the concept of teamwork impossible.

In addition to such struggles, the league, and in particular the Poughkeepsie team, came under regional scrutiny for an ugly incident that highlighted the racial intolerance prevalent at the turn of the century. On May 12, *Sporting Life* reported that "Lewis Padron, an infielder on the All-Cuban team, is coming on to join the Poughkeepsie team.... Padron, the Cuban, seems to be a good find."[90]

Lewis Padron was the Anglicized name of Luis Padrón, a multi-talented, multi-position player born in Matanzas, Cuba, in 1878, whose accomplishments during his long career in the Cuban Winter League earned him a place in the Cuban Baseball Hall of Fame. In his off-season (summer and fall), he played minor league ball for years along the U.S. East Coast. For example, in 1908 as a starter for New Britain of the Connecticut State League, he went 18–10 on the mound and hit .314. Of Afro-Cuban descent and dark-skinned, Padrón had to contend regularly with hostile, racially insensitive fans when playing in the United States. Playing for the Poughkeepsie Colts in early July 1905, Padrón found a unique way to silence the racial epithets hurled at him while playing an away game at Newburgh.

> On the 6th, at Newburgh, Padron, of the Poughkeepsie team, gave an exhibition of hitting seldom seen in any game. He went to the plate and the Newburgh rooters began to hurl the epithet of "nigger" at him time and time again. Padron is very dark, being a full-blooded Cuban, but has no negro blood. This seemed to make him mad, and with two men on bases he hit the first ball pitched for a home run. Several innings later he again went to the bat with two men on bases. The crowd called, "The nigger can't do it again." At this, Padron hit the first ball pitched for another home run in almost the identical spot, scoring six runs [on the two home runs] and winning the game for Poughkeepsie.[91]

Despite such incidents and other difficulties, the league season was completed, Hudson won its first and last league pennant, and former champion Poughkeepsie slipped to third in the standings.

The unsettled nature of the league in 1905 was mirrored in Brouthers' personal ups and downs during what would be a prematurely short season for him. He started out the campaign magnificently: "Old Dan Brouthers opened the season with the Poughkeepsie team on May 11 by knocking out a home run when he stepped to the plate in the first inning. He made another hit during the game."[92] As the season progressed, however, unspecified injuries limited the amount and the quality of his play. "Dan Brouthers ... will be out of the game for some time. The infirmities of age are beginning to tell on the old boy."[93] His old sensitivity to criticism returned, but on one occasion his bat work managed to silence the "cranks." "Big Dan Brouthers ... was hissed for alleged errors in the Poughkeepsie field to-day in a game between Poughkeepsie and Paterson, of the Hudson River League. The old man replied to his critics by batting out a home run. After ambling in, he combed down [silenced] the grand stand eloquently."[94] Despite this small victory, the constant carping forced him to contemplate retirement.

Local sportswriters actually encouraged the fans to criticize him, contending that this compelled him to improve his performance:

> It seemed to have done some good to prod up Capt. Brouthers for he played the game of his life. He stopped hard drives sent to first, picked them out of the dirt

and brought in the only run scored in the game, Fogarty being on second base because of McArdle's error and coming home on Dan's drive to right field. Brouthers caught a hard drive with one hand and made a double [play] at second base. He was the hero of the day and we take our hats off to Dan.[95]

By the time Dan returned to regular action in August, however, Poughkeepsie had slipped to fourth place in the five-team league and the old veteran seemed to have lost all his skill at first base.

> It was heart rendering [sic] to witness the game from the grand stand. There were cries for Fogarty to go on first base because of the work of Brouthers. Winning such a game and then having a man throw it away was more than the people could stand and every person who came out vowed that if Brouthers continued to play first base they would withdraw their patronage.[96]
>
> Alfy Williams was kept busy bringing in runs to make up for those given away by Brouthers and although Alfy did his best, Brouthers gave away more than Alfy could bring in.[97]

The *Poughkeepsie Daily Eagle* attributed Dan's poor play and frequent absences from the field, and similar behavior by a few of his teammates, to drunkenness and dissipation.

> The players, or at least three or four of them, have not kept their ends up.... A ball player cannot stay up all night, drink and carouse around town, and then go on the diamond the next day to play baseball. This was clearly proven in Wednesday's game with Kingston, when one pitcher was knocked out of the box and the man who belongs on first base [Brouthers] was not in his place.... It is impossible for a drinking baseball player to go into a game and cope with the respectable, sober man who is a credit to the game.[98]

The *Eagle* soon urged Manager McCabe to take action. "It is time to call a halt and that is just what Manager McCabe ought to do. He has not yet taken a cent from his players because of fines but it is now time to start."[99] The Colts' manager's response to public pressure was soon forthcoming: "Late Wednesday night ... McCabe ... fined Third Baseman Giesier $25 and suspended him indefinitely; Pitcher Smith was fined $25 and suspended indefinitely and Catcher McCarthy and Capt. Dan Brouthers were each fined $25."[100]

Despite the embarrassment caused him by the public notification of the fine, it took Brouthers another five days to resign, and even then it was not the revelation of his alcohol problem that prompted his withdrawal, but rather, another poor fielding performance. "Capt. Dan Brouthers retired from baseball Monday night and it was evident from his work in Monday's game that his baseball career in any league is over. Brouthers simply handed the game to Paterson ... by a score of 6 to 5. Four of the runs came in on Brouthers's errors."[101]

The path from praise and support to disdain and ridicule had been steep and swift. After a glorious season the previous year that once again brought his name and deeds on the diamond to national attention, Big Dan was now forced to retire from the 1905 season in disgrace.

Less than two months into 1906, however, when ice and snow were still blanketing the mid–Hudson Valley, the *Albany Evening Journal* reported that Brouthers was returning to his former league as a team owner and manager. "Dan Brouthers has secured the Newburgh franchise of the Hudson River League."[102] Why would Brouthers, whose exit the previous season was a humiliating embarrassment, and whose reputation for being very careful with his money was well known, return to the scene of his greatest failure in baseball, invest in a financially troubled franchise, and assume a professional role—owner and manager—for which he had no previous experience?

The most logical answer is that it was an effort to recover his good name. Unfortunately for him, his desperate gamble to restore his professional and personal reputation was a failure.

The Newburgh franchise, according to *Sporting Life*, "seemed pursued with an evil genius."[103] It had finished last or next-to-last every year since joining the league, and attendance was hindered not just by the club's poor record, but by its field's poor location. "The grounds were located at a distance from the city and the [trolley] car service was very bad."[104] The franchise ownership had changed hands five times in the previous two years, and many players had either jumped their contracts and signed elsewhere or simply retired from the game.

Consequently, a month after taking the helm, Dan Brouthers was forced to resort to a desperate tactic to try to fill his roster. In a letter published in *Sporting Life* in mid–March, he made his appeal: "I have secured the franchise of the Newburgh Club of the Hudson River League, and I am in need of a second baseman, shortstop, third baseman and first baseman. Any player that can fill the above positions, correspond with Dan Brouthers, Wappinger's Falls, N.Y. Players must be good batters as well as good fielders."[105] During his brief stint as team owner, Brouthers himself had to come out of retirement and play first base in nine games.

Decades earlier, as we have seen, the fates had played a cruel joke on Brouthers when the *New York Clipper* published his portrait and biography simultaneously with word of his second release by the Troy Trojans. A similar ironic counterpoise befell the great slugger in 1906. In April, *Sporting Life* published a humorous article purporting to be a dream that Brouthers recently experienced about his new Hudson River League franchise. "With the softly falling snow that enveloped Wappinger's Falls last Monday night came gentle sleep to the eyes of Big Dan Brouthers.... In Dan's dream it was the Fourth of July ... and ... the Newburgh team had played thirty games and won them all by scores that made the pennant look like a cinch."[106] As the dream continued, Brouthers received congratulatory telegrams from some of his former teammates and rivals, like Cap Anson, John McGraw, and Cal Griffith, and "then came the shouts of the crowds as they stamped and screamed on the grandstand.... Dan was bowing to the swelling crowd.... When Mrs Brouthers gave him a shake, saying, 'Dan, get up and shovel the snow. Your house and lands are all covered like the middle of December'.... Dan awoke, and after a long stretch began to shovel the snow from the sidewalks in front of his property, which took him all day long."[107]

The real events of July 4 in Newburgh were a far cry from those in the July 4 of that dream. Instead of bowing to the cheers of the Newburgh fans, Brouthers, after losing two games to Paterson on July 4 and with his team in last place, "announced he was done.... He threw up [quit] the job after vowing he had lost $500 in the venture and saying he would lose no more."[108]

Thanks to Brouthers' failures on the field and as a team owner in 1905–1906, and to the new public awareness of his bouts with alcohol, these years represent the low point in his long career. Despite such trials, however, the old veteran responded with the characteristic resilience with which he had met every other challenge over the years.

In October, a *Washington Post* article reported that Old Wappinger had moved with his family to New York City to begin a new baseball-related career. It would soon be revealed that John McGraw had hired him as a scout for the New York Giants. The 48-year-old Brouthers also served notice that he would still find some time to put in some work on the diamond. "Quit playing baseball?... Well, I guess not. I'll be playing until they cut the uniform off me, and you know, I can go some yet."[109]

Seven

The Once Famous Ball Player: 1907–1932

> Old Dan Brouthers ... stands guard at the press gate in the grandstand of the Polo Grounds, unheralded and unsung — and unrecognized by most of the fans who sit all around him. — *The Auburn Citizen*, July 29, 1911

Dan Brouthers' professional baseball career from the late 1870s to the early 1900s corresponds to a period of unprecedented growth and transformation in American society. When he first walked onto the diamond for the Wappingers Falls Actives, the telephone, the phonograph, the incandescent light bulb, motion pictures, the automobile and the airplane did not exist. When he resigned as owner of the Newburgh franchise of the Hudson River League in 1906, all of these inventions were in common use or well on their way to being so.

The technological advances of the era were accompanied by a demographic transformation of equal significance. Of 31 million Americans in 1860, one in five was a city dweller. By 1900, the country's population had more than doubled to 76 million, and nearly half (46 percent) called a city home.

No place in the nation exemplified such fundamental societal changes more than New York City — the poster child of the new urban, industrial age. Between 1870 and 1915, its population tripled, increasing from one and a half to nearly five million. In the decade that preceded the Brouthers family's move there, the city experienced rapid changes, thanks to non-stop construction and advances in public transportation. In 1898, Brooklyn and other surrounding areas were consolidated into the now familiar five boroughs of Manhattan, the Bronx, Queens, Brooklyn and Staten Island. Subway service began in

Seven. *The Once Famous Ball Player: 1907–1932*

October 1904, when the Interborough Rapid Transit Company's first line transported passengers from City Hall in lower Manhattan to Broadway and 145th Street in an unheard-of time of twenty-six minutes.[1] One week after its debut, ridership averaged 350,000 a day. Construction of other lines soon followed, including a 1908 route dug under the East River that linked Brooklyn with Manhattan.

Advancements in the arts and architecture kept pace with the city's growth. *The Adventures of Dollie*, the first motion picture directed by D.W. Griffith, premiered in New York in 1908. By 1910, New Orleans jazz musicians giving performances in town began referring to it as "The Big Apple," since their appearances elsewhere paid "little apples." The New York Public Library opened its doors in 1911, and two years later the new Grand Central Station—replacing the original built in 1871—opened at 42nd Street and Park Avenue. In February 1913, the New York Armory art exhibit introduced a scandalized American public to the Modernist works of Picasso, Matisse and Duchamp.

While New York City in the early 1900s served both as a model of technological advancement and a center for the arts, it also became associated with terrible accidents and horrific workplace-related tragedies that were an ugly byproduct of industrialization. On June 15, 1904, the steamship General Slocum caught fire and burned in the East River. On board were a church group of more than 1,400 from the Little Germany section of Manhattan, bound for their annual picnic grounds at Eaton's Neck, Long Island. Fire broke out onboard soon after the trip started, and terrified passengers discovered that the ship's emergency equipment was either missing or in disrepair. More than 1,000 would-be picnickers, mostly women and children, either drowned or were burned to death in the fire.

On March, 25 1911, fire broke out on the eighth floor of the Asch Building on Washington Square in Manhattan, site of the Triangle Shirt Factory. Because the managers had locked the doors to the stairwells, 146 garment workers, nearly all of whom were Jewish and Italian immigrant women, died either from the fire, smoke inhalation, or from jumping to their deaths. Until the destruction of the World Trade Center by Muslim extremists on September 11, 2001, the General Slocum Disaster and the Triangle Shirtwaist Factory fire were the two deadliest incidents in New York City history.

"Old" New York—prior to its consolidation of Brooklyn—hosted two major league baseball teams in the nineteenth century—the National League Giants, who started out in 1883 and were first nicknamed the New Yorks or the Gothams, and the Metropolitans, who were members of the American Association from 1883 until 1887.

At the end of the 1902 season, the American League Baltimore Orioles were sold and the franchise moved to New York, where they became the Highlanders. Eleven years later, the club adopted a new nickname—the Yankees. In June 1903, a boy of German immigrant stock was born in New York who would become famous playing for the Yankees. He was christened Henry Louis Gehrig.

In 1907, Dan Brouthers was hired by John McGraw as "chief scout"[2] for the Giants, and within a year he moved his family—except eldest daughter Anna Lillian, who had married in 1906—to New York City. The Brouthers settled on the 100 block of West 96th Street in Manhattan, an area known as the Upper West Side, where they would reside for nearly two decades. A narrow band of land bounded by the Hudson River on the west and Central Park on the east, the Upper West Side had experienced a building boom in the late nineteenth century, thanks to the relocation of Columbia University to a site just north of the area in 1890 and the opening of a subway station at 96th Street. Today this neighborhood is home to high-rise apartment buildings, but in Brouthers' era, four- and five-story brownstone row houses were the norm.

When the Brouthers family arrived in New York, the Upper West Side was one of the most attractive areas of the city. Construction of Riverside Park, located on the Hudson River from 72nd to 125th Streets, just a few blocks west of the family's new home, was nearing completion. Several blocks to the east lay the 843-acre green expanse of Central Park, designed by Frederick Law Olmsted and completed in 1873. Two blocks from the family's new home was the Gothic-style Church of the Holy Name of Jesus, built in 1890, which replaced St. Mary's Church in Wappingers Falls as their place of worship. Shortly after their move, the Brouthers were joined on the Upper West Side by eldest daughter Anna Lillian and her husband, John Fitzgerald, who moved to nearby Amsterdam Avenue in 1910. By 1915, the young couple had relocated to West 96th Street themselves, just a block from Dan and Mary Ellen's home.

Despite the attractive nature of the family's new surroundings, questions about the motivation for the move offer no easy answers. Relocating to New York would certainly be more convenient for Brouthers in his new role, but he would still be spending long periods away from his family while on the road, leaving them now to fend for themselves far from the familiarity and security of their Wappingers Falls home. Dealing with issues related to any properties or businesses that he might still have owned in Dutchess County from a distance of 80 miles away in New York City would also have been problematic.

The move would not have been an easy one for Mary Ellen or the three

SEVEN. *The Once Famous Ball Player: 1907–1932* 155

younger children, who in all likelihood had no prior experience in any city larger than Poughkeepsie, and who now would be far from relatives and friends. Despite his great love of the game, if Brouthers were well-off financially, it might not have been worth the effort for him, at age 49, to disrupt the lives of his entire family by moving them to New York just to work for the Giants as a scout.

Viewed in this context, the move was likely in response to a need to leave behind some unfortunate events or circumstances (public awareness of his drinking problem, forced retirement from the diamond due to poor play, financial failure as a club owner) and start anew. Additionally, as we shall see, his need to continue to work to support his family until he was in his seventies suggests that despite his thrift and the wealth he apparently had accumulated during his playing years, he found himself in financial difficulties as he neared his 50th birthday. As a former-teammate-turned-sportswriter delicately put it in 1911, "Dan once owned much real estate up in Wappinger Falls, and was credited as being a wealthy man, but real estate didn't prove as good a speculation as Dan anticipated."[3]

In the early days of professional baseball, player recruitment tended to be informal and haphazard, with teams relying on recommendations from current or former players, or close confidants of the manager. An example of this type of recruiting can be observed by reviewing the manner in which Dan Brouthers' contemporary, Buck Ewing, Giants catcher and future Hall of Famer, became a professional player.

Before joining the Reds, first baseman Long John Reilly, a Cincinnati native, had been Buck Ewing's teammate on the Queen City's semi-pro Mohawk Browns. After a Reds' game in Rochester, Reilly and another Red, second baseman Joe Gerhardt, met with the manager of their local opponent's club — none other than Horace Phillips — in a Rochester hotel. Phillips was in need of a catcher, and it was for the purpose of getting one that he called at the hotel to ask Reilly and Gerhardt where he could find one. "After a moment's thought, Gerhardt looked up and said, 'Why, wouldn't that young fellow Ewing do?' 'Just the man I was thinking about,' replied Reilly. The result was that Buck was telegraphed that night and caught the season out [with Rochester]."[4]

Around the time of Dan Brouthers' hire by John McGraw, *Sporting Life* noted that both in personnel and in the recruitment process itself, a change had occurred in baseball. "The employment of scouts for [discovering] playing talent by major league clubs is becoming general.... Many veteran players are now doing valuable summer work."[5]

Recruitment was now viewed as an investigative process in which former players acted as "secret agents"[6] and "sleuths,"[7] doing "detective work"[8] to discover new talent for their clubs. Some franchises made their scouts' names public. "Dan Brouthers is wearing rubber shoes in behalf of the Giants, and Brooklyn's scout is Tom Daly."[9] Other teams preferred to work surreptitiously. "The Cubs have men on the road whose identity is kept secret.... Connie Mack, [manager] of the Athletics, has half a dozen secret agents at work, and is believed to have strings tied to more than a hundred minor league players."[10]

After World War I, the scouts' ranks included far fewer former players, and emphasis shifted from looking for polished performers who could quickly ascend to the major leagues to an approach favored by men like Branch Rickey, who preferred to recruit raw talent that could later be honed on the franchise's farm teams.[11]

A few years after Brouthers was hired by John McGraw, the role of a baseball scout was still unclear to the public, and the press requested that the retired slugger offer an explanation of his role. His response was simple and straightforward:

> I've been asked to explain the duty of a baseball scout. The baseball scout is a man who during the playing season is constantly on the lookout for promising material for that club that employs him.... One day he may be watching a minor league player and the next be looking over some semi-professional who has never played with a league.... For many years I have been connected with the New York National [League] Club in that capacity, and in my time have recommended many youngsters who have turned out to be stars.[12]

Brouthers spent the 1907 season scouring the country for young talent, and by August was recommending players to McGraw or offering contracts to them on sight. Noting his travels and discoveries, the *Washington Post* suggested that unlike most scouts of the day, who worked on commission, Brouthers was a salaried Giants employee. In mid–August, he was reported to be "in Reading [Pennsylvania] on a scouting expedition for Manager McGraw.... He is especially interested in the work of the players of the Tri-State League teams. Brouthers gets a big salary from New York for going through the minor leagues after men."[13]

The pace and frequency of Brouthers' recruiting soon became unrelenting:

> "Harry Curtis, the Giants new catcher, was picked up by Dan Brouthers, who is scouting the country for talent"[14];
>
> "Dan Brouthers, the Giants' scout, has his eye on pitcher Frank Reed of the Albany Club"[15];
>
> "Dan Brouthers picked up 13 minor leaguers for a lump sum of $15,000 while attending the auction sales of ball players"[16];

SEVEN. *The Once Famous Ball Player: 1907–1932* 157

"McGraw sent 'Dan' Brouthers, the veteran ball player to watch [prospect Larry] Doyle at work. Brouthers was so impressed with the youngster's playing that he recommended purchasing his release. The Springfield [franchise] set the purchase price at $4,500 and the New York Club paid the money"[17];

"Scout Dan Brouthers has unearthed Merkle in ... Michigan, and he is said to be a Hal Chase 'in the rough' by the club's big scout."[18]

The latter two minor league prospects, Larry Doyle and Fred Merkle, would enjoy long, successful careers with the Giants and play a significant role in the team's consecutive pennants from 1911 to 1913. Doyle, a scrappy second baseman, spent 14 years in the major leagues, ten of them with the Giants. He twice led the league in hits while with New York (172 in 1909; 189 in 1915), and also topped the Senior Circuit in doubles (40 in 1915), triples (25 in 1911), and batting average (.320 in 1915). His respective .310 and .330 marks in 1911 and 1912 helped the Giants to win two pennants.

Merkle, a 6'1", 190-pound first baseman who hit and threw right-handed, spent ten seasons with the Giants and the remainder of his career with Brooklyn and Chicago. A lifetime .270 hitter, he hit .309 during New York's successful 1912 pennant run.

Merkle's steady, if unspectacular, career and reputation were forever tarnished by a mental error he made in a game late in the 1908 campaign, his second year in the major leagues. He had spent most of the season on the bench as a backup for the Giants regular first baseman, Fred Tenney. On September 23, with the Giants tied with the Cubs for first place, Merkle replaced Tenney, whose back was strained, in the lineup at the Polo Grounds. With two out in the ninth inning and Harry McCormick on first base, Merkle singled sharply down the right field line and McCormick advanced to third base. The next hitter, shortstop Al Bridwell, hit the first pitch from Cubs starter Jack Pfiester to center field for a single, and McCormick crossed the plate with what appeared to be the winning run. Seeing McCormick score the run and assuming the game was over, Merkle ran to the center field clubhouse without touching second base, apparently unaware of, or having forgotten, the rule in force that stated that a run is not scored if the runner crosses the plate during a play in which the third out is made.

As thousands of Giants fans rushed onto the field to celebrate an apparent victory, the Cubs' alert second baseman Johnny Evers, of "Tinker-to-Evers-to-Chance" fame, shouted to center fielder Solly Hofman to retrieve the ball, which he did. Hofman threw it to Evers, who touched second base for the third out. With Merkle forced at second, by the rules, McCormick's run did not count and the game remained tied. Owing to the controversy, the fans refused to leave the field and the game was called on account of darkness.

As a result of the tie, the Cubs and Giants finished the regular season with identical 98–55 records, and the teams were required to replay the tie game. On October 8, the Cubs defeated the Giants, 4–2, in the makeup game and were crowned National League champions. For the rest of his life, Fred Merkle was saddled with the nickname "Bonehead" after the press christened his momentary mental lapse in the crucial game.[19]

With Brouthers back in the national limelight, it was perhaps inevitable that some of the old "Jumbo" stereotypes used to characterize him in the past would resurface, although now in a slightly less direct manner. "A local wag tells a story at the expense of big Dan Brouthers, the Giants' chief scout. Someone loaned Dan a jockey badge for the races, and as he was about to pass into the enclosure, the gate-keeper asked him if he was a jockey. 'Sure,' remarked Dan without a smile. 'Well,' replied the gate-man, 'you are in the wrong place. We don't race elephants here.'"[20]

In light of Brouthers' feverish recruitment activity over the year and the financial largesse granted to him by the Giants in his endeavors, the press concluded that manager McGraw, with Brouthers' help, had abandoned the club's previous policy of dealing "only in developed players,"[21] in favor of a different approach:

> The activity of Scout Dan Brouthers indicates that a new policy is to prevail in the club. The development of raw material has now become an important part of the work of every ball club in the major leagues. The picking of men from the minors is very much of a lottery as sometimes a minor league star does not shine when transplanted to ... [major] league circles. On the other hand, men of lesser import in the smaller leagues sometimes flourish among the big fellows. Of course, it often depends on how they are handled."[22]

The most remarkable aspect of Big Dan's first year as chief scout for the Giants was the unshakable confidence that savvy McGraw had placed in him in his new role as scout. It was one thing to invite a retired major leaguer to put on the uniform one more time and play in an official game, as McGraw had done for him in September 1904. It was quite another to entrust him with complete responsibility for recruiting new players for the Giants and to provide him with all the financial resources to close deals with recruits and their teams.

At season's end, Brouthers joined other members of the champion 1894 Orioles at homecoming reunion ceremonies in Baltimore. The event consisted of a banquet and three exhibition games between the old-timers and an Eastern League Baltimore club. A feature of the banquet "was the presentation to veteran Dan Brouthers of the ball with which he made the longest hit ever made at old Union Park."[23] The blast referred to here was his previously mentioned home run that was hit both over the Baltimore fence and beyond an adjacent street during the 1894 campaign.

After sitting out the first exhibition game during the ceremonies, Brouthers returned to his familiar first base position in the second contest, singling once in four appearances, but also committing a costly error, thanks to being out of shape. "But for errors by big Dan Brouthers and [third baseman] Bill Clarke, both of whom had too much girth to move around, the youngsters [the opposing team] would have been shut out, 1 to 0."[24]

Early the following year, during an impromptu get-together of retired players at John McGraw's pool and billiard parlor, scout Brouthers made a series of comments on hitting in which he compared modern hitters favorably to their early-era counterparts.

> The man who can hit as good as .285 today would have hit far above the .300 mark in the old days.... Say what you please ... but the ballplayers of today are better than they were. More than that, they are better hitters.... It is true that the players of today do not finish the season with as good hitting averages as they did years ago, but that does not necessarily mean that they are not as good if not better batters. The players are up against a harder proposition now. The batters of today must contend with more scientific pitching as well as scientific fielding. The thickly padded [fielding] glove has hurt the batter immensely. In the olden days a fielder would not think of getting one of those bullet-like drives past third with his bare hand. Even if he went after it the chances were that it would bounce away and he could not recover in time to throw the man out, or he would come up with a broken finger. Now the batter has everything against him, and that makes the game more even. The pitcher hasn't got as much advantage as the general public would suppose. Of course he knows the good batters and works to deceive them, but at the same time the batters know the shortcomings of all the pitchers in the business equally well, and he waits until he gets what he wants. In nine cases out of ten, a battle of wits like this results in a draw. The fielder makes up the rest of the combination against the batter.[25]

These opinions "aroused the ire"[26] of the old-timers in his audience, "for it is mighty seldom that an oldtimer [sic] can be induced to agree that the players of this generation are better than those of 30 years ago."[27]

Just two years later, however, in conversation with fellow old-timer and Brotherhood rebel, Roger Connor, the Giants' fabled first baseman and home run king of baseball before the Ruth era, Brouthers reversed his position on the subject of old era players versus new era stars:

> "I can't see how the game has improved much, Dan!" said Connor. "In fact, I don't believe there's anybody excepting Lajoie, Cobb, Wagner and others, who can hit the ball any harder than we did!" "That's been my argument all along," replied Brouthers. "And furthermore the pitchers and fielders aren't a bit better. You don't see any greater stars than Ewing, Keefe, Clarkson, Ward, Anson,

Hardie [sic] Richardson, Radbourn, Kelly and Williamson, do you?" "You can bet your life on that," said Connor, with a grim smile.[28]

While such flip-flops on the subject of the merits of old-timers versus those of the modern players were dutifully recorded by the press, there were no accompanying reports of more Brouthers successes in the recruiting arena in 1908, and in August, *Sporting Life* broke the news that "Dan Brouthers, who rounded up the youngsters for [Giants owner] President Brush ... is out of a job as a discoverer of talent."[29] Once again, Old Wappinger had been embarrassed in the national press. Four months earlier, as we have seen, he had been selected to explain in an article the duties of a baseball scout to the fans. Now the recruiting "expert" had been relieved of his duties.

While no details of Brouthers' release were forthcoming, years later, comments that John McGraw made about Brouthers' replacement, scout Dick Kinsella, a former minor leaguer who would remain with the Giants for more than two decades, and whose finds included pitcher Carl Hubbell, hint at what might have been Brouthers weak point — recruiting too many players who failed to make good in proportion to those who were successful. "It isn't the fellows he [Kinsella] sends to me that makes him great.... It's the ones he keeps me from buying. He saves my ball club a lot of money every year by keeping me off the dead ones."[30]

Despite his being relieved of his full-time position, the press continued to publish sporadic reports of Brouthers' activity as a freelance scout, including work for the Giants and for minor league teams. Early in 1911, *Sporting Life* reported that "The Richmond Club [of the Virginia League], on the recommendation of Dan Brouthers, has signed 'Wee Willie' Martin as second baseman. Martin last year played semi-pro ball with ... the All-Collegiates of New York."[31] Four years after being dropped as a salaried Giants recruiter, it was noted that "Dan Brouthers is floating about New York occasionally doing some scouting for John McGraw."[32]

Although Brouthers once again found himself without a full-time job, early the following year, 1909, reports surfaced that he had organized a semi-pro team and that at age 51 he would again don the uniform, this time accompanied by his youngest son, Addison.

> Dan Brouthers, one of the great base ball players in his day — and it was a long day, too — has gone into training again. He is going to play baseball with an independent team next summer.... When Brouthers was in his prime he weighed close to 200 pounds.... He accumulated much weight after he retired from the diamond, but he is an active man still. Every day he circles the reservation, in Central Park, in New York City, several times, and is losing superfluous flesh.... Big Dan has two sons, one of whom is quite a ball player. The young man's

SEVEN. *The Once Famous Ball Player: 1907–1932*   161

name is Addison Gumbert Brouthers, and was named after "Ad" Gumbert, the old National League pitcher, now sheriff of the county in which Pittsburg is situated. Brouthers and Gumbert were members of the Pittsburg team [actually, the 1890 Players' League Boston Reds team] when "Ad" Brouthers was born.... The boy is now appearing with Christy Mathewson's indoor team.[33]

Indoor baseball, the progenitor of softball, was invented in Chicago in 1887 by members of the Illinois Farragut Boat Club. It featured a large, soft, 12-inch ball that was tossed underhanded, a slender bat and shortened base paths. Players wore rubber-soled shoes and heavily padded uniform pants for sliding on hard surfaces. In its early years the game had many names, including "mush ball," "pumpkin ball," and "kitten baseball," until the term "softball" was coined for the sport by Walter Hakanson of the YMCA.[34]

In organizing his own semi-pro team and christening it "Dan Brouthers' Colts," Brouthers was following the lead of Cap Anson, the retired Chicago White Stockings star. Standing six feet tall and weighing 220 pounds, Anson logged 27 seasons of major league play, including 22 with the National League White Stockings, collected 3,435 hits and compiled a lifetime .334 batting average. After leaving the professional circuit with no business skills other than those he learned on the diamond, Anson organized a semi-pro team, Anson's Colts, and with the remaining savings from his years as a star built a ballpark for the team on Chicago's South Side. It proved to be a money-losing venture, and he sold his team at the close of the 1909 season.

The similarity between Brouthers' new team and Anson's prompted the press to compare the two veteran contemporaries and to ask Brouthers about their first meeting.

> Brouthers and Anson were the ideals of the fans of 20 years ago. Both were big men and terrific hitters. Each was a first baseman.... The rivalry between Anson and Brouthers was great for several years. "I'll never forget the first time I ever saw Anson," said Dan. "Someone had told him there was a big bruiser ... just as big as he was and who could maul the ball just as hard. Anson bet that I wasn't as big as he, and when we were brought together we eyed each other for a minute, and then Anson admitted that I had him tied, anyhow. That was my first year in the league."[35]

Thirteen years after their retirement from major league baseball, Brouthers and Anson were reunited on an early February afternoon in 1909, at John McGraw's pool and billiard parlor in New York.

> Up at McGraw's yesterday there was a scene worthy of the pen of a descriptive expert and the brush of a painter. Dan Brouthers and Cap Anson, diamond warriors of two decades ago, stood together and talked of the old days. These two grim old gladiators towered above the fans who gathered around them. They were heroes of the days when big men were more powerful in baseball than now.

Both are now past the half century milestone, but those years of active life on the diamond have preserved them.... He is a gray haired fan now who can speak intelligently of the prodigious batting feats performed by Anson and Brouthers in the eighties.[36]

Anson had traveled east from Chicago in an effort to seek some protection from major and minor league clubs who were raiding his semi-pro team roster, taking away players he had developed without paying for their release. The former Chicago manager had arranged to meet with National League President Harry Pulliam to plead his case. He would not be successful, and would have to sell his team and exit baseball for good at the end of the 1909 season.

During Anson's chance meeting with Dan Brouthers in New York, however, the pair was joined by John McGraw for what was described as an "old fashioned fanning bee" [gab session], with the topic once again focused on comparing the old-time players with the moderns. "'I don't see anybody these days who has it on us,' declared Anson to Brouthers. 'They're good boys but they don't hit any better.' 'Nobody ever had it on your two fellows for weight,' kidded McGraw. 'No, nor with the bat,' retorted Anson. 'Eh, Dan?' 'Right you are,' asserted Big Dan."[37] For more than an hour, Anson and Brouthers reminisced and told each other that they were just as fit now as ten years earlier. "'I've been training every day this winter,' said Dan, 'and intend to play ball next summer.' Anson told about playing a benefit game in Chicago last summer. He came to bat and found that his eye was still good as he lined out a base hit."[38]

As an independent city in the 1850s and 1860s, Brooklyn was a hotbed of baseball activity. A half-century later, now incorporated into New York City, Brooklyn was home to dozens of semi-professional teams. "Brooklyn had many enclosed venues through the first half of the 20th century which hosted semi-pro and high level amateur ball. In a time before television dominated leisure hours, a walk or short trolley to a local ball game was a common weekend activity. These clubs played in front of crowds from a few hundred to a few thousand, and flourished at standards from near major league to neighborhood recreational."[39] The names of some of the long-forgotten clubs who played on early Brooklyn semi-pro fields form a litany that confirms the enduring popularity of the sport in the era: the Edison Club, the Dexters, the Marquette nine, the Bath Beach Field Club, the Empire City team and the Sterlings.

A surviving piece of Dan Brouthers' stationery from the early 1900s is preserved in the great slugger's Hall of Fame library file in Cooperstown. It contains a letterhead, reproduced here, that summarizes the old veteran's activities in his new position:

SEVEN. *The Once Famous Ball Player: 1907–1932*

Under Personal Management
Dan Brouthers' Colts
Home Grounds
Saratoga Park
Broadway and Halsey Street Brooklyn, N.Y.

The upper-left corner contains a photo of the veteran, under which appears his name, followed by the phrase, "Free Lance Scout for Major and Minor Leagues."[40]

Saratoga Park, a large lot bordered by Halsey and Macon Streets, Broadway and Saratoga Avenue, was run by an amusement company and used as Barnum and Bailey's Circus venue in Brooklyn from 1891 to 1905. In 1906, the park was enclosed and fitted with extensive stands behind the plate, down the foul lines, and in deep center field. The park was closed in 1912 and converted to housing lots. A small modern Saratoga Park, one block to the west, replaced the original park.

While extant records from Dan Brouthers' Colts' three seasons at Saratoga Park are fragmentary, they are sufficient to confirm that Dan and Addison did appear together in the team's lineup frequently, and that thanks to Dan's participation in games during the teams last season, 1911, he became one of few individuals who have played organized baseball in five decades.

On Sunday, March 28, 1909, the Colts made their semi-pro debut at Meyer-Rose Park in Brooklyn against the home-team Ridgewoods. Dan played first base and Addison played right field. Both Brouthers went hitless in a 12–4 loss. "Big Dan looked natural in a baseball uniform, and cavorted around the initial sack with something of his old-time vigor. His son played in [the] right garden [field] but had no chance to distinguish himself."[41]

The majority of news reports of the team are from 1911, owing at least partly to the notoriety of their new pitcher, Hank Mathewson. Younger brother of legendary Giants hurler Christy Mathewson, Hank was a tall (6' 3"), slender (175 pounds) right-hander who had brief, unsuccessful trials with the Giants in 1906 and 1907, pitching a total of 11 innings, surrendering eight hits and seven runs, and walking 14. Both Mathewson brothers died young after being stricken with tuberculosis—Christy at age 45 in 1925, and Hank at age 31 in 1924.

Although a failure as a major leaguer, Hank Mathewson's pitching skills proved excellent for semi-pro play:

"Hank Mathewson twirled a star game"[42];

"With Hank Mathewson in the box, Dan Brouthers' Colts had an easy time yesterday at Saratoga Park defeating the Pottstown team of Pennsylvania."[43];

"Hank Mathewson pitched a good game for the Colts, and would have held the home team [the Dexters] to fewer runs but for some loose playing in the infield."[44]

Playing regularly, Big Dan was ragged at first base, committing three errors, for example, against the Havana Red Sox in a mid–May contest. Although his long-ball hitting was now a thing of the past, he remained a regular contributor at the plate, banging out singles and occasional doubles, and on May 22, 1911, stealing a base against a Pottstown, Pennsylvania, team two weeks after celebrating his 53rd birthday.

Despite the Colts' winning ways, Brouthers' second venture into team ownership was no more successful financially than his first, and by the end of the 1911 season he found himself once again unemployed. Since losing his salaried scouting job for the Giants in 1908, he had no steady income, and his 1910 U.S. Census data indicates that he had been out of work for 20 weeks that year.[45] Sons Leo and Addison were both employed full-time by railroad companies as stenographers and were still living at home, but their incomes and Dan's sporadic scouting stipends were insufficient to maintain the family.

Humiliated and probably a bit desperate, Dan turned to John McGraw for help late in the 1911 season, and was not disappointed. The Giants manager offered him a position as night watchman at the Polo Grounds, and he gratefully accepted. Embarrassed by his lowly new position, he kept mum about it until it was discovered by the press.

> The mysterious disappearance of Big Dan Brouthers, once the champion batsman of the National League and first baseman of the old Detroits, Baltimores and Bostons, has been accounted for. Brouthers has been night watchman at the Polo Grounds since last summer, his sole companion being a dog. "I've been sleeping in the daytime for nearly a year," said Big Dan, "and my evening clothes, hanging in the locker, have grown rusty. But I'm getting a good salary and don't care about the sunshine. There's no chance for a beggar to cop the new grandstand while I'm around. You can bet on that."[46]

It was a steep, sad fall from the glory days as "the champion batsman of the country," but Big Dan accepted his lot with stoicism and characteristic grace. He was grateful for the opportunity, and would continue to work at the Polo Grounds in some capacity until the day before his death in 1932.

Brouthers enjoyed high visibility with the press in New York during his years as a Giants scout, semi-pro owner/manager and night watchman, ticket taker and press box attendant at the Polo Grounds. Consequently, in his later years he was frequently sought out as an elder statesman by local and out-of-town sportswriters who were developing articles about baseball's early era, or who simply had a column to write and needed a topic. Brouthers seemed pleased with the attention and willingly complied. Most of his extended

SEVEN. *The Once Famous Ball Player: 1907–1932* 165

comments on the game, therefore, date from this period in his life, and they offer interesting perspectives on less well-known aspects of early baseball and provide insight on Brouthers himself, who famously avoided the press during most of his career.

The first of these articles appeared in the *Washington Post* in late October 1910, and took the form of an interview with an anonymous sportswriter seeking Brouthers' opinion about the origin of alleged modern plays.

"How many plays have been discovered in baseball in the last twenty years?" asked the inquisitive man of Dan Brouthers.

"I don't know of any real new ones," replied the veteran. "They don't do much that they didn't do when I played ball. There is little difference. Some moves are made with more frequency, and teamwork is more common among clubs."

"How about the bunt?"

"Nothing to that! There is a man coaching for the New York baseball club who, twenty years ago, could bunt more skillfully than most players on the field today, and as skillfully as the experts, for all that I can see."

"You mean [Arlie] Latham, we may take it?"

"I certainly do. This squeeze play which they talk so much about I saw happen on the ball field, although the batter used to chop at the ball, rather than bunt it."

"How about the delayed steal?"

"Nothing to it. Old players used to do it, and they used to say they were blamed idiots for taking such chances on the bases. They weren't so critical then about picking plays and putting fancy names on them. If anything happened out of the ordinary — that is, the ordinary run of luck — they'd say after the game was over, 'That was a streak of luck, and the club was fortunate to get away with a victory.' That's what we used to get. None of your delayed steals and sacrifice killers and such things."

"But there wasn't any sacrifice [The sacrifice was not recognized as an official statistic until 1886]."

"No, there wasn't. That is, exactly in the manner that it is made today, although when managers saw the trend of the times, that baseball was getting more and more to be a game in which one run would be a great factor in winning, they trained their clubs to go after the sacrifice as much as any other play. Yet I have known times when we used to play out in the lake cities when we sacrificed. Did it deliberately, too. No picayune luck about it. Simply jumped in and took a chance on getting out [making an out] to get another fellow around. That's years ago, and that's why I tell you there are no new plays. They're all old — every one of them — and it's only the frequency of some of these so-called plays, against their scarcity in years gone by, which induces imaginative folks to think they see something we didn't know."[47]

Brouthers' folksy, informative approach to answering the interviewer's questions harkened back to the days when he was known as "Old Jed," and must have proven popular with the *Washington Post*'s readers and its editors, for two months later, prompted by the recent untimely death of former pitcher

Will White, the only nineteenth-century player who wore eyeglasses on the diamond, the *Post* asked Brouthers to comment on the trend toward greater use of spectacles by modern players.

Will White, brother of Deacon White, Brouthers' teammate and fellow Big Four member with the Detroit Wolverines, spent most of his ten-year big league career, which was shortened by arm problems, with Cincinnati's National League or American Association teams. He won 40 games or more four times, and won 30 or more twice. In August 1911, retired and on vacation, he suffered a heart attack and drowned while teaching his niece to swim.

Although discussion of whether ballplayers who need them should wear glasses — or contacts — for that matter, would be regarded as silly today, eyeglass use was often ridiculed in Dan Brouthers' era and was still considered controversial in the early 1900s. As late as 1912, for example, sportswriter Sam Crane viewed them as a "handicap" rather than an aid.[48] However, players who had gone without them due to either pride or embarrassment, later lamented not using them. In 1903, Brouthers' contemporary, ex–Giant Roger Connor, donned "goggles" for the first time in a minor league game, banged out a triple and two singles, and then lamented that "he had made the mistake of his life in not putting on glasses years ago. Had he done so, he would have never left the big leagues, he said."[49]

In his long discourse on the subject in the *Washington Post*, Brouthers managed to use nearly every nickname for eyeglasses, made indirect reference to his scouting days, demonstrated excellent powers of recollection and came out in favor of players using glasses:

> There are no players now in the fast company [major leagues] who wear glasses to remedy defects of the eyes.... Of course, the sun-fielders of every club wear glasses while chasing flies in the garden [outfield], but they are smoked glasses with plain lenses and have nothing to do with the sight of the performer. [Infielder Russell] Blackburne, of the White Sox, I am told, wears glasses now off the field, and if this is the case, his faulty sight may have been the cause of his poor showing both at the bat and in the field during the past season.
>
> No infielder or battery player in any league, as far as I have heard, wears glasses now, nor has there been a spectacle-wearer since the days of Will White.... And yet, it often seemed to me, that many good ball players could be added to the list of active stars if fellows who wore glasses were given consideration, or if their natural reserve or shyness did not keep them out of the game.
>
> A man who has properly fitted glasses can play just as good ball as anybody else. I shouldn't imagine that an infielder would get along well with goggles on — a bounding ball might put him out of business, and on a hot afternoon when the rims of the glasses get wet from perspiration, he might lose them while bending for a grounder. Still, why shouldn't an outfielder, if he could see better

SEVEN. *The Once Famous Ball Player: 1907–1932* 167

with lamps [glasses] on, wear them? And a catcher, with a good mask, would have his lenses perfectly protected.

I saw some college games in the last few years in which several lads wore glasses, and take it from me, these spectacled rah-rahs were as good as any of the others. Long ago I saw the second baseman of the University of Virginia, named McGuire, playing the infield with enormous spectacles, like those they put on German professors in caricature. And this McGuire was strong with the bat and on the middle station [second base]. He'd have made a crack professional, glasses and all, if he had wanted to go into the game.⁵⁰

His long discourse completed, Brouthers demonstrated why he recently had become so sought-after by the press by relating a story from the bygone days about the late Will White.

Will White, I suppose, was the last of the eye-glassed professionals. Nearsighted as Roosevelt — and Teddy could play a good game of ball, I'll bet — White was nevertheless a great pitcher. He had the curves, the speed, and all sorts of scientific trickery. As a batsman, White was the limit [terrible]. He batted, I think, about .003 each season. The poor fellow couldn't hit a blamed thing, and toward the latter part of his career, simply swung the bat three times and retreated benchward.

One afternoon, with the bases full and two out, Will came to bat. Up in the press box a discussion had been started about the chances of baseball, and one of the reporters remarked that even such a batsman as White was likely to soak [hit] a home run any time. Another man raised a loud guffaw and exclaimed: "Make a little bet with you. My gold watch, worth $200, against a nickel that White doesn't make a home run."

The watch and nickel were solemnly deposited in the hands of a good stakeholder, and just as the stakes were put up White made his third blind swing at the ball. And his bat struck the leather full and fair on the equator.

The ball rose high and floated out far beyond the farthest fielder. They ran and whooped and beckoned, and White steamed slowly on around the bases. Up in the press box a man who had staked his watch turned white as a ghost and his breath came in gasps of horror. And just as Will turned third, he stumbled, rolled over, and his glasses fell off. While he was groping for his glasses, the ball came in and they tagged him out.

The man who had staked his watch got up and pocketed the nickel. Then, still very pale, he raised his right hand. "Never again, so help me," said he, "shall I attend another game of ball." And he never did. He lived for 30 years after, as I heard the story, and never again set foot inside a ball park.⁵¹

Such anecdotes, related by Brouthers in his later years while managing a semi-pro team or taking tickets at the Polo Grounds turnstiles, reveal another side of the legendary player. The former "Champion Batsman of the World" and "Greatest Slugger in the Country," the player who reportedly never said a word during a game, was also a consummate story teller.

In December 1911, Sam Crane, ballplayer-turned-sportswriter who had teamed with Big Dan in Detroit, wrote a long, complimentary essay on the Wappingers Falls slugger as part of his series of stories on the "Fifty Greatest Ball Players in History." Describing Brouthers' swing, he verbalized for a new generation what may have appeared self-evident to the great slugger's former teammates and opponents: "I think that Dan Brouthers could hit a ball harder and further than any player I ever had the pleasure of playing with or against. Let him get a low ball or one between his waist and knee, and then watch the smoke of that clout."[52] Two weeks later, *Sporting Life* correspondent E. J. Lanigan mentioned Brouthers while dismantling an argument made by a reader that old-time players had it easier, since they could request either a high or low strike.

> Charley Radbourn and other old-time pitchers would, if they were alive, laugh heartily at the above pronouncement. No one who ever saw the old timers in action would accuse them of trying to pitch so the ball could be hit.... The expert pitchers, with the use of raise [rise] and drop balls, would try to get the batters to hit at a ball the batters didn't call for. And they were very successful. However, when the low and high ball rule was abolished, and a ball pitched between the knees and shoulders was fair, it did not handicap batters like Anson, Brouthers and other great hitters, who had been used to calling for a low or high ball. Brouthers always asked for a low ball, and when the rule was changed it was declared he would not be able to hit a high ball. All the pitchers kept the ball up around Dan's neck, but he hammered it just the same.[53]

Despite such praise for Brouthers in the press of the early teens, there also were signs that public awareness of his fame was fading, even among the younger players. In January 1912, the *Washington Times* published a brief story that illustrated this point well:

> Last spring when the Giants returned from the South, McGraw had several new faces in the squad. One afternoon, an hour before the game time, youngsters were taking batting practice. The only spectators were employees, the most interested being Brouthers. While watching the youngsters, he noticed one player with a glaring weakness. Walking across the field he called the youngster aside and explained how to remedy his fault. The youngster listened, nodding his head in assent. Brouthers was pleased, for he thought he had bumped into a youngster who didn't know it all. Just as Brouthers walked away, one of the veteran players joined the crowd. "Can you imagine that crazy bug telling me how to bat?" inquired the youngster of the vet, swelling with indignation. "If you ever hit like that fellow you won't have any trouble sticking up here, laconically replied the veteran. That is Dan Brouthers." The youngster almost keeled over. He wasn't as wise as he thought.[54]

En route to his second consecutive pennant in September 1912, John McGraw took the time to praise Big Dan, not for his hitting when a player,

SEVEN. *The Once Famous Ball Player: 1907–1932*

but for his abilities as a scout. Little Napoleon, as McGraw was nicknamed, was particularly pleased with Brouthers' decisions about Larry Doyle.

> Everybody has heard the story about Doyle. It was a good joke on "Jimmy" Callahan. He went to Springfield, Ill., and watched Doyle play. "Cal" [Callahan] was acting as the agent of the Highlanders. He sent word that he [Doyle] wouldn't do. I heard about Doyle and I also heard that three or four clubs were camping on his trail, intending to secure his release. I've confidence in "Dan" Brouthers' judgment of ballplayers. I couldn't leave the team to go to Springfield myself, so I sent for "Dan," told him to take the first train and get out on the bleachers wherever Doyle happened to be playing, and look him over. That was the time that we needed something to prop up second base, which was getting shaky. Dan went out to Illinois. In two or three days ... I received a telegram from Brouthers advising me to grab him. "There are a lot more [scouts] here, and they're putting up the ante fast," said "Dan." I telegraphed back to go about $500 higher than the last bid every time someone came to the front with a new offer. It took $4,500 to obtain Doyle's release.[55]

As the years passed, Brouthers' responsibilities at the Polo Grounds changed from night watchman to press box attendant to ticket-taker, and veteran sportswriters continued to make passing reference to some of the slugger's memorable home runs, like the mighty blast over the church steeple in Philadelphia[56] and the rocket that soared over the right-center field fence at Union Park in Baltimore in 1894, which continued to be described as "the longest hit ever made in baseball."[57] Such accolades, however, were accompanied by a return of the old, false stereotype of Brouthers as an awkward hitter, slow runner and clumsy fielder.

The worst of such fabrications appeared in the *Washington Post* in 1916 — ironically the same paper that had been regularly soliciting Brouthers' views in its sports columns. The anonymous article, "Brouthers Had to Hit 'Em Far in Order to Get to First Base,"[58] may hold claim to being the most inaccurate sports column ever written.

The author begins with the assertion that "Brouthers had to hit the ball a mile to get to first base, and with all his slugging proclivities Dan's record as a batsman fails to show where he made many home runs or triples."[59] The facts, as we know, are that among his nineteenth-century counterparts, he ranked second in triples and fifth in home runs, and averaged 25 steals per season.

In his next major error, the author asserts that in 1877, Brouthers ran into Fishkill second baseman McGlynn while trying to stretch a single into a double, and that the blow killed McGlynn. In actuality, as we have seen, the accident occurred in 1878, the victim's name was Quigley, his team was from Brooklyn, and he suffered the injury while catching.

The writer also asserts that after being released by the Troy Trojans in 1879, Brouthers took a job laying sewer pipe in Troy until he was discovered by Buffalo manager Jim O'Rourke, who offered him a job. The truth, as we have seen, is that after being released by Troy, Brouthers first played for Honest John Kelly's independent New Yorks in Manhattan, and then with the Brooklyn Atlantics. It was Brouthers' performance against Buffalo while he was with Brooklyn that convinced Jim O'Rourke to sign him for the Bisons.

Finally, the completely misinformed *Post* reporter asserts that Brouthers played his last major league season with Baltimore, when in actuality, after his year with the Orioles in 1894, he spent part of 1895 with Louisville and several months of 1896 with Philadelphia before retiring.

Early in 1914, Brouthers underwent successful surgery to repair an old baseball injury. Under the headline, "Hard Luck for Dan Brouthers," *Sporting Life* reported that "One of the old guard figured in the news yesterday. Dan Brouthers, fence-shattering hitter of two decades ago, left a hospital yesterday where he was successfully operated on. An injury of 25 years ago was recalled by Dan as the cause for the surgery."[60] Late in the 1884 season, while playing for Buffalo, Brouthers "was reported to have ruptured himself.... Such, however, is not the case. It was simply a temporary strain."[61] In all likelihood, however, this strain was a rupture or hernia, and the reason for the 1914 surgery.

There was much more happy news on the home front between 1915 and 1920. In quick succession, the remaining three single Brouthers children married (Leo in 1916, Margaret in 1917, and Addison in 1919), and before long there were more grandchildren to spoil: Leo's son, Dan, Margaret's boy, Charles, and Addison's daughter, Eileen. With their own children now grown and gone from the home, Dan and Mary Ellen took in boarders, usually three at a time, to make ends meet.

In successive weeks in July 1917, Brouthers authored two articles for the *Boston Globe*, the first an account of his long home run in Baltimore in 1894, the second on the subject of baseball superstitions. Under the long headline, "Longest Hit on Record: Dan Brouthers Knocked a Ball in 1894 That Didn't Stop Short of the Gulf of Mexico," Brouthers offered a lively account of his Union Park blast couched in the form of a tall tale:

> You never can tell what the old pill [ball] is going to do when it starts on its way. There are more freakish things about baseball than there are in a circus. You may not believe this, but just the same it is true.
>
> It has always been the aim of the boys to swat them where they ain't, but now and then the pill cuts up some caper that is decidedly peculiar.... The longest sail the pill over [ever] was given was directed by yours truly.
>
> It was back in 1894. I don't remember who we were playing, but it was on the old Baltimore Grounds. That pill looked good to me as it came slanting up and

I just took a fine bust at it. The center field was 500 yards from home plate, and it soared over that.

That was nothing, though, that being merely the first leg of the journey. It was some 15 years later that I next saw that ball. A reporter named Cummings who had been to the Tropics, attended a banquet of some old-time ballplayers in Baltimore. I was among those present, and what do you suppose came off?

Why, this gent, Cummings, after getting the go-ahead sign from the guy who was umpiring [acting as Master of Ceremonies], turned his attention to me, and after reeling off several yards of chatter, presented me with a water-soaked ball.

The ball, he said, was the one that I had slammed over the fence [,] and a sea captain friend of his found it in the Gulf of Mexico. Speaking about long hits, I guess that one of mine just about was the limit.

Of course, if you want to know how the sea captain know[s] that the ball he found in the Gulf was mine, you will have to put the quiz to him.[62]

Brouthers concluded his column with another tall tale about a four-bagger allegedly hit by Jim O'Rourke:

Being on the subject of long hits, recalls one made by Jim O'Rourke at the old Walpole Grounds some years ago. Jim's clout went over the left field wall, and that was all there was to it, for a while. However, as I said before, the ball does some crazy things.

You may doubt it, but that old pill Jim cuffed just intruded into the baggage car of a train. It nearly scared the baggage man to death. That train was running express to Providence, 44 miles away, so you will understand that the ball was given quite a ride by Jim.[63]

Superstitions among ballplayers are as old as baseball itself. Often called "hoodoos" by nineteenth-century players, they could be associated with animals, everyday objects or humans. Good luck objects quickly became temporary team mascots, although they did not necessarily need to be human: Boston's mascot for at least part of the 1886 season was a small Maltese kitten. "Mose," a ring-tailed monkey, served the same purpose for Buck Ewing's 1896 Cincinnati squad, sharing the honor with a good-luck turtle that had been donated by a local fan.[64]

A hoodoo that brought bad luck for baseball players was called a jinx. In his follow-up 1917 essay for the *Boston Globe*, Dan Brouthers addressed the issue of these troubling talismans.

A jinx may be any old thing, but a jinx above everything else is the bugaboo of the baseball player. A jinr [sic] may only be imaginary, but that is enough once a ballplayer gets the idea that one has been put on him.

When a player feels that he has been jinxed, he begins to worry, and believe me, he could not hit a barrel with a bed slat if it were rolled at him. Back of all this is the old story — that baseball players as a class are among the most superstitious men in the world.

Straw hats in center field are a jinx. A straw hat itself could not possibly be a jinz [sic] unless it had Charley Faust [a mascot for the 1911 Giants] under it. It is the glare that the straw hats produce that prevents the batsman from getting a good look at the pill.

If he fails to hit the first time, he will remember the straw hat brigade when he comes up later. They bothered him before and he suspects that they will bother him more. If he fails to get a hit that day he has the old alibi ready — jinxed by the straw hats....

I had an experience with a jinx myself. When I was playing with Detroit, John Clarkson, who was pitching for the Chicago club, used to beat us about every time he faced us. We might be hitting everybody else, but then along would come Clarkson and then good night.

Finally we got that jinx. We figured out that John had been fooling us, so this day instead of relying on the old plan of waiting him out, which often put us in a hole, we decided to slam away at everything that John served.

John pitched against us twice that day and say, when the double-header was over, his chin was at half-mast when he left the field.[65]

Although Big Dan Brouthers had left Wappingers Falls in 1907 for New York City, "he still called Wappingers Falls home and each year spent a vacation in the village."[66] In the summer of 1921, he made a special trip home to celebrate the anniversary of the founding of the Sweet-Orr overall company, where he had worked as a teenager prior to starting his baseball career. The quality and durability of the company's product was nationally known, and its logo featured several hefty men unsuccessfully trying to tear apart a pair of the company's overalls. A photo from the celebration featured 63-year-old Brouthers playfully tugging on one end of a pair of Sweet-Orr blue jeans, while four young ladies, employees of the company, tugged on the other. (See photo).

In 1925, Dan and Mary Ellen left the Upper West Side and moved in with their youngest daughter Margaret, her husband Charles Wilson, and their two young boys, Charles and Robert, in East Orange, New Jersey. Despite his age and the daily commute by train, Big Dan kept working at the Polo Grounds. In his 1923 *My Thirty Years in Baseball*, John McGraw asserted that "Dan is growing old, but he always will have a job."[67]

In June 1931, a New York daily published a conversation between Brouthers and contemporary Mickey Welch, a Giants pitching hero from the 1880s, 300-game winner, and future member of the Hall of Fame. Welch, like Brouthers, worked the gates at the Polo Grounds, thanks to the generosity of John McGraw. The conversation was framed by a short italicized narrative that explained to modern readers who the two old men were: "*Scene: the Polo Grounds. Amid the calm and quiet they sit in the centre field bleachers — Dan Brouthers, the Babe Ruth of the '80s and the Gay 90s, four times batting champion*

SEVEN. *The Once Famous Ball Player: 1907–1932*   173

Although Dan Brouthers moved to Manhattan's Upper West End in 1907, he often visited relatives and friends in Wappingers Falls. In April, 1921 he returned to the village to celebrate the fiftieth anniversary of the founding of the Sweet-Orr company. In the photo, Dan, who would turn 63 the following month, uses a pair of the company's overalls to engage in a playful tug-of-war against several young Sweet-Orr employees (author's collection).

of the National League, and Mickey Welch, the [Christy] Mathewson of the 80s, who won seventeen straight for the pioneer Giants in 1885. They're past 70 and work on the gates at the Harlem Park."[68]

The two old-timers began by complimenting each other on their accomplishments on the ball field a half-century earlier. However, Welch, still feisty at 72, was looking for some contemporary recognition of his work in the box: "I'm pretty sure no hurler of 1931 could turn the trick I performed in 1885.... I don't know why they haven't put the record in the books, but in 1885 I won three games in two days and allowed two runs in twenty-nine innings."[69] Brouthers was sympathetic, but made it clear that in his mind, a latter-day Giants pitcher, recently deceased, topped all the old hurlers: "Mickey.... I've been watching pitchers for more than sixty years, ever since I broke in at Wappinger's Falls. But Matty [Christy Mathewson] was the king."[70]

Welch conceded Brouthers' point, admitting, as did the Wappingers Falls veteran, that thanks to greater opportunities that all modern players had to learn the game while young, they were better at the game. "Yes, we had some dandies years ago. But the players now are better schooled. We [in the old days] took them off the lots. Now they are sent through years of preparation in the minors. Baseball has moved along like other sports."[71]

The conversation over, the story concluded with a short narrative similar to the one that had introduced it: *"And so they went, to talk of Mutrie* [a former Giants manager] *and the Giants and the 'good old days" in the calm of the centre field bleachers — veterans two, the Matty and the Ruth of yore, working on the gates.*[72]

In one of Brouthers' last interviews, conducted by Harold Burr of the *Brooklyn Eagle* in July, 1931 the veteran again changed his mind with regard to the superiority of modern players over the old-timers. He now declared that given the superior condition of their ball fields, the moderns should make fewer errors:

> Dan Brouthers, the first of the heavy hitters, admits that baseball has changed quite a bit since he was a boy up in Dutchess County, New York, breaking in with the Wappingers Falls amateurs. "But it hasn't changed either," the old fellow, a giant of a man in shirt sleeves and a straw hat contradicted himself. "I notice when the boys go out on the field nowadays they make just as many fumbles as we did, pull just as many bones.' This was quite an admission coming from one of the old Orioles — that those legendary ancients did make blunders. "Why," continued Dan, making the admission all right, "their playing fields are 100 percent better than ours were! I don't believe we'd ever had made an error if— But no matter. Do you know I never saw a groundkeeper until I played in Brooklyn in 1882 [actually, 1881]? He was a curiosity. I used to take a rake myself and clean up around first base just before the game started. Then I'd pass it along to the second baseman, the third baseman."[73]

The greatest revelation from this, perhaps Brouthers' last interview, however, was not about errors or field conditions, but rather, that the greatest slugger of the nineteenth century had no idea how many home runs he had hit in his career: "'There were so many of them, I can't remember,' said Brouthers simply."[74]

Although Dan Brouthers' published comments on baseball reveal no startling discoveries about the nature of the game, some offer interesting asides about less-discussed elements of the National Pastime in his era. Others reflect his ambivalence about conceding that modern players were superior to him or his peers. The real value of these stories and opinions resides in the glimpse they provide us of his true personality, a perspective that was often lacking or misrepresented in the press pronouncements of his era. The irony of their publication rests in the fact they were only produced and published after the great slugger had been reduced to working the most menial jobs late in life to support himself and Mary Ellen.

John McGraw, Dan Brouthers' teammate on the 1894 Orioles and manager of the New York Giants from 1902 to 1932. In 1907, McGraw hired Brouthers as his principal scout. When Brouthers fell on financial hard times a few years later, McGraw hired him as a night watchman, ticket taker and attendant at the Polo Grounds, where Brouthers worked until his death in 1932 (Library of Congress).

Although Brouthers turned 74 in May 1932, he continued his near-daily commute from East Orange, New Jersey, to Manhattan, assuming his place at the turnstiles during Giants home games or performing other duties on the grounds on off-days. New York was having a terrible year, and would finish the season tied with the Cardinals for sixth place.

On June 3, John McGraw, troubled by health problems and just tired out, resigned as the team's manager after three decades at the post. It was the end of an era. With their protector and benefactor, Little Napoleon, gone, it seemed unlikely that old-timers like Brouthers, Mickey Welch and famous Giants ace Amos Rusie, whom McGraw had hired to do odd jobs at the Polo Grounds, would retain their positions for long.

Brouthers worked the double header against Cincinnati on Sunday, July 31, delighted that the troubled

Dan Brouthers, circa 1932. This is the last know portrait of the famed slugger (**National Baseball Hall of Fame Library, Cooperstown, New York**).

Giants took both games from the Reds. Monday, August 1, was an off-day, but he still put in a day's work at the park. On Tuesday, August 2, he rose as usual, expecting to go to the ball park, but at breakfast complained of feeling ill. A doctor was called but the old veteran's condition deteriorated rapidly. At four o'clock in the afternoon, August 2, 1932, a heart attack took the life of Big Dan Brouthers, the greatest slugger of his age.

Epilogue:
The Grand Old Man
of the Game

Dan Brouthers ... was not taught to bat nor to do this thing or the other, eventually to master the art. He was art itself. — *New York World Telegram*, August 3, 1932.

Funeral services for Dan Brouthers were held at the Church of Our Lady of All Souls in East Orange, New Jersey, and the *Newark Star-Eagle* predicted that "prominent figures in baseball"[1.] would attend. After the requiem mass, however, the *New York Herald Tribune* reported that "no representatives of organized baseball were present at the services,"[2] although some had called at the family residence. Interment took place the following day at St. Mary's cemetery in Wappingers Falls, and the slugger's grave was banked high with floral tributes from the National League, the Giants and John McGraw. Dan's widow, Mary Ellen, survived him by only two weeks, dying at age 73 on August 16. The couple had been married for 48 years.

The portraits of Dan Brouthers offered in the obituaries that appeared shortly after his death ran the gamut from simple acknowledgments of his passing to high praise for his accomplishments, and from keen insights into his personality and baseball skills to tall tales and outright falsehoods.

Although Brouthers was hailed as a "baseball immortal"[3] by the *Boston Evening Transcript*, the *New York Mirror* felt that he "practically outlived the generation in which he was one of our national athletic heroes, for news of his death arouses only a faint stir of interest among fans who think only of Ruth and Jimmy Fox [sic] when the subject of slugging comes up."[4] The *Poughkeepsie Evening Star* and the *Newark Star-Eagle* respectively observed that "A modern generation knows him only through the legends of his prowess on the baseball diamond,"[5] and that "only the older fans appreciate what Dan Brouthers was to baseball."[6] The *New York American* proved these other newspapers correct when it mistakenly described Brouthers as "one of the great outfielders of baseball history."[7]

The most evocative statement acknowledging Brouthers' old-timer status, while at the same time affirming his place among the baseball greats, came from the *New York Herald Tribune*:

> The passing of Dan Brouthers must cause the mellow citizens of a proper baseball bringing up to feel old and yet feel young again. For he is indelibly in the picture of their lost youth, along with "Pop" Anson, Mike Kelly, Clarkson, Richardson, Rowe, "Deacon Jim" White, "Buck" Ewing, John M. Ward — no need to go on with names that boys of the 80s can rattle off. In the jumble of their earnest memories Dan Brouthers cannot be dislodged. They can forget him no more that the high-wheeled bicycle, the horse car, the mustache cup, the great blizzard [of 1888], Nick Carter [a popular dime-novel detective], Maud S. [a famous race horse], Jumbo [Barnum's famous elephant]. He had his place in the entertaining scene, the old man in charge of the press gate at the Polo Grounds.
>
> Dan Brouthers was a great all-around player and a mighty slugger. Let no one on the shadowed side of fifty believe that the current heroes of baseball are the masters of the old giants who still make the chords of memory tingle.[8]

There was near unanimity among obituary writers that no one in Brouthers' era hit the ball farther: "Only Ruth has hit the ball farther than Brouthers did, and there are veteran sportsmen who insist that if the ball had been livelier in his day as it is now, Brouthers would have out-slugged Ruth"[9]; "his record for distance has been exceeded only by Ruth, who, Brouthers' friends point out, had the advantage of the livelier ball."[10]

The opinion was unanimous that no one hit the ball harder: "He didn't hit as many home runs as his contemporary, Sam Thompson, but he hit them harder."[11] (At the time of Big Dan's death, it was believed that Thompson was the nineteenth-century home run king. Researchers in the 1970s, however, discovered that the true home run leader of the era was Giants slugger Roger Connor).

To confirm such assertions, sportswriters at the *New York Sun* sought out the opinion of recently retired Giants manager John McGraw, Brouthers' teammate on the Orioles, who for a quarter-century had been his supervisor at the Polo Grounds. McGraw stated "There is a general tendency to scoff at the record of the old timers, but most of them were the real thing. Brouthers really was a great hitter, one of the most powerful batters of all time. Big Dan in his prime, against present-day pitching and the modern lively ball, would have hit as many home runs as anybody. I don't think I ever saw a longer hitter."[12]

The *Poughkeepsie Evening Courier* attributed Brouthers' hitting success to "a keen eye and the tremendous driving power of his shoulders."[13] The *New York Sun* thought his long-ball-hitting ability was due to the combination of a powerful body and a long swing. "Brouthers was a picturesque figure at the plate. Powerfully built with great shoulders and a massive body, he looked the part of a slugger. His swing was a long one, and once he met the ball it traveled."[14]

Brouthers' ability to hit the ball hard and for distance without trying to kill it earned him the title of "pioneer" by the *New York World Telegram* for believing that "the old fashioned free swinging at the ball"[15] was not productive. The same daily offered comparisons between Ruth's and Brouthers' swings, declaring each slugger superior under specific circumstances:

The best "sample" of follow through in batting is furnished these days by Ruth. Brouthers dropped the end of his bat more toward the ground than Ruth drops it. The latter swings further back behind his shoulders than Brouthers did. Yet Ruth never has been able to scoop and hit a pitched ball as Brouthers could scoop it at about knee height and get long distance. Brouthers could outhit Ruth at that height, just as Ruth can loft a ball and gain distance with it when it is pitched to him around his waist.[16]

Dutchess County sportswriters, who were more familiar with Brouthers' personal history than their national counterparts, focused in their obituaries on the slugger's early determination to improve his originally weak playing skills. The *Poughkeepsie Evening Star* recalled that "When he started all the breaks apparently were against him; he couldn't field and he couldn't hit. But he had a consuming desire to excel, and through his indomitable will, the iron in his soul, and the granite in his character, he set out to correct his faults."[17] The *Poughkeepsie Sunday Courier* noted that while "a failure at the beginning, 'Dan' dedicated his life to baseball and fought his way to the top. He discovered his own mistakes, corrected them, and became a national figure through his own efforts ... and when his star had set he modestly stepped off the stage [so] that younger men might carry on."[18] The *New York Times* continued in this mode, asserting that "Big Dan Brouthers was not one to boast of his hitting or to think that great baseball ended when his fellow-players faded out.[19]

Given, as we have seen, that in his old age, Brouthers had a habit of weaving tall tales into comments he prepared for the press, it is perhaps appropriate that the press returned the favor on his passing. The *Bronx Home News*, the *Boston Evening Transcript*, the *New York Herald Tribune* and the *St. Louis Dispatch*, for example, all carried versions of a humorous tale about a pitcher victimized by Brouthers' bat in their obituaries. "Legend has it [that] he once was chased around the base[s] by a pitcher whose game he had ruined with a home run. 'You big bully,' the pitcher cried as he pursued Dan across the plate. 'You ought to be ashamed of yourself going around the country with a telegraph pole for a bat and knocking the bread and butter out of pitchers' mouths."[20]

It was likewise perhaps inevitable, given the many misrepresentations of Brouthers' skills or of events in his career that had crept into the accounts of his life, that some should reappear in his obituaries. This was the case with regard to the tragic on-field collision that caused the death of catcher John Quigley. Maclean Kennedy, of the *Detroit News*, felt compelled to refer to the incident in his tribute to Brouthers, adding more incorrect details to the already inaccurate version that had appeared during Brouthers' playing days.

It was while with the Troy club in 1879 that a peculiar accident happened in which Brouthers was one of the principals, and it resulted in the big slugger remaining out of the game for nearly two years. Brouthers, while running to second base, collided with McGlynn, the opposing second baseman. The impact and the falling of the big 200 pounder was so great that McGlynn died within a week of his injuries. Brouthers was heart broken and quit the game. Not until the latter part of 1881 could he be induced to return.[21]

In death, as in life, Dan Brouthers' baseball history continued to be inaccurately recorded by the press.

In 1945, 13 years after his death, Big Dan Brouthers was enshrined at Cooperstown. Only a handful of nineteenth-century players had been elected to the Baseball Hall of Fame during the first nine years (1936–1944) of its balloting. Although a Veterans' Committee had been established, it did not meet until 1945, prompting suggestions that early-era players were either being ignored or deliberately excluded from consideration.

Citing the lack of reliability of early records, the Committee on "Old Timers" tended to choose the majority of their nineteenth-century inductees not on the basis of their playing records, but on whether they had any subsequent twentieth-century major league managing records, which were deemed more reliable. This fact makes Brouthers' selection even more significant, since prior to 1961, there were only five nineteenth-century inductees who had no subsequent major league managing experience: Brouthers, Jim O'Rourke, Ed Delahanty, Hoss Radbourn, and Tommy McCarthy.

The incoming 1945 Hall of Fame class included Dan Brouthers, Roger Bresnahan, Fred Clarke, Jimmy Collins, Ed Delahanty, Hugh Duffy, Hugh Jennings, Mike Kelly, Jim O'Rourke and Wilbert Robinson. In reporting these players' selection, the *New York Times* inadvertently proved the contention some had made 13 years earlier, on the occasion of Dan Brouthers' death, that the memory of many of these players' deeds on the ball field had faded. A paragraph of the *Times* report was devoted to inductee Hugh Duffy, who at age 77, was still active with the Red Sox as a scout. Giants catcher Roger Bresnahan, who had died the previous year, likewise merited a paragraph, as did former Orioles Hughie Jennings and Wilbert Robinson, both of whom had managed in the major leagues for many years. The remaining five old-timers combined, including Dan Brouthers, merited just one sentence from the *Times*.[22]

Like many New England towns in the nineteenth century, Wappingers Falls needed immigrant labor to work in its mills and factories, but housed such workers far from the village's finer (and flatter) areas, which lay east of the waterfall that originally supplied the power to the mills. West of the falls and Wappingers Creek, on West Main Street, a high ridge causes the land to rise steeply, and it was here on the hillside that the laborers at the Print Works and other commercial plants lived. St. Mary's Church, which served the needs

Rena Corey, former Archivist for the Wappingers Falls Historical Society, stands at Dan Brouthers' grave at St. Mary's Catholic Church cemetery, Wappingers Falls, New York (author's collection).

of the largely Irish Catholic immigrant work force, sits near the top of this steep rise, a few blocks up West Main Street. Flanking the church to the southwest, partially hidden from view today by the church's elementary school, is the broad expanse of St. Mary's cemetery, where Dan Brouthers is buried.

No fine monument marks the grave of the greatest slugger of the nineteenth century, nor is there any reference on the small, rough-hewn granite grave marker to his Hall of Fame status or that he ever played baseball. All to be seen here are a cross, the Anglicized family name, "Brouthers," flanked by the names "Dan" and "Mary Ellen," and the simple statement, "At Rest." Here the great slugger slumbers, a Big Dan Brouthers' home run's distance from the approximate location of the original Wappingers Falls Actives' diamond, where, 135 years ago, young Dennis Bruther began his storied baseball career.

Appendix A: Dan Brouthers' Nicknames

Presented in chronological order:

The Young Giant *Cincinnati Daily Inquirer*, June 20, 1879.
The Goliath of the League, *Troy Daily Times*, July 15, 1879.
The Big Batsman, *New York Clipper*, April 30, 1881.
The Left-Handed Slugger, *Buffalo Daily Courier*, June 18, 1881.
The Kid, *Buffalo Courier*, July 29, 1881.
The Great Home Run Man, *Buffalo Courier*, July 30, 1881.
Jumbo, *Buffalo Commercial Advertiser*, June 1, 1882.
Reliable Dan Brouthers, *Buffalo Daily Courier*, June 15, 1883.
The Giant Brouthers, *Sporting Life*, October 8, 1883.
The Big 'Un, *Sporting Life*, October 8, 1883.
The Champion Batsman of the Country, *Sporting Life*, June 4, 1884.
The Jumbo First Baseman, *Milwaukee Sentinel*, May 4, 1885.
The Good Natured Giant, *Detroit Free Press*, April 26, 1886.
Gigantic Brouthers, *Detroit Free Press*, May 10, 1886.
Massive Brouthers, *Detroit Free Press*, May 19, 1886.
Big Brouthers, *Sporting Life*, May 22, 1886.
Big Dan Brouthers, *Detroit Free Press*, June 26, 1886.
The Redoubtable Brouthers, *Detroit Free Press*, September 11, 1886.
The Wappingers Falls Terror, *Sporting Life*, April 13, 1887.
The Tall First Baseman, *Buffalo Daily Courier*, June 2, 1888.
The Champion Batsman of the World, *Boston Daily Globe*, April 27, 1890.
Honest Dan, *Boston Daily Globe*, July 4, 1890.
The Greatest Living Batsman, *Sporting Life*, July 12, 1890.
Old Jed, *Sporting Life*, June 27, 1891.
The Greatest Slugger in the Country, *Milwaukee Sentinel*, September 20, 1891.
Big Brother with the Stick, *Sporting Life*, May 14, 1892.
Big Dennis, *Baltimore Sun*, June 6, 1894.

Giant Dan, *Sporting Life*, June 9, 1894.
The Wappingerian, *Baltimore Sun*, October 30, 1894.
Good Old Dan, *Sporting Life*, May 11, 1895.
The Mighty Irish King, *Sporting Life*, December 21, 1895.
Old Wappinger, *Philadelphia Inquirer*, April 5, 1896.
Gladstone, *Springfield Republican*, May 4, 1897.
The Wappingers Falls Boy, *Denver Post*, May 11, 1897.
Wappinger Dan, *Wilkes-Barre Record*, August 10, 1897.
The Old Man, *Springfield Daily Republican*, September 22, 1897.
The Sage of Wappingers Falls, *Sporting Life*, May 20, 1899.
The Great Brouthers, *Sporting Life*, February 8, 1902.
The Terror of All Pitchers, *Boston Daily Globe*, February 21, 1904.
The Big Fellow, *Poughkeepsie Daily Eagle*, May 14, 1904.
Old Dan, *Boston Daily Globe*, June 6, 1904.
The Immortal Dan, *New York Evening Telegram*, June 14, 1904.
The Old War Horse, *Ithaca Daily News*, August 2, 1905.
The Once World Famous Ball Player, *Sporting Life*, April 7, 1906.
Aged Dan Brouthers, *Washington Post*, October 21, 1906.
Scout Dan Brouthers, *Sporting Life*, September 28, 1907.
The Grand Old Man of the Game, *Utica Herald-Dispatch*, January 18, 1909.
Demon Dan, *Oswego Daily Palladian*, May 3, 1916.
The Fence-Smasher of the 80's, *New York Evening Post*, May 15, 1925.
The Babe Ruth of His Day, *Schenectady Gazette*, June 25, 1925.
Thundering, Ball Murdering Dan, *Daily Star* (Queens, New York), January 30, 1928.
The Mighty Slugger, *New York Herald Tribune*, August 3, 1932.
The Big Man with the Terrific Swing, *Philadelphia Inquirer*, August 4, 1932.

Appendix B: Dan Brouthers' Longest Hits

Playing for the National League Troy Trojans:

• July 2, 1879, at Star Park, home of the National League Syracuse Stars. Hit off Jim McCormick. "Broedders [Brouthers] made the longest hit ever seen on the Syracuse grounds yesterday. The ball struck the centre field fence within a foot of the top and rebounded to the infield. If the ball had gone a foot higher, Broeders would have made a home run." *Troy Daily Times*, July 3, 1879.

Playing for the National League Buffalo Bisons:

• June 17, 1882, at Recreation Park, Philadelphia, home of the independent Philadelphia Quakers. Hit off Jack Neagle. Hit "over the fence at right centre ... it being the longest hit ever made on the grounds." *New York Clipper*, June 24, 1882.
• August 5, 1882, at Recreation Park, Philadelphia, home of the independent Philadelphia Quakers. Hit off Hardie Henderson. "His last hit was the longest and highest hit ever seen on the ground[s], and probably the longest ever made. The ball went over the centre-field fence, fully one hundred feet above it, and landed far away in the vacant lots beyond the ball ground." *New York Clipper*, August 12, 1882.

Playing for the National League Detroit Wolverines:

• June 12, 1886, at Recreation Park, Detroit, home of the Detroit Wolverines. Off Charlie Sweeney of the St. Louis Maroons. "I think that Dan Brouthers could hit a ball harder and further that any player I ever had the pleasure of playing with or against ... about the longest drive I ever saw Dan make was in Detroit, when he hit a ball through the branches of a tree deep in centrefield. The ground was hard as flint at the time and the leather shot through the tree like a rifle ball and never did stop until it struck a fence that separated the ball field from a cricket grounds, a half mile away if I remember rightly." Sam Crane, *New York Journal*, December 11, 1911.

- May 17, 1887, at the Huntingdon Street Grounds, Philadelphia, home of the National League Philadelphia Phillies. Hit off Dan Casey. "The home run [over the right field fence] made by Brouthers was the longest ever made on the new grounds." *Sporting Life*, May 18, 1887.
- June 1, 1888, at the Huntingdon Street Grounds, Philadelphia, home of the National League Philadelphia Phillies. Hit off Dan Casey. "What a terrific blast it was! The ball went sailing a hundred feet over the fence and must have dropped a square block beyond the right field fence of the local grounds. There was no doubt about it being the largest hit ever made on the new grounds." *Detroit Free Press*, June 2, 1888.

Playing for the National League Boston Reds:

- May 6, 1889, at the Swampoodle Grounds, Washington, D.C., home of the National League Washington Statesmen. Hit off Egyptian Healy. "It was the first time the ball ever had been hit over the [center field] fence. The same hit would have cleared the centre field fence at the Boston grounds. It never raised over 25 feet high at any time." *Boston Daily Globe*, May 7, 1889.
- June 11, 1889, at the St. George Grounds, Staten Island, New York, temporary home of the National League New York Giants. Hit off Mickey Welch. "Welch shot one at him with a spin. Dan met it square on the trademark, and away she went, on a bee line, straight for the centre field fence. [Center fielder George] Gore stood up against the fence as the ball went sailing over his head for a home run, and the longest hit ever made on the grounds." *Boston Daily Globe*, June 12, 1889.

Playing for the American Association Boston Reds:

- August 9, 1891, at Recreation Park, Columbus, Ohio, home of the American Association Columbus Solons. Hit off John Dolan. "His home run in the sixth was a record breaker, and was without a doubt the longest hit ever witnessed on the home grounds. It cleared the center field fence and this feat has never before been performed. *Boston Daily Globe*, August 9, 1891.
- August 21, 1891, at the Congress Street Grounds, home of the American Association Boston Reds. Hit off Ice Box Chamberlain of the Philadelphia Athletics. "Dan Brouthers opened the eighth with the longest hit ever seen on these grounds, the ball going over the right field fence within fifty feet of the corner. *Boston Globe*, August 22, 1891.

Playing for the National League Baltimore Orioles:

- May 4, 1894, at Union Park, home of the National League Baltimore Orioles. Hit off Dan Daub of the Brooklyn Bridegrooms. "It is not stretching things to say that Mr. Brouthers made a hit. It was the longest hit ever made at Union

Park. The ball went over the right field fence, fifty feet from the foul line. Tom Burns, the Brooklyn right fielder, who was the last man to see the ball, says it was at least twenty feet from [above] the top of the fence when it went over.... The point over which Mr. Brouthers' hit passed over the fence is 365 feet from home plate. The ball touched mother earth sixty feet from the fence on the outside of the grounds." *Baltimore Sun*, May 5, 1894.
- June 16, 1894, at Union Park, home of the National League Baltimore Orioles. Hit off Ted Breitenstein of the St. Louis Maroons. "Brouthers' [home run] was made on a hit over the centre-field fence, which sent the ball to twenty-third street. The drive is believed to be the longest ever made on the grounds. The ball struck the sidewalk on Guilford avenue [sic], four doors below twenty-fourth street." *Baltimore Sun*, June 18, 1894.

Playing for the Eastern League Springfield Ponies

- April 3, 1895, at Athletic Park in Raleigh, North Carolina, against a Wake Forest College team. Hit off Wake Forest Pitcher Wynn. "'Big Four' Brouthers put the ball into the Cemetery [,] the longest hit ever made on the grounds." *The News and Observer* (Raleigh), April 4, 1895.
- August 28, 1896, at Springfield, against the Scranton Red Sox. "In the fourth he knocked a home run and sent the ball traveling farther than it ever traveled in the history of baseball in this city (Springfield). *Springfield Republican*, August 29, 1896.

Playing for the Hudson River League Poughkeepsie Colts

- June 1, 1904, at the Saugerties Driving Field, Saugerties, New York. Two home runs, described to John Thorn by eyewitness Merce Farrell as "the longest balls anyone in the town had ever seen or would see." John Thorn, "Baseball's First All-Star Game," ourgame.mlblogs.com/2012/09/09/baseballs-first-all-star-game.

Appendix C: Dan Brouthers' Major League Statistics

Bold Italics = League Leader
* Here I follow Bill Jenkinson's home run logs, which correctly indicate two home runs in 1890.
Source: baseball-reference.com

Dan Brouthers' Major League Statistics

Year	Tm	Lg	G	AB	R	H	2B	3B	HR	RBI	SB	BA	OBP	SLG	OPS
1879	TRO	NL	39	168	17	46	12	1	4	17	-	.274	.278	.429	.707
1880	TRO	NL	3	12	0	2	0	0	0	1	-	.167	.231	.167	.397
1881	BUF	NL	65	270	60	86	18	9	8	45	-	.319	.361	*.541*	.902
1882	BUF	NL	84	351	71	129	23	11	6	63	-	*.368*	*.403*	*.547*	*.950*
1883	BUF	NL	98	425	85	159	41	17	3	97	-	*.374*	*.397*	*.572*	*.969*
1884	BUF	NL	94	398	82	130	22	15	14	79	-	.327	.378	*.563*	*.941*
1885	BUF	NL	98	407	87	146	32	11	7	59	-	.359	.408	*.543*	*.951*
1886	DET	NL	121	489	139	181	40	15	11	72	21	.370	.445	*.581*	*1.026*
1887	DET	NL	123	500	*153*	169	*36*	20	12	101	34	.338	*.426*	.562	*.988*
1888	DET	NL	129	522	*118*	160	*33*	11	9	66	34	.307	.399	.464	.862
1889	BSN	NL	126	485	105	181	26	9	7	118	22	*.373*	.462	.507	.969
1890	BSN	PL	123	460	117	152	36	9	2*	97	28	.330	*.466*	.454	.921
1891	BSN	AA	130	486	117	170	26	19	5	109	31	*.350*	*.471*	*.512*	*.983*
1892	BRO	NL	152	588	121	*197*	30	20	5	*124*	31	*.335*	.432	.480	*.911*
1893	BRO	NL	77	282	57	95	21	11	2	59	9	.337	.450	.511	.961
1894	BAL	NL	123	525	137	182	39	23	9	128	38	.347	.425	.560	.985
1895	BAL	NL	5	23	2	6	2	0	0	5	0	.261	.292	.348	.639
1895	LOU	NL	24	97	13	30	10	1	2	15	1	.309	.380	.495	.874
1896	PHI	NL	57	218	42	75	13	3	1	41	7	.344	.462	.445	.907
1904	NYG	NL	2	5	0	0	0	0	0	0	0	.000	.000	.000	.000
TOTALS			1673	6711	1523	2296	460	205	107	1296	256	.342	.423	.519	.942

Chapter Notes

Chapter One

1. "Town of Beekman: St. Denis Church," 3.
2. Ibid.
3. U.S. Census, Town of Beekman, Dutchess County, NY, 1860.
4. U.S. Census, Town of Fishkill, Dutchess County, NY, 1870.
5. *Denver Post*, May 11, 1897.
6. *Sporting Life*, April 13, 1887.
7. *Sporting Life*, May 20, 1899.
8. *Philadelphia Inquirer*, April 15, 1896.
9. *Baltimore Sun*, October 30, 1894.
10. Edgar Popper, *The Birth and Growth of an Old Village: Wappingers Falls* (Millbrook, NY: Central Press, 1991), 2.
11. Ibid., 5.
12. *Poughkeepsie Eagle-News*, August 3, 1932.
13. Popper, 14.
14. Ibid., 13.
15. *Poughkeepsie Eagle-News*, January 5, 1925.
16. *Poughkeepsie Eagle-News*, October 22, 1928.
17. *New York Clipper*, July 7, 1877.
18. Joseph Poilucci, *Baseball in Dutchess County* (Danbury, CT: Rutledge, 2000), 98.
19. *New York Clipper*, August 28, 1880.
20. *Boston Daily Globe*, October 11, 1887.
21. *Poughkeepsie Eagle-News*, August 3, 1932.
22. *Sporting Life*, March 12, 1910.
23. *Poughkeepsie Eagle-News*, August 3, 1932.
24. *Boston Daily Globe*, February 21, 1904.
25. *Poughkeepsie Eagle-News*, August 3, 1932.
26. Ibid.
27. Ibid.
28. Connie Mack, *My 66 Years in the Big Leagues* (Mineola, NY: Dover, 2009), 118.
29. Ernest Lanigan, undated article, Dan Brouthers player file, National Baseball Hall of Fame, Cooperstown, NY.
30. *Poughkeepsie Eagle-News*, August 3, 1932.
31. *The Textile Worker*, Volume 9, No. 1, (1921) 242.
32. *New York Clipper*, August 4, 1877.
33. *New York Clipper*, May 18, 1878.
34. *Poughkeepsie Eagle-News*, July 7, 1877.
35. Ibid.
36. Ibid.
37. Ibid.
38. *The Dutchess Farmer*, August 21, 1878.
39. *Boston Daily Advertiser*, September 1, 1887; *Sporting Life*, September 9, 1888.
40. *Daily Inter-Ocean*, May 15, 1890; *Washington Post*, June 26, 1899.
41. *Poughkeepsie Eagle-News*, August 14, 1877.
42. *New York Clipper*, September 15, 1877.
43. *Buffalo Express*, March 3, 1924.
44. *New York Clipper*, July 13, 1878.
45. Franklin Ellis, *History of Columbia County* (Philadelphia: Everts and Ensign, 1878), 354.
46. *New York Clipper*, July 20, 1878.
47. *New York Clipper*, September 7, 1878.
48. *New York Clipper*, June 14, 1879.
49. *New York Clipper*, July 5, 1879.
50. Don Rittner, *Troy: A Collar City History* (Charleston, SC: Arcadia, 2002), 88.
51. *New York Times*, August 2, 1889.
52. *Troy Daily Times*, June 24, 1879.
53. *Troy Daily Times*, July 3, 1879.
54. While baseball-reference.com, *The Baseball Encyclopedia*, and other sources put Brouthers' home run total at 106, the actual number is 107. Left out of original calculations is a home run hit off Pittsburgh's John Tener at Boston on July 11, 1890, in a regularly scheduled game, confirmed by *Sporting Life*, July 12, 1890, and by the *Boston Daily Globe*,

July 12, 1890. Bill Jenkinson is the only historian to have noted this home run previously.
55. *Troy Daily Times*, August 2, 1879.
56. *Troy Daily Times*, July 15. 1879.
57. *New York Clipper*, August 16, 1879.
58. Ibid.
59. *Troy Daily Times*, August 12, 1879.
60. *New York Clipper*, August 9, 1879.
61. *New York Clipper*, August 30, 1879.
62. *New York Clipper*, June 28, 1879.
63. *New York Clipper*, August 16, 1879.
64. *Sporting Life*, May 12, 1894.
65. *Daily Inter-Ocean*, May 15, 1890.
66. Ibid.
67. *Washington Post*, June 26, 1899.
68. *New York Clipper*, August 23, 1879.
69. *New York Clipper*, September 20, 1879.
70. *New York Clipper*, April 3, 1880.
71. *New York Clipper*, April 10, 1880.
72. *New York Clipper*, May 1, 1880.
73. *New York Clipper*, May 15, 1880.
74. *New York Clipper*, June 5, 1880.
75. *New York Clipper*, July 24, 1880.
76. *New York Clipper*, August 28, 1880.
77. Ibid.
78. Ibid.
79. Ibid.
80. *Sporting Life*, June 14, 1884.
81. *Boston Daily Globe*, February 2, 1904.
82. *Sporting Life*, December 21, 1895.

Chapter Two

1. *El Paso Herald*, March 18, 1916.
2. Ibid.
3. *New York Clipper*, May 14, 1881.
4. *New York Clipper*, May 28, 1881.
5. Ibid.
6. *New York Clipper*, May 21, 1881.
7. Ibid.
8. Mike Roer, *Orator O'Rourke: the Life of a Baseball Radical* (Jefferson, NC: McFarland, 2005), 92.
9. *New York Clipper*, June 4, 1881.
10. Joseph Overfield, "The First Great Minor League Club," research.sabr.org/journals.
11. *New York Clipper*, June 18, 1881.
12. *Buffalo Daily Courier*, June 10, 1881.
13. *Buffalo Daily Courier*, July 3, 1881.
14. *New York Clipper*, July 19, 1881.
15. *Buffalo Daily Courier*, June 29, 1881.
16. *Brooklyn Eagle*, July 9, 1881.
17. *Buffalo Daily Courier*, July 31, 1881.
18. *Buffalo Daily Courier*, August 6, 1881.
19. *New York Journal*, December 11, 1911.
20. David Nemec, *Major League Baseball Profiles*, Vol. 2 (Lincoln: University of Nebraska, 2011), 226.
21. Ibid.
22. *Buffalo Daily Courier*, April 17, 1881.
23. Frank Vaccaro, "Hugh Daily," www.sabrbioproj.org/person/8d8c99e4.
24. *Buffalo Daily Courier*, July 25, 1881.
25. *Buffalo Daily Courier*, April 10, 1882.
26. *Buffalo Daily Courier*, May 18, 1882.
27. *Buffalo Daily Courier*, June 17, 1882.
28. *New York Clipper*, June 17, 1882.
29. *New York Clipper*, July 29, 1882.
30. Rich Westcott, *Philadelphia's Old Ballparks* (Philadelphia: Temple University, 1996), 12.
31. *New York Clipper*, August 12, 1882.
32. *Buffalo Daily Courier*, August 6, 1882.
33. *Scranton Tribune*, April 12, 1897.
34. *Sporting Life*, January 29, 1910.
35. *Buffalo Daily Courier*, July 30, 1882.
36. *Buffalo Daily Courier*, September 27, 1883.
37. *Sporting Life*, August 6, 1883.
38. *Sporting Life*, January 29, 1910.
39. Peter Morris, *A Game of Inches* (Chicago: Ivan R. Dee, 2006), 251.
40. quoted in the *Troy Daily Times*, July 15, 1879.
41. *New York Clipper*, April 30, 1881.
42. *Buffalo Daily Courier*, June 16, 1883.
43. Ibid.
44. *Buffalo Daily Courier*, October 8, 1883.
45. *Buffalo Daily Courier*, October 15, 1883.
46. *New York Clipper*, April 7, 1883.
47. *Buffalo Daily Courier*, May 17, 1883.
48. *New York Police Gazette*, April 27, 1889.
49. *Sporting Life*, May 30, 1888.
50. *Sporting Life*, November 7, 1883.
51. *Buffalo Daily Courier*, April 20, 1884.
52. *Buffalo Daily Courier*, April 26, 1884.
53. *Buffalo Daily Courier*, April 30, 1884.
54. *Buffalo Daily Courier*, May 3, 1884.
55. *Cleveland Herald*, May 8, 1885.
56. *Buffalo Daily Courier*, June 7, 1884.
57. *Buffalo Daily Courier*, June 14, 1884.
58. *Buffalo Daily Courier*, October 16, 1884.
59. Ibid.
60. *Sporting Life*, June 25, 1884.
61. *Buffalo Daily Courier*, June 20, 1884.
62. Morris, 334.
63. *Sporting Life*, July 16, 1884.
64. *Buffalo Daily Courier*, July 12, 1885.
65. *Sporting Life*, July 22, 1885.
66. Ibid.

67. *Sporting Life*, July 16, 1885.
68. *Sporting Life*, September 23, 1885.
69. Harold Seymour, *Baseball: the Early Years* (New York: Oxford, 1960), 170.
70. *Sporting Life*, September 23, 1885.
71. Ibid.
72. *Spalding Official Base Ball Guide*, 1890.
73. *Buffalo Daily Courier*, August 1, 1885.

Chapter Three

1. *Poughkeepsie Sunday Courier*, August 7, 1932.
2. *Washington Post*, September 11, 1910.
3. *Detroit Free Press*, April 28, 1886.
4. *Boston Daily Globe*, February 2, 1891.
5. *New York Herald*, April 7, 1912.
6. *Washington Post*, August 6, 1916.
7. *Brooklyn Eagle*, July 3, 1893.
8. *Detroit Free Press*, August 29, 1888.
9. *Sporting Life*, June 8, 1894.
10. *Poughkeepsie Sunday Courier*, August 6, 1932.
11. Both Dan Brouthers' online page at the National Baseball Hall of Fame and his statistical record in *The Baseball Encyclopedia* (MacMillan) list his playing weight at 207 pounds.
12. *New York Sun*, August 4, 1932.
13. *Sporting Life*, April 22, 1893.
14. *Baltimore Sun*, April 5, 1893.
15. *Milwaukee Sentinel*, May 4, 1885.
16. *Boston Daily Globe*, February 21, 1904.
17. *Boston Daily Globe*, August 23, 1889.
18. *Sporting Life*, October 24, 1888.
19. *Sporting Life*, May 29, 1889.
20. *Boston Daily Globe*, September 10, 1890.
21. *Yenowine's News*, September 2, 1890.
22. *Sporting Life*, June 20, 1891.
23. *Brooklyn Eagle*, July 18, 1894.
24. *Daily Picayune*, June 23, 1894.
25. *Troy Daily Times*, July 15, 1879.
26. *New York Clipper*, August 28, 1880.
27. *Boston Daily Globe*, February 21, 1904.
28. *Sporting Life*, May 25, 1887.
29. *New York Clipper*, June 11, 1891.
30. *Detroit Free Press*, July 7, 1886; *New York Clipper*, June 18, 1881.
31. *Buffalo Daily Courier*, July 8, 1886; *Detroit Free Press*, July 27, 1887.
32. Peter Morris, *A Game of Inches* (Chicago: Ivan R. Dee, 2006), 82.
33. Ibid., 211.
34. Ibid., 212.
35. David Nemec, *Major League Baseball Profiles*, Vol. 2 (Lincoln: University of Nebraska, 2011), 18.
36. *Boston Daily Globe*, July 4, 1890.
37. *Boston Daily Globe*, April 2, 1890.
38. *Boston Daily Globe*, May 23, 1890.
39. *Boston Daily Globe*, June 5, 1890.
40. *Boston Daily Globe*, October 17, 1890.
41. *Boston Daily Globe*, June 12, 1889.
42. *Baltimore Sun*, April 24, 1894.
43. *Boston Daily Globe*, February 21, 1904.
44. *New York Journal*, November 12, 1911.
45. *New York World*, August 5, 1932.
46. *The Sentinel* (Milwaukee), October 15, 1883.
47. *Sporting Life*, July 28, 1894.
48. E-mail communication from Sue MacKay, Director of Collections, Baseball Hall of Fame, August 8, 2012.
49. *Auburn Citizen*, August 30, 1912.
50. *Boston Daily Globe*, July 6, 1899.
51. *Boston Daily Globe*, February 21, 1904.
52. *Atchison Daily Globe*, July 6, 1889.
53. *New York Herald*, April 7, 1912.
54. *New York World*, August 4, 1932.
55. *Atchison Daily Globe*, July 6, 1889.
56. *Boston Daily Globe*, June 5, 1889.
57. *Brooklyn Eagle*, April 30, 1893.
58. *Brooklyn Eagle*, June 7, 1892.
59. *Boston Daily Globe*, May 8, 1892.
60. *Boston Daily Globe*, September 3, 1891.
61. *Sporting Life*, May 3, 1902.
62. *Sporting Life*, July 27, 1912; May 9, 1908; August 4, 1906; December 3, 1904.
63. David Voigt, *American Baseball* (State College: Pennsylvania State University, 1992), 12.
64. Ibid., 113.
65. Nemec, 104.
66. Ibid.
67. Ibid.
68. Ibid.
69. Richard Bak, "Before They Were Tigers: A Primer on Early Detroit Baseball," blog.detroitathletic.com/2012/06/11/before-they-were-tigers-a-primer-on-early-detroit-baseball/
70. Don Thompson, "Sam Thompson," sabr.org/bioproj/person/b3e0fab8.
71. *Detroit Free Press*, June 22, 1886.
72. *Detroit Free Press*, April 26, 1886.
73. Nemec, 9.
74. *Detroit Free Press*, April 26, 1886.
75. *Detroit Free Press*, May 22, 1886.
76. *Detroit Free Press*, May 24, 1886.
77. *New York Journal*, December 11, 1911.
78. Voigt, 179.
79. *Detroit Free Press*, June 19, 1886.

80. *Detroit Free Press*, July 5, 1886.
81. *Detroit Free Press*, July 4, 1886.
82. Bak, 25.
83. *Detroit Free Press*, May 10, 1886.
84. *Detroit Free Press*, May 19, 1886.
85. *Detroit Free Press*, September 26, 1886.
86. *Detroit Free Press*, June 24, 1886.
87. *Milwaukee Sentinel*, September 11, 1886.
88. *Detroit Free Press*, September 11, 1886.
89. *Detroit Free Press*, September 23, 1886.
90. *Sporting Life*, May 18, 1887.
91. *Detroit Free Press*, August 5, 1887.
92. *Detroit Free Press*, August 17, 1887.
93. *Sporting Life*, October 5, 1887.
94. *Detroit Free Press*, October 12, 1887.
95. *Sporting Life*, October 19, 1887.
96. *Sporting Life*, October 26, 1887.
97. Ibid.
98. *St. Louis Globe Democrat*, October 2, 1887.
99. *Detroit Free Press*, April 3, 1888.
100. *Detroit Free Press*, April 7, 1888.
101. Ibid.
102. *Sporting Life*, April 25, 1888.
103. Ibid.
104. *Detroit Free Press*, April 21, 1888.
105. *Detroit Free Press*, April 10, 1888.
106. *Detroit Free Press*, June 2, 1888.
107. Ibid.
108. *New York Times*, June 9, 1888.
109. *Detroit Free Press*, June 13, 1888.
110. Ibid.
111. Ibid.
112. *Sporting Life*, July 18, 1888.
113. *Detroit Free Press*, July 22, 1888.
114. *Detroit Free Press*, August 29, 1888.
115. *Detroit Free Press*, August 10, 1888.
116. *Sporting Life*, October 24, 1888.
117. *Detroit Free Press*, October 14, 1888.

Chapter Four

1. Brian McKenna, "John Clarkson," sabr.org/bioproj/person/47feb015.
2. *Boston Daily Globe*, November 18, 1888.
3. *Boston Daily Globe*, May 2, 1889.
4. *Boston Daily Globe*, May 7, 1889.
5. *Boston Daily Globe*, June 2, 1889.
6. *Boston Daily Globe*, August 8, 1889.
7. *Boston Daily Globe*, June 12, 1889.
8. *New York Times*, August 15, 1932.
9. *Morning Oregonian*, July 29, 1889.
10. *St. Louis Dispatch*, July 15, 1896.
11. *Boston Daily Globe*, June 30, 1889.
12. *Boston Daily Globe*, August 12, 1889.
13. Marty Appel, *Slide, Kelly Slide* (Lanham, MD: Scarecrow Press, 1999), 142.
14. Ibid., 143.
15. Ibid., 144.
16. Ibid.
17. David Nemec, *The Great Encyclopedia of 19th Century Major League Baseball* (New York: Donald I. Fine, 1997), 372.
18. *Sporting Life*, June 24, 1885.
19. David Voigt, *American Baseball* (State College: Pennsylvania State University, 1992), 57.
20. Ibid., 177.
21. James Hardy, *The New York Giants Base Ball Club: 1870 to 1900* (Jefferson, NC: McFarland, 1996), 97.
22. Ed Koszarek, *The Players League* (Jefferson, NC: McFarland, 2006), 81.
23. retrosheet.org, baseball-reference.com, and the Macmillan *Baseball Encyclopedia* incorrectly state that Brouthers hit only one home run in 1890.
24. *Boston Daily Globe*, April 26, 1890.
25. David Nemec, *The Official Rules of Baseball Illustrated* (Guilford, CT: Lyons Press, 2006), 59.
26. *Boston Daily Globe*, May 31, 1890.
27. *Boston Daily Globe*, July 11, 1890.
28. *Boston Daily Globe*, July 12, 1890.
29. Ibid.
30. *Boston Daily Globe*, July 18, 1890.
31. *Boston Daily Globe*, July 19, 1890.
32. *Boston Daily Globe*, February 23, 1890.
33. *Boston Daily Globe*, December 11, 1889.
34. *Boston Daily Globe*, July 12, 1890.
35. *Boston Daily Globe*, August 17, 1890.
36. *Boston Daily Globe*, July 26, 1890.
37. *Boston Daily Globe*, February 1, 1891.
38. Charles Alexander, *Our Game* (New York: Henry Holt, 1991), 58.
39. *Milwaukee Sentinel*, February 12, 1891.
40. Koszarek, 353.
41. *Boston Daily Globe*, April 9, 1891.
42. *Boston Daily Globe*, April 11, 1891.
43. *Boston Daily Globe*, July 12, 1891.
44. *Boston Daily Globe*, May 29, 1891.
45. *Boston Daily Globe*, August 9, 1891.
46. *Boston Daily Globe*, August 10, 1891.
47. *Sporting Life*, September 22, 1894.
48. *Boston Daily Globe*, August 19, 1891.
49. *Boston Daily Globe*, August 22, 1891.
50. *Sporting Life*, June 27, 1891.
51. *Boston Daily Globe*, July 17, 1891.
52. *New York Dramatic Mirror*, May 18, 1889.

53. *Bangor Daily News*, August 11, 1909.
54. Ibid.
55. *Milwaukee Sentinel*, September 20, 1891.
56. *Sporting Life*, November 14, 1891.
57. Ibid.
58. Ibid.
59. Ibid. Song copyright, 1883, by William A. Pond, Inc.
60. *Sporting Life*, November 14, 1891.
61. Ibid.
62. *Inter-Ocean*, February 17, 1892.

Chapter Five

1. *Brooklyn Daily Eagle*, August 28, 1892.
2. David Voigt, *American Baseball* (State College: Pennsylvania State University, 1992), 234.
3. Harold Seymour, *Baseball: the Early Years* (New York: Oxford, 1960), 268.
4. Bill James, *The New Bill James Historical Baseball Abstract* (New York: The Free Press, 1988), 52.
5. Bryan Di Salvatore, *A Clever Base Ballist* (Baltimore, MD: Johns Hopkins, 1999), 344.
6. *Brooklyn Daily Eagle*, April 9, 1892.
7. *Brooklyn Daily Eagle*, April 14, 1892.
8. *Sporting Life*, May 14, 1892.
9. *Brooklyn Daily Eagle*, June 4, 1892.
10. *Brooklyn Daily Eagle*, May 31, 1892.
11. *Brooklyn Daily Eagle*, June 2, 1892.
12. *Brooklyn Daily Eagle*, June 18, 1892.
13. *Brooklyn Daily Eagle*, June 21, 1892.
14. Charles Alexander, *Our Game* (New York: Henry Holt, 1991), 63.
15. *Brooklyn Daily Eagle*, July 17, 1892.
16. *Brooklyn Daily Eagle*, July 27, 1892.
17. *Brooklyn Daily Eagle*, July 30, 1892.
18. *Brooklyn Daily Eagle*, August 5, 1892.
19. *Brooklyn Daily Eagle*, August 14, 1892.
20. *Brooklyn Daily Eagle*, September 2, 1892.
21. *Sporting Life*, July 16, 1892.
22. *Brooklyn Daily Eagle*, August 2, 1892.
23. *Brooklyn Daily Eagle*, August 6, 1892.
24. Ibid.
25. *Brooklyn Daily Eagle*, August 13, 1892.
26. *Sporting Life*, August 6, 1892.
27. *Sporting Life*, September 17, 1892.
28. *Brooklyn Daily Eagle*, October 1, 1892.
29. *Brooklyn Daily Eagle*, October 7, 1892.
30. *Brooklyn Daily Eagle*, October 12, 1892.
31. *Brooklyn Daily Eagle*, October 8, 1892.
32. *Brooklyn Daily Eagle*, October 13, 1892.
33. Thomas Schlereth, *Victorian America* (New York: Harper Collins, 1991), 171.
34. *Brooklyn Daily Eagle*, April 10, 1893.
35. *Brooklyn Daily Eagle*, April 8, 1893.
36. *Brooklyn Daily Eagle*, April 19, 1893.
37. *Sporting Life*, April 8, 1893.
38. *Brooklyn Daily Eagle*, April 15, 1893.
39. *Sporting Life*, April 22, 1893.
40. *Sporting Life*, May 13, 1893.
41. *Brooklyn Daily Eagle*, June 4, 1893.
42. *Sporting Life*, June 9, 1893.
43. *Brooklyn Daily Eagle*, July 17, 1893.
44. Burt Solomon, *Where They Ain't* (New York: The Free Press, 1999), 30.
45. Ibid., 34.
46. *Brooklyn Daily Eagle*, August 6, 1893.
47. Ibid.
48. *Sporting Life*, August 12, 1893.
49. *Sporting Life*, August 26, 1893.
50. *Brooklyn Daily Eagle*, August 17, 1893.
51. *Brooklyn Daily Eagle*, August 27, 1893.
52. *Sporting Life*, October 7, 1893.
53. *Sporting Life*, November 11, 1893.
54. Solomon, 45.
55. David Nemec, *The Great Encyclopedia of 19thCentury Major League Baseball* (New York: Donald I. Fire, 1997), 521
56. *Sporting Life*, April 7, 1894.
57. Solomon, 57.
58. Ibid., 58.
59. Ibid., 55.
60. Ibid., 69.
61. *Baltimore Sun*, April 24, 1894.
62. *Baltimore Sun*, May 5, 1894.
63. *Baltimore Sun*, July 18, 1894.
64. Ibid.
65. Ibid.
66. Ibid.
67. Bill Jenkinson, *Baseball's Ultimate Power* (Guilford, CT: Lyons Press, 2010), 63.
68. *Baltimore Sun*, May 17, 1894.
69. *Baltimore Sun*, August 2, 1894.
70. *Baltimore Sun*, August 15, 1894.
71. *Baltimore Sun*, June 6, 1894.
72. Ibid.
73. *Baltimore Sun*, June 1, 1894.
74. *Sporting Life*, November 3, 1894.
75. *Brooklyn Daily Eagle*, February 19, 1894.
76. *Sporting Life*, October 21, 1893.
77. *Sporting Life*, February 24, 1894.
78. Ibid.
79. *Sporting Life*, July 21, 1894.
80. *Washington Post*, March 10, 1896.
81. Solomon, 89.

82. *Sporting Life*, June 2, 1894.
83. *Sporting Life*, March 9, 1895.
84. *Baltimore Sun*, July 6, 1913.
85. *Baltimore Sun*, April 6, 1895.
86. *Sporting Life*, May 4, 1895.
87. *Sporting Life*, May 11, 1895.
88. Ibid.
89. Ibid.
90. *Baltimore Sun*, June 15, 1895.
91. *Boston Daily Globe*, June 21, 1895.

Chapter Six

1. Fran Zimniuch, *Going, Going, Gone!* (Lanham, MD: Taylor, 2008), 24.
2. *Philadelphia Inquirer*, April 1, 1896.
3. *Washington Post*, May 10, 1896.
4. *Philadelphia Inquirer*, April 5, 1896.
5. *Philadelphia Inquirer*, April 6, 1896.
6. *Sporting Life*, April 11, 1896.
7. *Philadelphia Inquirer*, April 24, 1896.
8. *Brooklyn Eagle*, July 19, 1992.
9. *Sporting Life*, May 2, 1896.
10. *Penny Press*, May 9, 1896.
11. *Sporting Life*, June 20, 1896.
12. Ibid.
13. Ibid.
14. *Sporting Life*, July 11, 1896.
15. *Sporting Life*, August 8, 1896.
16. *Sporting Life*, November 14, 1896.
17. *Sporting Life*, July 11, 1896.
18. David Voigt, *American Baseball* (State College: Pennsylvania State University, 1992), 289.
19. *Queens Daily Star*, January 30, 1928.
20. *Milwaukee Sentinel*, September 20, 1891.
21. *Springfield Republican*, July 17, 1896.
22. Steven Reiss, *Touching Base* (Westport, CT: Greenwood Press, 1980), 159.
23. Ibid., 169.
24. *Penny Press*, February 9, 1894.
25. *Washington Post*, January 24, 1897.
26. *Springfield Saturday Evening Union*, July 18, 1896.
27. *Springfield Republican*, July 19, 1896.
28. *Springfield Republican*, July 22, 1896.
29. *Springfield Republican*, August 16, 1896.
30. *Springfield Republican*, August 29, 1896.
31. *Springfield Republican*, July 22, 1896.
32. *Springfield Republican*, July 19, 1896.
34. *Sporting Life*, August 18, 1896.
34. *Springfield Republican*, August 14, 1896.
35. *Springfield Republican*, July 22, 1896.
36. *Springfield Republican*, May 4, 1897.
37. *Springfield Republican*, August 10, 1897.
38. *Springfield Republican*, September 22, 1897.
39. Edgar Popper, *The Birth and Growth of an Old Village* (Millbrook, NY: Central Press, 1991), 43.
40. *Sporting Life*, April 13, 1887.
41. *Denver Post*, May 11, 1897.
42. *Wilkes-Barre Record*, August 10, 1897.
43. Rena Corey, "Rush's Hotel: the Pulse of Wappingers in the Late 1890's," *Southern Dutchess News*, 3B.
44. *Rochester Democrat and Chronicle*, March 24, 1898.
45. *Sporting Life*, April 2, 1898.
46. *Sporting Life*, April 23, 1898.
47. *Sporting Life*, May 7, 1898.
48. Ibid.
49. Ibid.
50. Ibid.
51. *Sporting Life*, June 4, 1898.
52. *Boston Daily Globe*, July 6, 1898.
53. *Hartford Courant*, June 22, 1899.
54. *Boston Daily Globe*, July 6, 1899.
55. I am indebted to Rena Corey, former Archivist at the Wappingers Falls Historical Society, for verifying through Society records that Dan Brouthers was never the mayor of the village.
56. recorded in the Dutchess County Assessor's Office, Poughkeepsie, New York.
57. *Poughkeepsie Daily Eagle*, April 2, 1900.
58. Ibid.
59. Ibid.
60. Ibid.
61. *Sporting Life*, December 8, 1900.
62. *Sporting Life*, February 8, 1902.
63. *Sporting Life*, March 8, 1902.
64. *Sporting Life*, April 19, 1902.
65. *Poughkeepsie Daily Eagle*, May 9, 1902.
66. *Sporting Life*, May 11, 1902.
67. *Sporting Life*, December 20, 1902.
68. Ibid.
69. John Thorn, "Baseball's First All-Star Game," ourgame.mlblogs/2012/07/09, 3.
70. Ibid.
71. Ibid.
72. Joseph Poilucci, *Baseball in Dutchess County* (Danbury, CT: Rutledge, 2000), 17–18.
73. Vern Luse, "The 1903 Hudson River League," research.sabr.org/journals/1903-hudson-river-league.
74. *Sporting Life*, July 18, 1903.

75. *Sporting Life*, July 25, 1903.
76. *Poughkeepsie Daily Eagle*, June 11, 1903.
77. *Poughkeepsie Daily Eagle*, May 14, 1904.
78. *Poughkeepsie Daily Eagle*, May 23, 1904.
79. *Poughkeepsie Daily Eagle*, June 2, 1904.
80. Thorn, 4.
81. *Boston Daily Globe*, June 6, 1904.
82. *Los Angeles Times*, August 9, 1904.
83. Poilucci, 19.
84. Quoted in *Sporting Life*, June 11, 1904.
85. *Boston Daily Globe*, February 21, 1904.
86. *New York Evening Telegram*, June 14, 1904.
87. Charles Alexander, *John McGraw* (New York: Penguin, 1988), 209.
88. Mike Roer, *Orator O'Rourke* (Jefferson, NC: McFarland, 2005), 233.
89. *Sporting Life*, October 15, 1904.
90. *Sporting Life*, May 12, 1904.
91. *Sporting Life*, July 22, 1905.
92. *Sporting Life*, June 3, 1905.
93. *Sporting Life*, June 17, 1905.
94. *Washington Post*, June 12, 1905.
95. *Poughkeepsie Daily Eagle*, June 12, 1905.
96. *Poughkeepsie Daily Eagle*, August 29, 1905.
97. Ibid.
98. *Poughkeepsie Daily Eagle*, August 24, 1905.
99. *Poughkeepsie Daily Eagle*, August 29, 1905.
100. Ibid.
101. Ibid.
102. *Albany Evening Journal*, February 5, 1906.
103. *Sporting Life*, September 22, 1906.
104. Ibid.
105. *Sporting Life*, March 10, 1906.
106. *Sporting Life*, April 7, 1906.
107. Ibid.
108. *Sporting Life*, July 14, 1906.
109. *Sporting Life*, October 21, 1906.

Chapter Seven

1. *New York Times*, October 28, 1904.
2. *Sporting Life*, November 30, 1907.
3. *New York Journal*, December 11, 1911.
4. *New Hampshire Register*, June 27, 1889.
5. *Sporting Life*, August 21, 1909.
6. Ibid.
7. Ibid.
8. Ibid.
9. Ibid.
10. Ibid.
11. Mitchell Clark, "The Scouting History of Baseball," www.livestrong.com/article/355609-the-scouting-history-of-baseball//.
12. *El Paso Herald*, April 30, 1910.
13. *Washington Post*, August 20, 1907.
14. *Washington Post*, September 1, 1907.
15. *Sporting Life*, September 28, 1907.
16. *Chicago Daily Tribune*, November 15, 1907.
17. *Sporting Life*, December 7, 1907.
18. *Sporting Life*, September 28, 1907.
19. Trey Strecker, "Fred Merkle," www.sabr.org/bioproj/person/372b4391.
20. *Sporting Life*, November 30, 1907.
21. *Sporting Life*, October 26, 1907.
22. Ibid.
23. *Sporting Life*, October 19, 1907.
24. *Sporting Life*, October 26, 1907.
25. *Auburn Citizen*, December 17, 1908.
26. Ibid.
27. Ibid.
28. *Sporting Life*, November 12, 1910.
29. *Sporting Life*, August 1, 1908.
30. *Milwaukee Sentinel*, April 17, 1930.
31. *Sporting Life*, April 1, 1911.
32. *Sporting Life*, January 4, 1913.
33. *Utica Herald-Dispatch*, January 18, 1909.
34. "History of Softball," www.athleticscholarships.net/history-of-softball.htm.
35. *Utica Herald-Dispatch*, January 18, 1909.
36. *Auburn Citizen*, February 5, 1909.
37. Ibid.
38. Ibid.
39. "Brooklyn's Semipro Fields," www.covehurst.net/ddyte/brooklyn/semipro_parks.html.
40. Unsourced article, Dan Brouthers player file, National Baseball Hall of Fame, Cooperstown, NY.
41. *Brooklyn Eagle*, March 29, 1909.
42. *Brooklyn Eagle*, May 15, 1911.
43. *Brooklyn Eagle*, May 22, 1911.
44. *Brooklyn Eagle*, June 5, 1911.
45. U. S. Census, Borough of Manhattan, New York, April 21, 1910.
46. *Syracuse Journal*, May 9, 1912.
47. *Washington Post*, October 23, 1910.
48. *New York Evening Journal*, February 6, 1912.

49. *Sporting Life*, May 23, 1903.
50. *Washington Post*, December 18, 1910.
51. Ibid.
52. *New York Journal*, December 11, 1911.
53. *Sporting Life*, December 23, 1911.
54. *Washington Times*, January 24, 1912.
55. *New York Evening Telegram*, September 27, 1912.
56. *Sporting Life*, December 30, 1911.
57. *Auburn Citizen*, September 19, 1913.
58. *Washington Post*, August 6, 1916.
59. Ibid.
60. *Sporting Life*, January 24, 1914.
61. *Sporting Life*, October 15, 1884.
62. *Boston Daily Globe*, July 8, 1917.
63. Ibid.
64. Roy Kerr, *Buck Ewing: a Baseball Biography* (Jefferson, NC: McFarland, 2011), 62.
65. *Boston Daily Globe*, July 15, 1917.
66. *Poughkeepsie Sunday Courier*, August 7, 1932.
67. John McGraw, *My Thirty Years in Baseball* (Lincoln: University of Nebraska, 1995), 68.
68. Unsourced newspaper article, June 21, 1931, Dan Brouthers player file, National Baseball Hall of Fame, Cooperstown, NY.
69. Ibid.
70. Ibid.
71. Ibid.
72. Ibid.
73. *Brooklyn Eagle*, July 19, 1931.
74. Ibid.

Epilogue

1. *Newark Star-Eagle*, August 4, 1932.
2. *New York Herald Tribune*, August 5, 1932.
3. *Boston Evening Transcript*, August 3, 1932.
4. *New York Evening Mirror*, August 3, 1932.
5. *Poughkeepsie Evening Star*, August 4, 1932.
6. *Newark Star-Eagle*, August 4, 1932.
7. *New York American*, August 3, 1932.
8. *New York Herald Tribune*, August 4, 1932.
9. *New York World Telegram*, August 3, 1932.
10. *Newark Star-Eagle*, August 4, 1932.
11. *New York Herald Tribune*, August 3, 1932.
12. *New York Sun*, August 4, 1932.
13. *Poughkeepsie Evening Courier*, August 7, 1932.
14. *New York Sun*, undated, Dan Brouthers player file, National Baseball Hall of Fame, Cooperstown, NY.
15. *New York World Telegram*, August 11, 1932.
16. Ibid.
17. *Poughkeepsie Evening Star*, August 4, 1932.
18. *Poughkeepsie Sunday Courier*, August 7, 1932.
19. *New York Times*, August 15, 1932.
20. *St. Louis Post-Dispatch*, August 3, 1932.
21. *Detroit News*, August 4, 1932.
22. *New York Times*, April 26, 1945.

Bibliography

Articles

Bak, Richard. "Before They Were Tigers: A Primer on Early Detroit Baseball." blog.detroitathletic.com/2012/06/11/before-they-were-tigers-a-primer-on-early-detroit-baseball//.

Bevis, Charlie. "Congress Street Grounds." sabr.org/bioproj/park/33169c79.

"Brooklyn's Semipro Fields," www.covehurst.net/ddyte/brooklyn/semipro_parks.html.

Clark, Mitchell. "The Scouting History of Baseball." www.livestrong.com/article/355609-the-scouting-history-of-baseball/.

Constantelos, Stephen. "Nap Lajoie." sabr.org/bioproj/person/ac9dc07e.

Corey, Rena. "Rush's Hotel: The Pulse of Wappingers in the Late 1890's." *Southern Dutchess News*, April 25, 2012.

Healy, Paul. "Pynchon Park." www.projectballpark.org/history/na/alt/pynchon.html.

"History of Softball." www.athleticscholarships.net/history-of-softball.htm.

Jensen, Don. "John McGraw." sabr.org.bioproj/person/fef5035f.

Lesch, R. J. "Larry Doyle." sabr.org/bioproj/person/3b7d0b88.

"Luis Padrón." http://www.baseball-reference.com/bullpen/Luis_Padr%C3%B3n.

Luse, Vern. "The 1903 Hudson River League." research.sabr.org/journals/1903-hudson-river-league.

McKenna, Brian. "John Clarkson." sabr.org/bioproj/person/47feb015.

Overfield, Joseph M. "The First Great Minor League Club." research.sabr.org/journals/first-great-minor-league-club?tmpl=componentnn&print=1&page=.

_____. "When Baseball Came to Richmond Avenue." *Niagara Frontier*, Vol. 2, No. 2, 1955.

Potts, Mindy. "Historic Stottville and its Distinctive Businesses." freepages.genealogy.rootsweb.ancestry.com/cliffamere/History/col/Stottville.ColCo.htm.

"St. Mary's Church. Our Lady of the Falls." *www.catholic-church.org/saintmarys/history.htm*.

Strecker, Trey. "Fred Merkle." sabr.org/bioproj/person/372b4391.

Thompson, Don. "Sam Thompson." sabr.org/bioproj/person/b3e0fab8.

Thorn, John. "Baseball's First All-Star Game." ourgame.mlblogs.com/2012/07/09/baseballs-first-all-star-game.

"Town of Beekman: St. Denis Church," http://www.beekmanhistory.com/id43.html.

Triscuit, Zach. "Ned Hanlon." sabr.org/bioproj/person/1e360183.

"Union Park in Central Baltimore: Before They Took Out the Ball Game." www.writingcentralbaltimore.com/wcb_spring10/doku.php?id=union_park.

Vaccaro, Frank, "Hugh Daily." sabr.org/bioproj/person/8d8c99e4.

Baseball Periodicals

Baseball Magazine
Spalding's Official Base Ball Guide, 1890
Sporting Life
The Sporting News

Books

Alexander, Charles. *John McGraw*. New York: Penguin, 1988.

___ *Our Game: An American Baseball History.* New York: Henry Holt, 1991.
Appel, Marty. *Slide, Kelly, Slide: The Wild Life and Times of Mike "King" Kelly, Baseball's First Superstar.* Lanham, MD: Scarecrow Press, 1999.
Di Salvatore, Bryan. *A Clever Base-Ballist: The Life and Times of John Montgomery Ward.* Baltimore: Johns Hopkins, 1999.
Ellis, Franklin. *History of Columbia County.* Philadephia: Everts and Ensign, 1878.
Fleitz, David L. *More Ghosts in the Gallery: Another Sixteen Little-Known Greats at Cooperstown.* Jefferson, NC: McFarland, 2007.
Hardy, James E. *The New York Giants Base Ball Club, 1870 to 1900.* Jefferson, NC: McFarland, 1996.
James, Bill. *The New Bill James Historical Baseball Abstract,* revised edition. New York: The Free Press, 1988.
Jenkinson, Bill. *Baseball's Ultimate Power: Ranking the All-Time Greatest Distance Home Run Hitters.* Guilford, CT: Lyons Press, 2010.
Kerr, Roy. *Buck Ewing: A Baseball Biography,* Jefferson, NC: McFarland, 2011.
_____. *Sliding Billy Hamilton: The Life and Times of Baseball's First Great Leadoff Hitter.* Jefferson, NC: McFarland, 2010.
Koszarek, Ed. *The Players League: History, Clubs, Ballplayers and Statistics.* Jefferson, NC: McFarland, 2006.
Mack, Connie. *My 66 Years in the Big Leagues.* Mineola, NY: Dover, 2009.
McGraw, John J. *My Thirty Years in Baseball.* Lincoln: University of Nebraska, 1995.
Morris, Peter. *A Game of Inches: The Stories Behind the Innovations That Shaped Baseball.* Chicago: Ivan R. Dee, 2006.
Nemec, David. *Major League Baseball Profiles.* Volumes 1 & 2. Lincoln: University of Nebraska, 2011.
_____. *The Great Encyclopedia of 19th-Century Baseball.* New York: Donald I. Fine, 1997.
_____. *The Official Rules of Baseball Illustrated.* Guilford, CT: Lyons Press, 2006
Popper, Edgar A. *The Birth and Growth of an Old Village: Wappingers Falls, New York, 1707–1977.* Millbrook, NY: Central Press, 1991.
Poilucci, Joseph V. *Baseball in Dutchess County: When It Was a Game.* Danbury, CT: Rutledge: 2000.
Reiss, Steven A. *Touching Base: Professional Baseball and American Culture in the Progressive Era.* Westport, CT: Greenwood Press, 1980.
Rittner, Don. *Troy: A Collar City.* Charleston, SC.: Arcadia, 2002.
Roer, Mike. *Orator O'Rourke: The Life of a Baseball Radical.* Jefferson, NC: McFarland, 2005.
Schlereth, Thomas J. *Victorian America: Transformations in Everyday Life.* New York: Harper Collins, 1991.
Seymour, Harold. *Baseball: The Early Years.* New York: Oxford, 1960.
Solomon, Burt. *Where They Ain't: The Fabled Life and Untimely Death of the Original Baltimore Orioles, the Team That Gave Birth to Modern Baseball.* New York: The Free Press, 1999.
Voigt, David Quentin. *American Baseball: From the Gentleman's Sport to the Commissioner System.* Volume I. State College: Pennsylvania State University, 1992.
Westcott, Rich. *Philadelphia's Old Ballparks,* Philadelphia: Temple University, 1996.
Zimniuch, Fran. *Going, Going, Gone! The Art of the Trade in Major League Baseball.* Lanham, MD: Taylor, 2008.

Census, Archives and Directories

U.S. Federal Census, Dutchess County, New York, 1860, 1870, 1880, 1900.
U.S. Federal Census, Manhattan, New York, 1910, 1920.
New York State Census, Manhattan, 1915.
U.S. Federal Census, Essex County, New Jersey, 1930.
City Directory, Orange, New Jersey, 1932.
Office of the County Clerk, Dutchess County, Poughkeepsie, New York.

Newspapers

Albany Evening Journal
Atchison Daily Globe
Auburn Citizen
Baltimore Sun
Bangor Daily News

Boston Daily Globe
Boston Evening Transcript
Brooklyn Eagle
Buffalo Express
Chicago Daily Tribune
Cleveland Herald
Daily Picayune
Denver Post
Detroit Free Press
Detroit News
The Dutchess Farmer (Dutchess County, New York State)
Hartford Courant
Inter-Ocean (Chicago)
Los Angeles Times
Milwaukee Sentinel
Morning Oregonian
Milwaukee Sentinel
Morning Oregonian
New York Clipper
New York Dramatic Mirror
New York Evening Telegram
New York Evening Journal
New York Herald
New York Journal
New York Police Gazette
New York Sun
New York Times
New York World
New York World Telegram
Milwaukee Sentinel
Morning Oregonian
El Paso Herald
Penny Press (Minneapolis)
Poughkeepsie Daily Eagle
Poughkeepsie Eagle-News
Poughkeepsie Sunday Courier
Queens Daily Star
Rochester Democrat and Chronicle
St. Louis Dispatch
St. Louis Globe Democrat
Scranton Tribune
The Sentinel (Milwaukee)
Springfield Republican
Springfield Saturday Evening Union
Syracuse Journal
The Textile Worker
Troy Daily Times
Utica Herald-Dispatch
Washington Times
Washington Post
Wilkes-Barre Record
Yenowine's News (Milwaukee)

Online Resources

retrosheet.org.
baseball-reference.com.
ancestry.com.
19Cbaseball.com.
baseballhalloffame.org.
baseballalmanac.com.
bioproj.sabr.org
research.sabr.org.journals
baseballindex.org

Unpublished Sources

Dan Brouthers, player file, National Baseball Hall of Fame, Cooperstown, New York.
Dan Brouthers, player file, Bill Jenkinson, Willow Grove, Pennsylvania.
Dan Brouthers, photo file, National Baseball Hall of Fame, Cooperstown, New York.
Dan Brouthers, home run logs, Bill Jenkinson, Willow Grove, Pennsylvania.
E-mail communication from Sue MacKay, Director of Collections, Baseball Hall of Fame, August 8, 2012.

Index

Aaron, Henry 40
Alexander, Charles 90
Andrews, Ed 63
Anson, Adrian "Cap" 20, 54, 62, 151, 161–62
Appelby, S.C. 110

Baldwin, Charley "Lady" 61, 64, 67, 69
Bancroft, Frank 20
Barnes, Ross 76
Bennett, Charley 60, 71, 74, 79, 86, 87, 90
Birkenmeyer, Alfred 146
Boggs, Wade 125
Bond, Tommy 12, 19
Bradley, George 20–21
Bresnahan, Roger 180–81
Bridewell, Al 157
Briody, Charles "Fatty" 67
Brodie, Steve 108
Brouthers, Anna Lillian 64, 89, 154
Brouthers [Brooder], Annie 4, 7
Brouthers, Daniel Leo 74, 89, 170
Brouthers, Dennis Addison 43, 89, 163, 170
Brouthers [Brooder], Ellen 5, 170, 172
Brouthers, James 4, 14, 41
Brouthers [Brooder], Margaret 5, 170, 172
Brouthers [Brooder], Martin 4
Brouthers, Mary Ellen 133, 154, 172, 174, 177
Brouthers [Brooder], Michael 4–6
Brouthers, Paul 104
Brown, Tom 80, 90, 136
Buffinton, Charlie 38, 73, 90, 91
Burkett, Jesse 128
Burns, Thomas "Oyster" 99, 127
Burr, Harold 174
Byrne, Charles 48–49, 99, 102–3

Carew, Rod 125
Carey, George 116

Carter, Nick 249
Cartwright, Alexander 8
Casey, Dan "Kid" 65, 72, 120
Caylor, O.P. 17
Chamberlain, Elton "Ice Box" 40
Chapman, Jack 44
Clarke, Bill 159
Clarke, Fred 117, 180
Clarkson, John 62, 65, 77–79, 82–82, 86–87, 90, 172
Clements, Jack 120
Cleveland, Grover 72
Cobb, Ty 125–26
Cogswell, Joseph 8
Collins, Hubert "Hub" 97, 99
Collins, Jimmy 180
Comiskey, Charles 53
Connor, Roger 23, 47, 57, 99, 128, 159, 178
Conway, Pete 45, 69
Corbett, "Gentleman Jim" 48
Corey, Rena 134
Cosgrove, Dr. James M. 12
Crane, Ed "Cannonball" 79, 105, 130
Crane, Sam 30, 69,, 61
Crawford, Sam 126, 167–68
Croak, James 43
Croak, Margaret 43
Croak, Mary Ellen 43
Croak, William 43
Cross, Lave 120, 123
Curtis, Harry 156

Daily, Bill 82–83
Daily, Cornelius "Con" 97, 99
Daily, Hugh "One Arm" 35–36, 40
Dauvray, Helen 49
Dawson, Andre 57
Dean, Jay Hanna "Dizzy" 46
DeLaney, Daniel 3–4

Delehanty, Ed 120, 123–24, 180
Derby, George 32
Devlin, Jim 12
Dolan, Jack 92
Doscher, Herman "Herm" 18
Doyle, Larry 157
Duffy, Hugh 90, 180–81

Esper, Charles "Duke" 108
Evers, Johnny, 157
Ewing, William "Buck" 25, 79

Farrell, Charles "Duke" 90
Farrell, Jack 38
Farrell, Merce 145
Ferguson, Bob 20–23, 26–27, 32
Fitzgerald, John 152
Flint, Frank "Silver" 38
Fogarty, Jimmy 80
Foley, Curry 29, 31
Force, Davy 33, 39, 42
Foutz, Dave 97–99, 104–6, 109

Galvin, Jim "Pud" 29, 35–36, 38–39, 41, 43–45, 73
Ganzell, Charlie 71, 112
Gastright, Hank 57
Gehrig, Lou 154
Geier, Phil 123
Gerhardt, Joe 154
Getzein, Charley 61, 64, 69, 73
Gill, William 93
Gleason, William "Kid" 108
Golden, Richard 93
Gore, George 38, 81, 85
Griffin, Mike 97, 99
Griffith, Clark 92
Griffith, D.W. 154
Gumbert, Addison 53, 87,, 90, 100, 161
Gwynn, Tony 125

Haddock, George 90–91, 97, 99
Hakanson, Walter 161
Hallman, Bill 120
Hamilton, Billy 85, 100, 105, 119–20
Hanlon, Edward "Ned" 46, 50, 60, 68, 71, 74, 85, 88, 107–9, 115–17, 135, 141
Hart, Bill 98
Hart, Jim 79, 82
Hawke, Bill 108
Healy, John "Egyptian" 40, 80
Hoffman, Solly 157
Hornsby, Rogers 125
Hough, Frank 37
Hulbert, William 16

Irwin, Art 21, 80, 87, 90–91, 119, 135

Irwin, John 91

Jenkinson, Bill 111
Jennings, Hughie 107–8, 115–17, 180–81
Johnston, Dick 89
Jones, Charley 19

Kantzsh, George 135
Keefe, Tim 23, 56, 74, 85
Keeler, Willie 105–8, 115
Kelley, Joe 107–8, 115
Kelly, "Honest John" 27–28, 40
Kelly, Mike 38, 49, 57, 62, 76–80, 82–83, 90, 92, 180
Kennedy, Maclean 180
Kennedy, Ted 144
Kilrain, Jake 81–82
Kinsella, Dick 160
Kinslow, Tom 97, 105

Lajoie, Napoleon "Nap" 125
Lanigan, Ernest 11, 168
Lansing, Wellington "Wallie" 9
Latham, Arlie 49
Leadley, Bob 46, 74
Lucas, Henry V. 34
Lush, Bill 135

Mack, Connie 11
Madden, Joseph "Kid" 82
Marks, Abe 111
Martin, Willie 160
Mathews, Bobby 19
Mathewson, Christy 147, 163
Mathewson, Hank 163–64
McCabe, William 141, 143–44, 149
McClusky, John 117–18
McCormick, Harry 157
McCormick, Jim 64
McGraw, John 55, 107–8, 111, 114–15, 117, 146–47, 151, 154–55, 158, 160–62, 164–69, 172, 176–78
McMahon, John "Sadie" 91, 107, 109, 112
McQuaid, John 83
Meekin, Jouet 100, 114
Meinke, Frank 43
Merkel, Fred 157–58
Mertes, Sam 123
Morrill, John 78
Morris, Peter 43
Mountain, Frank 32
Murnane, Tim 21–22, 82–83
Murphy, Morgan 87, 90
Musial, Stan 125
Mutrie, Jim 20
Myers, H.C. 22

Index

Nash, Billy 78, 88, 90, 119, 123–24
Nemec, David 88
Nichols, Charles "Kid" 41

O'Brien, Darby 97, 103
O'Bruádair, Daíbi 5
O'Leary, Dan 60
O'Rourke, Jim 29, 31, 33, 37, 43–44, 76, 18, 146–47, 170–71, 180
Orth, Al 120, 123
Ortiz, David 40

Padrón, Luis [Lewis Padron] 147–48
Peitz, Henry "Heinie" 107–8
Pfeffer, Fred 40–41
Phillips, Horace 15–18, 21, 26–29, 34
Pike, Lipman "Lip" 24
Poilucci, Joseph 143
Powell, Martin 60
Prince, Charles 91
Purcell, William "Blondie" 90

Quigley, John 12–14, 180
Quinn, Joe 78, 90

Radbourn, Charles "Hoss" 38, 63, 65, 78–79, 82, 87, 90, 168, 180
Ramsey, Henry 141
Reach, Al 119, 123–24
Reed, Frank 136
Reilly, C.E. 23
Reilly, John "Long John" 155
Richardson, Danny 103, 105
Richardson, Hardy 31–32, 37, 42, 45–46, 58–59, 61, 72–72, 83, 90–91
Richter, Francis 123
Rizzuto, Phil 40
Robinson, Wilbert 107–8, 180–81
Rogers, John I. 119, 123–24
Rowe, Jack 31–32, 37, 45–46, 58–59, 72, 74
Rusie, Amos 41, 81, 109, 114
Ruth, Babe 50, 125, 178
Ryan, Jimmy 59

Selee, Frank 20
Serad, Billy 41, 45

Seymour, Harold 46
Shindle, Billy 107
Shriver, Harry "Pop" 80
Smith, Tom 119
Soden, Arthur 90
Sole, Asa 24, 29
Spalding, Al 85
Stearns, Frederick Kimball 58, 67
Stein, Ed 97
Stockdale, Otis 112
Stott, Jonathan 14
Stovey, Harry 87–88, 105
Sullivan, John L. 48, 81–82
Sunday, Billy 42
Sweeney, Charlie 61

Taylor, Jack 120
Tebeau, Oliver "Patsy" 20
Tenney, Fred 157
Thompson, Sam 57, 60, 64, 71, 74, 119–20, 124, 178
Thorn, John 141, 145
Treadway, George 107
Twitchell, Larry 64

Van Haltren, George 73
Von der Ahe, Chris 67

Wagner, Honus 125–26
Ward, John 49, 55, 79, 84–86, 95, 97–99, 103, 107, 128, 135, 141
Watkins, Bill 67–68, 71, 73–74
Weidman, George "Stump" 64
Welch, Mickey 23, 79, 81, 172–74
White, Jim "Deacon" 29, 33, 37, 43, 45–46, 58–59, 69, 71–74, 76
White, Will 18, 166–67
Whitney, Jim 38
Williams, Alfie 48
Wilson, Charles 172
Wolf, William "Chicken" 40
Wood, Pete 45
Wright, George 76, 117
Wright, Harry, 20, 76, 119

Young, Cy 41, 56, 100